MW01073170

NET ASSESSMENT AND MILITARY STRATEGY

NET ASSESSMENT AND
MILITARY STRATEGY

Retrospective and Prospective Essays

EDITED BY

Thomas G. Mahnken
with an introduction by
Andrew W. Marshall

Rapid Communications in Conflict and Security Series
General Editor: Geoffrey R.H. Burn

CAMBRIA
PRESS

Amherst, New York

Copyright 2020 Cambria Press

All rights reserved.
Printed in the United States of America

No part of this publication may be reproduced, stored in or introduced
into a retrieval system, or transmitted, in any form, or by any means
(electronic, mechanical, photocopying, recording, or otherwise),
without the prior permission of the publisher.

Requests for permission should be directed to
permissions@cambriapress.com, or mailed to:
Cambria Press
100 Corporate Parkway, Suite 128
Amherst, New York 14226, USA

Library of Congress Cataloging-in-Publication Data on file.

ISBN: 978-1-62196-539-8

TABLE OF CONTENTS

LIST OF FIGURES

ACKNOWLEDGMENTS

This book was a long time coming. It grew out of a project on "Net Assessment: Past, Present, and Future" that I initiated in 2012 when I was the Jerome E. Levy Chair of Economic Geography and National Security at the U.S. Naval War College. That project included workshops in September 2012 at George Mason University in Fairfax, VA and March 2014 at The Johns Hopkins School of Advanced International Studies (SAIS) in Washington, D.C. to explore the conduct of net assessment in retrospect and prospect and discuss a series of draft papers. I would like to thank those who participated, including Dmitry (Dima) Adamsky, Robert Angevine, Eliot Cohen, Jaymie Durnan, Jacqueline Deal, Eric Edelman, Tom Ehrhard, Fritz Ermarth, Jim FitzSimonds, Karl Haslinger, Jerry Hendrix, I. Lewis Libby, Steve Lukasik, Robert Martinage, Andrew May, Jeffrey McKitrick, Williamson Murray, Michael Pillsbury, Jim Roche, Stephen P. Rosen, Abram Shulsky, Bob Silano, John Schutte, Jan van Tol, Michael Vickers, Barry Watts, and Enders Wimbush. The workshops, and the feedback they generated, helped guide the authors of the chapters that appear in this volume.

Andrew W. Marshall expressed his desire to write a foreword for this book at the project's inception. When I finally gave him the complete manuscript, he asked whether he could instead contribute a chapter. The result of that effort, which he undertook with the assistance of Jacqueline Deal, appears as the introductory chapter of this volume.

I would like to express my gratitude to Andrew May and Jeff McKitrick for their support throughout this long process and to Robert Silano for his editorial assistance, which went far beyond the norm.

Andy Marshall did not see net assessment as an arcane art. From the beginning, this project was conceived as an aid to those who seek to understand net assessment, with a particular focus on the rising generation of future strategists. I leave it up to the reader to determine whether this volume ultimately serves that purpose.

Thomas G. Mahnken

Acronyms and Abbreviations

C3	command, control, and communications
C4I	command, control, communications, computers, and information
CIA	Central Intelligence Agency
CILTS	Commission on Integrated Long-Term Strategy
DARPA	Defense Advanced Research Project Agency
DDR&E	Director of Defense Research and Engineering
DIA	Defense Intelligence Agency
DOD	Department of Defense
FOFA	follow-on forces attack
FY	fiscal year
GNP	gross national product
ICBMs	intercontinental ballistic missiles
IEDs	improvised explosive devices
IT-RMA	information technology-revolution in military affairs
LRRDPP	Long-Range Research and Development Planning Program
LRA	long-range aviation
MTR	military-technical revolution
NAG	Net Assessment Group

NATO	North Atlantic Treaty Organization
NESC	Net Evaluation Subcommittee
NIE	national intelligence estimate
NSC	National Security Council
NSAM	National Security Action Memorandum (Kennedy/ Johnson Administrations)
NSDD	National Security Decision Directive (Reagan Administration)
NSDM	National Security Decision Memorandum (Nixon/Ford Administrations)
NSSD	National Security Study Directive (Reagan Administration)
NSSM	National Security Study Memorandum (Nixon/Ford Administrations)
ONA	Office of Net Assessment
OSS	Office of Strategic Services
PA&E	Program Analysis and Evaluation
PDB	President's Daily Brief
PGMs	precision-guided munitions
R&D	research and development
RMA	[the] Revolution in Military Affairs; [a] revolution in military affairs
RSO	reconnaissance-strike organizations
SESC	Special Evaluation Subcommittee
SMEs	subject matter experts
SSBN	ballistic missile submarine

Net Assessment and Military Strategy

Introduction

The Origins of Net Assessment

Andrew W. Marshall

The Office of Net Assessment (ONA) was responsible for carrying out three programs in the Department of Defense from November 1973 until the collapse of the Soviet Union:

- Net assessment, which focused on selected warfare areas and theaters, to support the leaders of the defense establishment in making decisions for the extended competition with the Soviet Union;

- An effort to correct the apparent underestimation of the Soviet defense burden, that is, the percentage of the Soviet gross national product (GNP) devoted to its military forces and other national defense goals; and

- Special tasks, including lessons learned efforts, for instance, following the Yom Kippur and Falklands Wars; discussions with other military establishments such as Israel, France, and Japan; and especially in the 1980s, efforts to prepare projections of the future security environment, and to explore the effects of space-based missile defense systems.

It should be added that during the 1990s ONA focused on the nature and likely consequences of a revolution in military affairs (RMA) for the United States as well as the similar prospect for the People's Republic of China. Other studies analyzed past experiences of large-scale changes in defense analogous to a contemporary RMA, and insights on why some military organizations do well in such periods and others do not.

This chapter reviews ONA's work on the first two programs and also traces the origins of that work to approaches and concepts developed by the RAND Corporation from the mid-1950s to the late 1960s. Those intellectual precursors included studies of trends and asymmetries in the defense policies of the United States and the Soviet Union as well as the framework of the Cold War as a long-term competition in order to outlast the Soviet Union.

The goal of the particular kind of net assessment that ONA performed was to provide the Secretary of Defense and the service chiefs with insights to help them make better decisions on long-term competition with the Soviet Union than would otherwise be possible. Such assessments depended on a shared belief in the existence of an extended competition with the Soviet Union, a perspective that was far from universal at the time.

Each net assessment sought to illuminate both trends and asymmetries in the behavior of the United States and its allies in contrast to the behavior of the Soviet Union and its allies. The goal was to provide as good a picture as possible of the key competitions and contrasting strategies of both sides as they had evolved over the previous 20 to 30 years. These assessments sought to identify the ways in which Soviet conduct differed from ours as a result of geography, culture, history, organizational structure, or other factors. Special attention was paid to the asymmetries that favored the United States or that provided opportunities for U.S. strategy to exploit. Assessments in most areas were repeated every few years and improved as understanding of competitions and practices of both sides improved and analytic methods were developed or refined.

This kind of net assessment process was not the only type that could be done. Indeed, when asked in 1972 to establish or re-establish a net assessment group on the National Security Council (NSC) staff, I enquired what sort of net assessment was needed. The answer was developing a means of scoring outcomes of prospective near-term wars or campaigns such as a European conflict or an all-out war in multiple theaters. That prompted me to question whether existing models of warfare were good enough and how many alternative scenarios leading to war should be examined.

For various reasons, I did not believe that this could be done well enough or be that useful. Then I happened to meet General James H. Polk, USA, who had just come home after commanding US Army Europe. He mentioned his efforts to obtain intelligence from his staff on how good Soviet ground forces actually were. He failed to get much information, but his endeavor to get anecdotal stories on the various operational problems experienced by the Soviet Union during training and exercises allowed him to form his own judgment. The Soviet military had many problems, mainly arising from inferior skill levels among conscripts. When I indicated that my preference in the net assessment process included analytic methods to look for critical asymmetries, he was encouraged.

I do not think that such a process could have succeeded at the National Security Council. My subsequent move over to the Pentagon did make it possible because Secretary of Defense James R. Schlesinger and I agreed on what would or could be useful, given the time required to develop databases and analytic methods. My move to the Department of Defense resulted from a deal struck by Henry A. Kissinger, the National Security Advisor to the President, and Schlesinger. After seeing a report on the first net assessment of US and Soviet ground forces conducted under the interagency process roughly one year earlier, Schlesinger indicated that he wanted three assessments on the strategic nuclear, maritime, and

Central Front in Europe. In addition, ONA activities would include special studies—for example, reviews of lessons learned from recent conflicts and, as discussed below, broader measures to assess the ability of the Soviet Union to compete with the United States. Schlesinger decided that these net assessments must be frank in reporting problems and that he would decide who should get these reports.

Thus began the production of diagnostic net assessments that might assist Schlesinger and his successors to make better decisions. I thought that the most effective way of developing such assessments was to use some of the methods that Joseph E. Loftus had introduced to me when he came to RAND in the autumn of 1954. Loftus had served in Air Force intelligence from 1950 to mid-1954. While in the RAND Washington office, he read the internal RAND paper entitled "The Next Ten Years." Written by Bernard Brodie, Charles J. Hitch, and me, it attempted to provide ideas on major questions deserving of attention. In December 1954, Loftus wrote a short paper, "Ten Minutes on the Next Ten Years," dissenting from some of our conclusions.

Loftus became my colleague in the Economics Department at RAND when he moved out to California in early 1955. We began talking in detail about his reasons for claiming that "The Next Ten Years" was too pessimistic, which were based on his reconstruction of Soviet history and American behavior within the bounds of what today is called the strategic nuclear balance. Loftus highlighted efforts by Joseph Stalin to initiate several major programs to bridge the Soviet strategic offensive and defensive gaps during and immediately after World War II together with special organizations to manage them. The efforts needed substantial outlays of resources that suggested that the Soviet Union faced major challenges unlike the United States, and also that it was pursuing the competition with the United States in quite different ways.

Shortly after the end of World War II, the Soviets began what would become an expensive program to develop air defenses. In addition to covering major cities such as Moscow, this effort included protecting investments made under another major post-war initiative, Stalin's drive to build nuclear weapons. The Soviet Union had obtained US bomb designs and then set people to work on their own designs around 1943. Since no fissile material was available, a special program was initiated to produce it. Soviet fissile material sites were protected by air defense units. Loftus had reason to believe that in 1947 half of the concrete and three quarters of the stainless steel made in the Soviet Union was going to support the construction of nuclear facilities.

Loftus inferred another major asymmetry in the competition from his observation of Soviet investments in bombers and missiles. He came to believe in the early 1950s that the Soviets were committed to developing intercontinental ballistic missiles (ICBMs) rather than using bombers to potentially mount nuclear attacks on targets in the United States. This meant that at a time when most American analysts considered that Soviet bombers could pose nearly as serious a threat as US airpower posed to the Soviet Union, Loftus perceived Soviet capabilities for intercontinental strikes were more limited. Loftus and I speculated that a lack of trust in Soviet pilots, a deficit of bases to refuel and recover their damaged aircraft in proximity to the United States, the absence of a tradition of valorous pilots from World War II, or perhaps some combination of these factors accounted for the asymmetry. Even though the Atomic Energy Commission initially had custody of nuclear weapons, and some were deployed by 1952 at Strategic Air Command bases and later on bombers on airborne alert, the Soviets never delegated custody to their forces.

Loftus' approach was very different from that of other RAND colleagues. To assist the Air Force, RAND needed to produce projections of Soviet forces and their posture over the next 10 to 15 years. Some people believed that such intelligence and projections should be based on data including stolen plans. Loftus and I held that something more systematic was possible and needed. The central task was identifying trends in the Soviet allocation of resources. As economists, we knew resources were finite. Thus, when the Soviet Union was pouring money into air defenses, it meant that other capabilities such naval forces could not be as well financed. The World War II US Strategic Bombing Survey had shown that notwithstanding the activities of the Wehrmacht across Europe, one third of German expenditures were spent on air defense. This reinforced the sense that such investments in air defenses could be costly and that identifying the patterns of expenditures by an adversary over time could be illuminating with regard to its future prospects and asymmetries in the competition.

The diagnostic net assessment approach was further informed by studying organizational behavior. During the late 1950s, Loftus and I considered the improvements being made in our predictions. In looking at trends in allocating resources, we were studying how resources were allocated by—and to—Soviet organizations. It led us to ask what was known about their behavior. I was aware of the collaboration of Herbert A. Simon and James G. March, but I reread their work on organizations and also visited them and their colleagues at Carnegie Mellon. This helped me refine my thinking on how to make improvements in our projections.

Most important for my future thinking on strategy, I got to know Joe Bower and Roland Christensen at the Harvard Business School during this period, which trained future chief executive officers to compete in their respective sectors. From them I learned that the students were being taught to ask the following questions:

- What business are you really involved in?
- Who are your competitors in that business?
- What are your relative strengths and weaknesses?

These questions were designed to help corporate leaders develop a strategy to gain market share at the expense of their competitors and perhaps even drive them out of business. This academic orientation later informed my thinking on a framework for approaching long-term competition with the Soviet Union in the development of the net assessment process.

Loftus was my major collaborator until 1963, when I went to Paris to work on a project that Secretary of Defense Robert S. McNamara assigned to RAND. While I was gone, Loftus retired. But just before I left for Europe, Schlesinger joined RAND and, once I returned in the spring of 1965, we began to collaborate on what became the idea of a long-term competition framework. Consistent with the formulation of the strategy of containment by George F. Kennan, Schlesinger arrived at RAND with the idea that the object was outlasting the Soviets and encouraging them to devote resources to activities that were less threatening or even favorable to the United States. He had already become skeptical of estimates made by the Intelligence Community that the share of Soviet GNP allocated to the military, the so-called *defense burden*, was six to eight percent. Schlesinger thought that this percentage was a serious underestimate. Therefore, he encouraged adopting a focus not only on respective US and Soviet approaches to particular warfare areas but also to the broader comparison of our respective defense burdens.

I succeeded Schlesinger as the Director of Strategic Studies at RAND, a position that Henry S. Rowen had created, and which Schlesinger has occupied for about a month before joining the Nixon transition team in late 1968. In that position I wrote the paper on long-term competition, which I completed in the late spring or early summer of 1969 and which RAND published in 1972. It presented terms of reference for a small group tasked with developing a candidate approach to strategic nuclear competition. I laid out thoughts on how to formulate a strategy and goals based on some initial ideas about relative strengths and weaknesses. I had intended to use its results to initiate discussions on implementing US strategy. But after an extended vacation with my wife in late summer and early autumn 1969, I moved to Washington around Thanksgiving, having been recruited by Kissinger to conduct studies for the National Security Council.

When I moved to the Department of Defense, Schlesinger wanted me to continue working on developing alternative Soviet GNP estimates and defense spending as well as assessments on strategic nuclear, maritime, and the Central Front in Europe. Several other net assessments were quickly added, including a so-called investment balance: assessing the share of defense spending by both the United States and the Soviet Union on capital stock (for example, military hardware) versus consumables (for example, fuel and ammunition). Eventually we did theater assessments of the Korean Peninsula, the northern flank of the North Atlantic Treaty Organization (NATO), and a broader Asian balance. Moreover, we looked at areas of warfare such as anti-submarine warfare, command and control, and power projection. Overall, about a dozen net assessments were conducted, several of which were done multiple times. We did not deserve an "A" on the Central Front assessment until about 1986 and the strategic nuclear balance also was a little like that. Somehow, finally, these efforts came together in a better way.

Because work on Soviet GNP and military spending were conducted in parallel with the net assessments, it corroborated the suspicion that Schlesinger and I thought the defense burden was larger than commonly believed. Igor Birman, a Soviet economist, who came to the United States in the mid-1970s, raised questions over the Soviet GNP estimate by the Intelligence Community. At the time, it was generally accepted that Soviet GNP was roughly 50 to 55 percent of US GNP and slowly increasing. In fact, most American economists thought the Soviet Union was catching up and some even predicted it would surpass the United States by the 1990s. These economists largely failed to exercise independent, critical judgment on this topic.

By the late 1970s, the demographer Murray Feshbach was identifying problems with Soviet conscripts. As a result, ONA sponsored a project to interview Russian emigrés to understand the recruitment system. Feshbach indicated that although the Soviet military traditionally was mostly of Slavic descent, Russians from Central Asia formed an increasing annual share of new conscripts. Interviews revealed that men of Central Asian ethnicity or descent were assigned to non-combat roles such as working as railway and construction troops or as cooks and bottle washers in line units. They did not serve as members of tank crews because they were not trusted to fight or were not fluent in Russian. Statements made by those involved in military training complained of the physical and mental skills of conscripts. Feshbach connected the complaints to contamination of the environment including the presence of heavy metals in the water supply.

Eventually, the relatively low skill level of Soviet recruits affected equipment maintenance and basic abilities in such areas as driving and map reading, which the US military did not face. This reinforced an insight that General Polk shared with me in the early 1970s about constraints on the Soviet military. By the early 1980s, a growing number of obstacles troubled the Soviets. When Ronald W. Reagan entered the White House, these findings matched to his inclination to drive home the advantages of the United States in the long-term competition.

It is notable that net assessments conducted at the time reflected the long-term competition framework that evolved from my work at RAND with Loftus and, especially, Schlesinger. This explains the character of the assessments; they were designed to assist the Secretary of Defense and the service chiefs in making decisions about the future. Though not necessarily the only kind of assessment that could be done, much experience was gained in conducting them. The long-term competition framework became useful in drawing attention to questions on the capability of competitors to sustain their effort. Addressing that question requires investigating the size of the military effort and other areas to maintain power at home, manage an empire, and further project power abroad. In regimes where protecting the leadership and its control over the institutions of state is paramount, there may be a tendency to spend more on defenses.

* * *

The lessons that I learned from Loftus suggest the sort of insight you can get from a careful review of the past. His reconstruction of Soviet behavior beginning at the end of World War II indicated enduring handicaps and asymmetries that characterized its approach during the Cold War. Above all, his insights revealed how different the Soviets were, underscoring the need to do thorough research and not assume that the competition was like us.

Chapter 1

What is Net Assessment?

James G. Roche and Thomas G. Mahnken

Net assessments utilize a multidisciplinary approach to defense analysis to capture the dynamics of national or coalition military strengths and weaknesses for comparison with the capabilities of competitors and adversaries. They offer insights to senior leaders on the relative military power of the United States vis-à-vis potential adversaries over time. Furthermore, assessments provide the basis of strategic decision-making. This chapter examines the concept of net assessment with special reference to developing strategy, presents alternative definitions of net assessment, and outlines the characteristics of an assessment. It concludes with an examination of the role of net assessment within the defense establishment over the years by focusing on the rivalry between the superpowers during the Cold War and its aftermath in the ensuing decades.

The Concept

While the term *net assessment* only entered the vernacular in the 1970s, the concept is quite old. Indeed, perhaps the earliest record of net assessments can be found in speeches by the Athenian *strategos* Pericles and Spartan leader Archidamus prior to the Peloponnesian War. Each of them, in turn, calculated the relative social, political, economic, and military strengths and weaknesses of both Athens and Sparta, examined various scenarios, and diagnosed the situation. Pointedly, they addressed their people and shared a basic assessment of the situation. But they differed in their prescriptions derived from net assessments: on one hand, Archidamus urged caution while, on the other, Pericles came out in favor of going to war against the Spartans.[1]

It is worth noting the characteristics that Archidamus and Pericles had in common.[2] First, both men were responsible political leaders with every incentive to examine a situation as clearly as possible. Moreover, each served as a political and military leader. Second, they acted on their own; they did not administer large bureaucracies. Third, they did not have staffs but spoke based on personal observations and information gleaned from conversing with trusted parties. What is more, one man could comprehend essentially all relevant details on geographic and political factors, military forces, methods of warfare, and partisan objectives. Fourth, they considered the situation as a whole and were not confined by artificial limitations. Finally, they did not rely on others to assess the strengths and weaknesses of their potential adversaries.

Those characteristics are worth remembering since practitioners of assessments likely face a different situation: they cannot personally understand all the relevant facts and they depend on large, enmeshed bureaucracies to process and control vital information. Both organizational and bureaucratic constraints on assessments are more evident today than in the past.

The concept of net assessment figures into classical strategic thought, even if the same term was not used. It is worth noting that the title of the first chapter of *the Art of War* by Sun Tzu can be translated as "On Assessments."[3] Indeed, the concept of net assessment lies at the heart of one of his now famous maxims: "Know the enemy and know yourself; in a hundred battles, you will never be in peril."[4] Accordingly, a reliable net assessment forms the bedrock of military success. *The Art of War* goes on to consider the nature of a net assessment:

> To gauge an outcome of war we must compare the two sides by assessing their relative strengths. This is to ask the following questions: Which ruler has the way? Which commander has the greater ability? Which side has the advantage of climate and terrain? Which army follows regulations and obeys orders more strictly? Which army has superior strength? Which officers and men are better trained? Which side is more strict and impartial in meting out rewards and punishments? On the basis of this comparison I know who will win and who will lose.[5]

Two things stand out in this description. First, it is the balance between the two sides and not the absolute capabilities of adversaries that matter. Second, many dimensions of military power that were identified by Sun Tzu are qualitative and not amenable to quantitative analysis.

The concept also is found in *On War* by Carl von Clausewitz where it emerges from the inquiry by the Prussian soldier-scholar into decisions on the use of force:

> To discover how much of our resources must be mobilized for war, we must first examine our own political aim and that of the enemy. We must gauge the strength and situation of the opposing state. We must gauge the character and abilities of its government and people and do the same in regard to our own. Finally, we must evaluate the political sympathies of other states and the effect the war may have on them. To assess these things in all their ramifications and diversity is plainly a colossal task. Rapid and correct appraisal of them clearly calls for the intuition of a

genius; to master all this complex mass by sheer methodological examination is obviously impossible.[6]

Despite the tradition of conducting net assessments, the process only began during the Cold War for several reasons. First, the United States faced a single, overwhelming threat that resulted in a focus on defense planning. Second, the threat was long-term: it became clear over time that the Cold War represented an enduring feature of the international order which required sustained effort. Third, nuclear weapons gave urgency to understanding the military balance: any missteps would be grave. Last, reductions in defense spending at the end of the Vietnam War questioned the long-term effectiveness of US strategy and put a premium on strategic thinking.

DEFINITIONS

Although no single definition of net assessment exists, a Department of Defense (DOD) directive describes it as the "comparative analysis of military, technological, political, economic, and other factors governing the relative military capability of nations."[7] Its purpose is identifying the issues that deserve the attention of senior officials. While capturing its essence, the description fails to portray the origin and evolution of the concept. Senior officials have a compelling need to assess the posture of the United States vis-à-vis potential adversaries taking into account of the relevant non-military variables. In fact, the comparisons should include more non-military variables, but typically that is too difficult. When allies are involved on both sides, such variables can become incommensurate to a degree that assumptions about them only provide background. But there are some major exceptions. Economics, demographics, education, etc., are sectors in which military comparisons can benefit greatly from an understanding of nonmilitary factors.

When asked in March 1972 to define the concept of a net assessment, Andrew W. Marshall who served on the National Security Council staff characterized it as "a comparison between the US and some rival nation in terms of some aspect of our national security activity" and "the most comprehensive form of analysis in the hierarchy of analysis." It should diagnose "problems and opportunities rather than recommending actions [and] provide an objective and comprehensive comparative analysis."[8] Two elements of this definition are notable. The first is that assessments should be comprehensive and multidisciplinary and the second that they should be diagnostic rather than prescriptive to understand the military balances rather than recommending courses of action. Writing five months later in August 1972, Marshall described net assessment as

> . . . a careful comparison of US weapon systems, forces, and policies in relation to those of other countries. It is comprehensive, including description of the forces, operational doctrines and practices, training regime, logistics, known or conjectured effectiveness in various environments, design practices and their effect on equipment costs and performance, and procurement practices and their influence on cost and lead times. The use of net assessment is intended to be diagnostic.[9]

Thus, net assessments comprise multidisciplinary analyses that are comparative, diagnostic, and forward-looking—the framework for evaluating military balances and strategic competition. Often, they are operationalized to diagnose strategic asymmetries between competitors and also identify opportunities and challenges in support of policymakers. As Marshall indicated in 1992, "I see the function of net assessment being to provide to top leadership a frank, well thought out, unbiased diagnosis of major problem areas and issues that they should pay more attention to."[10] Therefore net assessment is the precursor for strategic decision-making.

The net assessment approach has been influenced heavily by practice over the decades. As Paul Bracken noted: "The best way to define net assessment is to understand that it is a practice. It isn't an art (like military judgment), nor is it a science (like chemistry). Rather, it's a way of tackling problems from certain distinctive perspectives."[11] The scope of net assessment suggests the use of a different set of analytic techniques and tools than those employed by other analytical approaches. That is, because assessments look at large issues, the techniques used are different than those used in business, cost-benefit, or decision analyses. But there may be useful overlaps between net assessment and business and decision analysis. For example, whereas assessments seek to understand military balances and identify fields of long-term competitive advantage, the successful company devotes considerable energy to trying to understand where the firm stands relative to the competition. Similarly, where assessments seek to identify sources of uncertainty in military balances, business leaders operate under conditions of uncertainty over which they have little or no control, but which they must take into account. Markets are affected by actions and decisions but also by events outside the market, especially by governmental policies on tax, trade, currency, and education to name only a few. Thus, large business firms need to assess both current and potential effects of policies which influence decisions on research and development, location of production, distribution channels, labor, and operating costs.

NET ASSESSMENT CHARACTERISTICS

The approach used in net assessments can be characterized by a number of key features. The first is an emphasis on competitive interaction of national security organizations.[12] The approach may assume that relations among states and other participants are distinguished by neither conflict nor cooperation but instead by competing actors with differing objectives. Moreover, it assumes that the competitors are not strategically autistic but interactive and, similarly, that they may perceive the world differently and act accordingly. In military terms, this means different countries might have similar hardware but use it differently. In addition, it recognizes that the nature of military leadership involves national culture as well as military capabilities. For example, both Egypt and Syria acted differently than the Union of Soviet Socialist Republics (USSR) despite being armed with its equipment, trained in its operational doctrine, and advised by its mentors.[13]

Net assessments seek to incorporate such considerations into analyses as much as possible. The key aspect of net assessments during the Cold War was developing in-depth understanding of the way the Soviet armed forces thought about military power and warfighting. Soviet military operations were formed by the Marxist theory that the objective laws of war would yield success. As a result, operational art was formulated and executed from the top down.

Strategic geography also influenced Soviet thinking. For example, while the United States and, many years later, the Soviet Union developed aircraft carriers, they did this for different reasons. Carriers were means of power projection for the US Navy whereas they were sea-denial weapons for the Soviet Navy. However, one of the authors was told privately by a Soviet naval officer that his nation's first carrier was being built for the same purpose as American carriers: that is, power projection. Also, Soviet amphibious forces were intended for rapid operations against neighbors especially in the Baltic rather than for distant power-projection missions. Thus, the net assessment approach is based on the notion of a competitor who thinks differently about neighboring states than the United States, the trustworthiness of its forces, and national objectives.

A second major characteristic of the net assessment process is its emphasis on bureaucratic, organizational, and cultural factors that often result in sub-optimal behavior by both sides. It has been noted that, as humans, we think and act as we are organized. Soviet doctrine required harsh centralized control of operations. Devolved decision-making was not a critical part of the way of war for the Soviet Union. By contrast, the United States was comfortable devolving the decision-making process down to junior officers and senior enlisted men. Israeli armored forces borrowed parts of Russian doctrine and concepts of operation. Israeli tank commanders were amazed when exercising with American junior officers who were free, even required, to think on their own and lead their units in ways that supported the mission. Israeli officers waited until their leaders told them what to do next. In the Beka Valley, this led at times to small units ignoring their leaders to do what they wanted independently of the overall mission. These considerations are all the more important in an era of joint and combined warfare. How potential adversaries integrate different sorts of combat power can influence the overall effectiveness of their militaries. Concepts such as Air-Land Battle during the 1970s and 1980s and, more recently, Air-Sea Battle will influence the outcome of future conflicts, particularly when the fog of war is thickest.

A third characteristic of net assessment is the fact competitors enjoy limited resources and operate on the basis of imperfect information. Net assessment, like managerial economics and decision analysis, must deal with uncertainty. It also is comfortable using qualitative as well as quantitative data unlike, for example, systems analysis or cost-benefit analysis.[14] An example of early operations research was found in the equations of Frederick W. Lanchester wherein forces were evaluated based on numbers and particular rules used to determine or predict outcomes of military engagements.[15] Because of the difficulty in sensibly representing qualitative data with quantitative measures, this effort to structure conflict proved to be little more than an academic exercise. Decades later, the US Army Combat Analysis Agency developed a system known as *weapons effectiveness indicators/weighted unit values* or WEI/WUV to measure the potential of a given military force by quantifying firepower, mobility, and survivability of Soviet weapons as compared to selected US weapons. Similar to the Lanchester equations, this system attempted to measure the probability of combat success of opposing forces. By assigning different values to different weapons, it moved past the Lanchester analysis of World War I but was not compelling when measured against important historic roles of command and control, doctrine, morale, and leadership. For example, under either formulation, Israel should have lost every war to the Arabs because they were utterly outnumbered. Moreover, the Soviets should have won at Kiev against the Germans. But Israel won every war and Germany captured more than a half a million troops at Kiev although the Soviet forces were well equipped and fed, just not well led.

Analysis by the Soviets found battle outcomes are influenced by many qualitative factors and attempted to capture them in their *correlation of forces* analyses.[16] Although understanding the complexity of modern combat, the Soviets were unable to operationalize the concept of the correlation of forces. How to account for the morale and different levels of commitment of the belligerents? Or the value of the ingenuity and vision of opposing commanders? Or the relative value of command and control? Or the value of deception? To take one example, because of the effective deception campaign by the United States against Japan in World War II, the Imperial General Staff kept some 10,000 aircraft based in Hokkaido to counter American invasion forces coming from the north. In the event, the US military campaign to the south was considered by the Japanese to be a mere faint in preparation for a real assault from the north.

A fourth characteristic of net assessment flows from the three previous characteristics. It is an emphasis on asymmetry. One output of net assessment analyses is understanding *asymmetries* in doctrine, concepts of operations, and effectiveness of military systems and forces. Where are the key differences? What might be their impact on a conflict? Which ones could be useful for us? Which ones must we take into account and either counter or avert? Asymmetries often create opportunities for one side or the other when strategies are developed. A military that puts a premium on control of subordinate units can offer opportunities for adversaries to manipulate data available to the high command. Or, disrupting digital lines-of-communications can disrupt decision-making. Alternatively, some asymmetries should lead to the development of counter measures long before engaging in conflict. For example, technically unsophisticated adversaries relied on improvised explosive devices (IEDs) as a primary weapon which was extensively used. Few understood that *only* 12 percent of devices targeting Allied forces in Iraq and Afghanistan were effective. Initially, this meaningful asymmetry was not recognized and the IEDs extracted a high price in casualties, delayed movements, and upset operational planning. Eventually, supply routes were altered, drones inspected activity on the ground, time interval data was able to reconstruct where the IEDs were made, and those facilities were subsequently attacked.

A fifth characteristic of net assessment involves thinking in time, often over two to three decades. This approach attempts to reflect the time dimension of national military strengths and weaknesses relative to a potential adversary. As a result, net assessment places a heavy emphasis on analyzing long-term trends, including but not limited to those in the military sphere.

Eventually, the poor economics of the Soviet Union were overwhelmed by an ever-growing demand for technology and weapons considered necessary to compete with United States. By the late 1980s, the burden placed on the Soviet economy by the military was perhaps 40 percent, the Soviet gross national product came to only a quarter of that estimated by the United States, and the Soviet economy stopped growing. One could argue Americans outpaced the Soviets because of its superior education system, mobile workforce, positive demographics, and the meritocracy of capitalism. Thus, the Soviet Union lost the long-term, peacetime competition and, because of the nuclear arsenals of the superpowers, neither side met the other on the battlefield.

In assessing long-term trends, net assessments try to capture the pace and intensity of long-term competition. Rapid development of weapons and other capabilities, changes in the concept of operations over time (such as the Soviet notion of supplying forces by air which only evolved from flying large aircraft to a wholesale-retail model of flying large aircraft to hubs, transferring material to smaller aircraft, and flying closer to deployed forces), and exploratory deployments of troops, aircraft, and naval forces indicated the determination to operate far from Russia.

Managerial economics or business analysis and net assessment require understanding one's corporate strategy as well as that of current, close competitors, possible barriers to entry for some emerging competitors, and governmental attitudes toward these strategies. This is not easy. And it often represents major uncertainties highlighted or masked in business analysis. What are the enduring corporate interests? What of the interests of competitors? Where do competitors stand relatively in the marketplace? Are the strategies of the competitors reasonable? Will the firm be able to match any inroads by the competition that might affect its market share?

In military affairs, gaining an understanding the strategy of potential adversaries is equally or more complicated and often is gleaned from inferences drawn by the Intelligence Community. To better understand existing or emerging strengths and weaknesses of adversaries, assessments will seek to examine possible game changers or revolutions in military affairs. How are conflicts changed when precision weaponry is the rule rather than the exception?[17] Also, do sophisticated technology advances require a dramatic change in the capability to maintain them? For example, 35 years ago concern arose over outnumbered but superior Israeli forces confronting less-well-trained Arab militaries, which were often armed with sophisticated weapons. However, it actually turned out that potentially available sophisticated target-acquisition systems may have helped the Arabs, but that maintenance and care of such hardware greatly overstressed them.

Sixth, net assessment emphasizes multidisciplinary analysis. It includes considerable use of scenario analysis and wargaming to assess military balances. Normally, business analysis tries to capture information from a set of variables. What might appear as a simple problem of finding business or manufacturing facilities requires understanding the current and future business climate; state and federal taxes, labor, environmental, and regulatory policies; and infrastructure to support business. In some cases, quality of education or living standards become critical variables. Where will the skilled workers come from? To what extent do the local schools help or hinder obtaining and retaining talent? Similarly, net assessments take nonmilitary variables into account if they are germane to developing long-term strategy and decisions to implement it. In what might appear to be a simple problem, military decisions on which systems to build, where to build them, and where to deploy forces require consideration of variables running from quality of life to the political implications inherent in such decisions. For example, decisions on where to base forces, so-called force *bed-down* decisions, are among the most emotional decisions facing senior military leaders and are not typically susceptible to cost-benefit analyses.

Finally, net assessments are meant to be descriptive rather than prescriptive. Specifically, they set out to highlight two or three emerging problems or opportunities in given areas on which to enable senior officials such as the Secretary of Defense to base decision-making. This emphasis placed on emerging challenges and opportunities represents a unique feature of the approach.

One great virtue of any net assessment is limited aspirations. It does not attempt to predict the outcome of a particular battle or campaign. It does, however, seek to enumerate and evaluate the strengths and weaknesses of each side over time. And, it suggests answers for the future if it unfolds in particular ways in comparative strengths and weaknesses; stated or implicit strategies and interests; and quality of forces and their weapons and doctrine. By studying trends in forces, economics, demographics, and other factors, it looks for indicators of hostile strategic intent and compares them to what an adversary states and does over time. The underlying purpose to offer decision makers inputs for developing or adjusting long-term military strategy.

NET ASSESSMENT IN PRACTICE

Since the early 1970s, the ONA approach has been operationalized primarily by developing so-called *military balances* prepared for the Secretary of Defense. Each one was a specific net assessment. The subjects addressed indicated the comprehensiveness needed in calculating the position of the United States vis-à-vis real or potential adversaries. Most balances were updated every few years including strategic nuclear arms, US-USSR naval capabilities, Central Europe, power projection, anti-submarine warfare, command and control, the Middle East, Northeast Asia, and space. The development of studies required excursions into many areas to understand larger issues including how the Soviet Union assessed competition with the United States (scenarios, metrics, technical calculations, etc.); dollar-ruble modeling of the Soviet macro economy conducted by the Central Intelligence Agency; Soviet tank design, production, and operation; the implications of changing Soviet demographics; long-term changes in weather and their impact on the Soviet economy; and the influence of new technology on aging weapons systems.

Although these balances were being developed and the specific supporting studies and war games completed, the Pentagon had another office that focused on Net Technical Assessments of Research and Development, which concerned manufacturing, sustainability, and reliability of weapons systems. It worked closely with ONA and contributed relevant insights to net assessments. In addition, some effort was devoted to operational net assessments focused on differing military strategies, doctrine, tactics, and operational concepts of opposing forces. Such assessments were done by Air Force analysts and focused on the situation in Korea during the late 1970s.

The need will always exist for cost-benefit analyses in order to identify the pros and cons in selecting weapons systems and making budgetary decisions. What is more, it will be necessary to evaluate the position of the United States relative to current or potential adversaries. Where will adversaries place the focus of their efforts to succeed over time? How might their strengths and weaknesses eventually develop? How might their military capabilities be complemented by those of allies? And what actions can be taken to affect their strategic decisions? As the net assessment process continues to evolve, it will provide information and insights to assist decision-makers in the formulation and development of US military strategy.

Notes

1. Robert B. Strassler, ed., *The Landmark Thucydides* (New York: The Free Press, 1996), 1.80–81, 1.141–42.
2. The authors are grateful to Abram N. Shulsky for these insights.
3. Sun Tzu, *The Art of War*, trans. Roger Ames (New York: Ballentine Books, 1993), chapter 1.
4. Sun Tzu, *The Art of War*, trans. Samuel B. Griffith (Oxford; Oxford University Press, 1963), 84.
5. Sun Tzu, *The Art of War*, Ames trans., 103–104.
6. Carl von Clausewitz, *On War*, ed. and trans. Michael Howard and Peter Paret (Princeton, NJ: Princeton University Press, 1989), 585–86.
7. Department of Defense Directive 5111.11, "Director of Net Assessment" (December 23, 2009), 1.
8. Andrew W. Marshall, "The Nature and Scope of National Net Assessment," draft National Security Council memorandum, March 26, 1972, 2.
9. Andrew W. Marshall, "The Nature and Scope of Net Assessments," National Security Council memorandum (August 16, 1972), 1.
10. Interview of Andrew W. Marshall by Alfred Goldberg and Maurice Matloff (July 2, 1992), 20.
11. Paul Bracken, "Net Assessment: A Practical Guide," *Parameters* (Spring 2006): 91.
12. Stephen Peter Rosen, "Net Assessment as an Analytical Concept," in *On Not Confusing Ourselves*, ed. Andrew W. Marshall, J. J. Martin, and Henry S. Rowan (Boulder, CO: Westview Press, 1991), 283–301.
13. See Michael J. Eisenstadt and Kenneth M. Pollack, "Armies of Snow and Armies of Sand: The Impact of Soviet Military Doctrine on Arab Armies," in *The Diffusion of Military Technology and Ideas*, ed. Emily O. Goldman and Leslie C. Eliason (Palo Alto, CA: Stanford University Press, 2003).
14. On this comparison, see Eliot A. Cohen, "Net Assessment: An American Approach," memo 29 (Tel Aviv: Jaffee Center for Strategic Studies, 1990).
15. See Frederick W. Lanchester, *Aircraft in Warfare: The Dawn of the Fourth Arm* (London: Constable and Co., 1916); see also John W. R. Leppingwell, "The Laws of Combat?" *International Security* 12 (Summer 1987): 89–134.
16. See Michael J. Deane, *The Soviet Concept of the "Correlation of Forces"* (Arlington, VA: SRI International, 1972).

17. See, for example, Thomas G. Mahnken, "Weapons: The Growth and Spread of the Precision Strike Regime" in *The Modern American Military*, ed. David M. Kennedy (Oxford: Oxford University Press, 2013).

Chapter 2

Net Assessment in the Era of Superpower Competition

Barry D. Watts

One byproduct of the Cold War was interest at the highest levels of the US government in *net* comparisons of the respective military capabilities of the United States and the Soviet Union. An early manifestation of this was President Harry Truman's establishment of a Special Evaluation Subcommittee (SESC) under the National Security Council (NSC) on his final day in the Oval Office. By then it was becoming apparent that the growing nuclear capabilities of the Union of Soviet Socialist Republics (USSR) would eventually pose an existential threat to the United States. The new committee's task was to assess the "net capability of the USSR to inflict direct injury," including radioactive fall-out, on the Continental United States and key US installations overseas through July 1955.[1] Subsequently, under President Dwight Eisenhower, the SESC was renamed the Net Evaluation Subcommittee (NESC) and the NESC continued to provide annual assessments of the likely effects of a general nuclear war between the United States and the USSR through 1964.

Today the secretive NESC has been largely forgotten and net assessment has become identified with the Pentagon's Office of Net Assessment (ONA) and its long-serving first director, Andrew W. Marshall. Appointed by his close friend and former RAND colleague, then Secretary of Defense (SecDef) James R. Schlesinger, Marshall took up the job as the Pentagon's Director of Net Assessment in October 1973. The NESC was a precursor of Marshall's net assessment office but not the only one. Besides the NESC other antecedents included: the *net estimate* made by the Central Intelligence Agency and the Joint Staff in 1954; technical net assessments for the Director of Defense Research and Engineering (DDR&E) in the mid-1960s; early efforts by Marshall to assess the overall US-USSR military balance in 1970; and a national assessment of US and USSR ground forces by the NSC's Net Assessment Group (NAG) in 1973–1974. These various attempts to compare the military capabilities of the United States and its allies with those of the Soviet Union and its allies were all fundamentally motivated by the nuclear threat the USSR's nuclear forces posed to the United States during the Cold War.

This chapter has two aims. First, it reviews the principal antecedents to the Pentagon's Office of Net Assessment (ONA) in the Office of the Secretary of Defense (OSD). Second, it describes Marshall's development and use of diagnostic net assessment through the end of the Cold War.

The position Marshall occupied for some four decades was established by Secretary of Defense Melvin R. Laird in response to President Richard M. Nixon's restructuring of the US Foreign Intelligence Community in 1971.[2] Nixon's implementing memorandum included establishing a Net Assessment Group within the National Security Council. The NAG was intended to help Kissinger monitor reforms of US foreign intelligence and to oversee national net assessments.[3] Laird, however, balked at turning over responsibility for assessing military balances to the National Security Council and did not appoint a Director of Net Assessment during his tenure as SecDef. Instead he assigned the function to Colonel Donald S. Marshall, USA (Ret.).[4] Colonel Marshall headed a long-range planning element in the Executive Secretariat of the Office of the Secretary of Defense and had responsibility for net assessments from 1971 until late 1972 or early 1973.[5]

Andrew Marshall was the first to be officially appointed to fill to the position established by Laird in 1971, although Colonel Marshall could plausibly claim the distinction (if only briefly) of having been the Pentagon's original net assessor. But from 1973 to 2015 Andrew Marshall was the Pentagon's first and only Director of Net Assessment. When he retired at the age of 93 in early 2015, he had served 13 Secretaries of Defense starting in the Nixon administration. His extraordinary tenure explains why the net assessment enterprise has been so closely identified with him ever since.

THE NSC's NET EVALUATION SUBCOMMITTEE

Truman's establishment of the SESC was prompted by the perception in Washington that the Soviets were moving rapidly to deploy long-range bombers capable of striking the American homeland with atomic weapons. In August 1949 the Soviet Union had successfully detonated its first fission device, a copy of the implosion weapon (nicknamed Fat Man) dropped on Nagasaki in August 1945. In response to the USSR's first nuclear detonation (RDS-1, nicknamed Joe-1), on January 31, 1950, Truman announced that he had directed the Atomic Energy Commission to "continue its work on all forms of atomic weapons, including the so-called hydrogen or superbomb."[6] Two years later, in July, RAND researchers with close connections to the Los Alamos National Laboratory determined that both superpowers would be able to produce large numbers of thermonuclear (fusion) bombs with multiple megaton yields in the not too distant future.[7] Their prediction was validated four months later when the United States detonated a staged, radiation-implosion, 82-ton thermonuclear device (Mike) that yielded a 10.4-megaton (MT) explosion. In November 1955 the Soviets followed suit with their first true (staged) fusion bomb (RDS-37). This 3MT weapon, dropped from a Tu-16 medium bomber, was scaled down to 1.6 MT for the November test.

When Truman created the SESC, Soviet long-range aviation (LRA) did not possess bombers with a range to strike targets in North America from bases in Russia and then return home, although Western European targets were within reach and one-way bombing missions against the Continental United States were possible.[8] For its initial analysis the SESC assumed that Tu-4s, Russian reversed engineered copies of the US B-29, could reach any target in the United States on one-way missions.[9] In fact, the Tu-4's actual performance was so inferior to the B-29's that even on one-way missions the Soviet bomber could not reach the northeast United States with a 5-ton fission bomb.[10] Nevertheless, it was logical to assume that Soviet intercontinental range bombers would eventually be fielded, and nuclear-capable regiments of long-range Bison B bombers and Tu-95 Bear bombers entered service in 1956 and 1957, respectively.[11]

The SESC issued its first report in June 1953. The document assumed LRA would target bomber bases in the United States, Europe, and the Far East as well as mount the "heaviest possible attack . . . upon major population, industrial and control complexes in the continental United States."[12] It warned that in such an attack, 24 to 30 percent of Soviet bombers would be lost, the US population would suffer between 9 and 12.5 million casualties (half fatal), and the industrial base would initially be paralyzed in the targeted areas.[13] Nevertheless, the report concluded that the damage inflicted on the United States "would not be such as to prevent delivery of [a] powerful initial retaliatory atomic air attack, continuation of [the] air offensive, and *successful prosecution of the war*" [emphasis in the original].[14]

Through 1964, the NESC continued conducting annual studies of the "net capabilities of the USSR, in the event of general war, to inflict direct damage upon the United States and to provide a continual watch for changes that would significantly alter those net capabilities."[15] However, in December 1964 Secretary of Defense Robert S. McNamara advised President Lyndon B. Johnson that the NESC's studies had outlived their usefulness because they did not provide "a basis for planning guidance."[16] According to McNamara, the Special Studies Group on the Joint Staff and the annual project lists issued by the Secretary of Defense were more useful in illuminating the specific problems associated with structuring and budgeting US strategic-nuclear forces. As a result, in March 1965 the Net Evaluation Subcommittee was judged to have served its purpose and discontinued. [17] Yet within a few years General Leon W. Johnson, USAF (Ret.), who had headed the NESC from 1961 to 1964, began advocating the restoration of a similar evaluation group on the NSC.[18]

THE 1954 NET ESTIMATE

At a meeting of the National Security Council in early 1954, President Eisenhower lamented that the foreign intelligence he received neither clearly distinguished between Soviet capabilities and intentions nor weighed their capabilities against estimates of US capabilities.[19] Instead he wanted net evaluations comparable to the commander's estimate that Major General Sir Kenneth Strong had prepared for him during World War II. Therefore, he tasked Allen W. Dulles, the Director of the Central Intelligence (DCI), and Admiral Arthur W. Radford, USN, the Chairman of the Joint Chiefs of Staff, to prepare a net estimate of the probable outcome of a general war with the Soviet Union. Dulles delegated the task to Lieutenant General Harold R. Bull, USA, of the National Estimates Board, who in turn chose Ray S. Cline to work on the estimate at the Pentagon. Radford detailed Rear Admiral Thomas H. Robbins, USN, to oversee the effort by the Joint Staff. However, Robbins delegated this responsibility to staff officers who reportedly had no clue initially what to do.[20] The upshot was that Cline both structured the analysis and wrote the estimate.

Cline invoked the authority of the Chairman of the Joint Chiefs of Staff to gain use of a first-generation, vacuum-tube computer in the basement of the Pentagon and to have experienced military wargamers in the Washington area detailed to Pentagon.[21] Additionally, he reduced the interaction between the attacking and defending sides to formulas that enabled the "war" to be "fought" on the computer. These developments resulted in what Cline later called interesting discoveries, the main ones being that it would be an act of desperation for the USSR to attack with substantially inferior long-range airpower and that America's extensive radar warning systems would make it impossible for LRA to achieve surprise.[22]

The 1954 estimate overseen by Cline did not develop into a standing organization to conduct periodic net assessments. Nevertheless, the implications of the net estimate were more sensible than those implied by the damage estimates in the SESC's 1953 report (NSC 140/1), although not for the reasons Cline later cited.[23] In the wake of the Berlin blockade and the Korean War, many in the American national security community worried that the Soviet Union would soon resort to direct military action in the hope of achieving world domination. Looking back in 1976 Cline argued that both the 1954 net estimate and the national intelligence estimates (NIEs) of that period "succeeded in reducing the Soviet military threat to the United States to reasonable proportions in the minds of war-planning staffs," thereby using analysis to render an invaluable service to the Nation.[24]

In the case of Cline's 1954 net estimate, his analytic conclusions regarding the Soviet threat were, according to his own account, grounded on computer analysis of the likely outcome of a US-Soviet nuclear war. Even today, however, there are compelling reasons to doubt the ability of even the most advanced computer models to predict actual war outcomes with confidence. As RAND's Paul Davis observed in 1988, "war outcomes are sensitive to scores of factors, rather than the handful regularly discussed," and this sensitivity generates such massive uncertainty that it is meaningless to talk about "best-estimate" outcomes.[25] After studying the results of a conflict between the North Atlantic Treaty Organization

(NATO) and the Warsaw Pact in the 1980s using a state-of-the-art wargaming model (namely, the RAND Strategy Assessment System), Davis concluded that:

> The results of . . . multiscenario analytic war gaming defy reductionist analysis: simulated war outcomes often change drastically with what might naively be considered to be small changes of assumption, and even the relative value of alternative improvement measures varies substantially from scenario to scenario. Measures or capabilities critical in some circumstances are almost irrelevant in others.
>
> These wild fluctuations are not analytic artifacts, but rather a manifestation of something that professional military officers and historians have known since time immemorial, that war is an incredibly complex phenomenon characterized by uncertainty—except, for example, in instances where one side has overwhelming force (a situation that does not obtain in Europe). Moreover, tactics, strategy, and other human factors matter *greatly*.[26]

Notwithstanding huge uncertainty inherent in computer predictions of war outcomes, reasons existed in the 1950s to doubt that Soviet leaders were on the brink of unleashing LRA to mount a surprise atomic attack on the United States, as Cline had concluded in the net estimate in 1954. At the time, communications intelligence would have given American leaders ample warning of LRA preparations for such an attack. To highlight a fundamental asymmetry in the nuclear postures of the US and USSR, Soviet leaders were unwilling to trust their bomber crews with nuclear-armed bombers, fearing that disgruntled pilots might turn them on the Bolshevik regime. Nuclear weapons were not even stored at LRA bases and, during the 1950s, it would have taken LRA regiments between six and eight hours to load bombs on board waiting Soviet planes once the weapons had arrived.[27] By contrast, early in the Cold War US political leaders not only permitted Strategic Air Command (SAC) to store nuclear weapons at SAC bases but trusted its aircrews to sit 15-minute ground alert with nuclear-armed bombers and, during the 1960s, fly airborne alert missions with B-52s carrying nuclear weapons.[28]

After Moscow had begun deploying intercontinental ballistic missiles (ICBMs), Marshall with his RAND colleague, Joseph Loftus, concluded that even the Soviet ICBM force "had not been designed for quick reaction," a capability that was central to SAC's deterrent posture throughout the Cold War.[29] This difference over the control of nuclear weapons revealed weaknesses in Soviet nuclear posture that were rarely exposed in comparisons of US and Soviet strategic forces.[30] Thus, the reduction of the Soviet threat in Cline's 1954 net estimate was justifiable, though not for the quantitative force-exchange calculations usually cited.

NET TECHNICAL ASSESSMENT

John S. Foster, Jr., who served as DDR&E from 1965 to 1973, brought in Nils Fredrick Wikner to be his special assistant for comparative threat assessments of US and Soviet military weaponry and to track the evolution of Soviet advances to minimize the risks of technological surprise.[31] Because of this focus, the resulting net technical assessments were narrower than the kinds of military balances Marshall's ONA produced later. When Marshall became Schlesinger's Director of Net Assessment in 1973 the two men quickly decided that ONA should concentrate on three principal areas of military competition: the US-USSR strategic-nuclear balance because of the overriding US goal of deterring nuclear war; the NATO-Warsaw Pact military balance because a conventional war in Europe was the most likely trigger for an all-out US-USSR nuclear exchange; and the US-USSR maritime balance as catch-all for power projection and strategic mobility.[32] By August 1974, a fourth major area was added to ONA's core portfolio: a military-investment balance that compared the defense economics of the United States and the USSR, with emphasis on Soviet research and development (R&D) as a leading indicator of future Soviet capabilities. This fourth balance area was added because of Schlesinger's skepticism (shared by Marshall) regarding CIA's insistence that the USSR's military burden—military and military related spending as a percentage of Soviet gross national product (GNP)—was similar to America's. Schlesinger's doubts over this estimate peaked during his brief tenure as Director of Central Intelligence in the first half of 1973. He and Marshall, being economists, saw the inconsistency of CIA's burden estimate with two other CIA judgments: first, that the USSR's GNP was at least half of US GNP; and, second, that Soviet military expenditures had to be 150-160 percent greater than what the United States was spending.[33] Taken together, these two judgments argued that the USSR's burden was at least double that of the United States. Nonetheless, CIA analysts were adamant that, in the early 1970s, the USSR's military burden, like that of the United States, was around six or seven percent of GNP.[34]

The USSR's military burden exemplifies the kinds of the broader, contextual factors ONA's military balances sought to incorporate. The strategic-nuclear, NATO-Warsaw Pact, and maritime balances not only aimed to compare the quantities of men and equipment of various types on the opposing sides but aspired to take into account the doctrine, geography and terrain, mobilization capabilities, training, logistics, and other qualitative factors likely to affect war outcomes. Technical comparisons of weapon systems could be included in ONA's assessments, but the former were much narrower than the latter. Perhaps the one area of overlap between ONA's US-USSR investment balance and DDR&E's technical assessments was in estimating the dollar costs of Soviet weapon systems. If representative of Soviet weaponry in general, the estimate that the F-4 cost four times as much as the MiG-21 had implications for the quantities of front-line equipment the United States and the USSR could afford to field in the long run.

Aside from issues of breadth and scope, the other reason for mentioning DDR&E's net technical assessments is that they simulated Andrew Marshall to begin thinking about what would be involved in conducting comprehensive net assessments. Wikner asked RAND to evaluate US-

USSR RDT&E [research, development, test and evaluation] programs, systems, and technologies.[35] Marshall got the assignment and in 1971 concluded that the existing methodologies for net assessments of any sort were inadequate, the requisite databases were poor, and no single comparison was sufficient.[36] However, if the United States wanted to pursue a more selective R&D strategy in order to become a more effective long-term competitor, assessing the various areas of military technology in comparison with Soviet weaponry would be beneficial.[37] The need for such a strategy, he argued, was that the Soviets were "overtaking us or challenging us in a number of areas in which the U.S. was previously comfortably ahead" and, consequently, "some broad diagnostic assessments" must be developed to understand in detail how the United States was "doing relative to the Soviets."[38] This idea would become a central theme in Marshall's subsequent development of diagnostic net assessment.

KISSINGER, THE SPECIAL DEFENSE PANEL, AND MARSHALL'S "FIRST" NET ASSESSMENT

In September 1969 Henry Kissinger asked Marshall to meet with him in Washington to discuss intelligence matters. When they met, Kissinger explained that President Nixon was unhappy with the intelligence reaching the White House and asked Marshall to look into the matter.[39] This encounter eventually resulted in the revival of net assessments by the National Security Council. Marshall became a part-time NSC consultant at the end of 1969 and got involved in other initiatives that culminated in moving to the Pentagon to set up a net assessment program for Schlesinger.

One of these initiatives was Kissinger's Special Defense Panel. It was undertaken in 1970 after Marshall presented his report on the intelligence reaching the Oval Office. It sprang from attempts to negotiate a strategic arms control agreement with the Soviet Union. President Lyndon Johnson had first suggested negotiations to limit both sides' nuclear forces in

1967. The two superpowers agreed to talks in the summer of 1968, and full-scale negotiations began in November 1969 under Kissinger in Washington and the head of the Arms Control and Disarmament Agency, Gerard Smith, in Helsinki. However, by late 1970 Kissinger became concerned that Moscow might stonewall the talks or otherwise misbehave. Accordingly, he organized the Special Defense Panel under K. Wayne Smith to develop options to pressure the Soviets if they started dragging their feet on arms control. In addition to Marshall, the Special Defense Panel included Andrew J. Goodpaster, Charles M. Herzfeld, Frederic S. Hoffman, William W. Kaufmann, Laurence E. Lynn, Jr., and Schlesinger. Early on Herzfeld suggested that an assessment be done of the overall US-USSR military balance, including long-term trends, as context for the panel's recommendations.[40] Marshall and Schlesinger volunteered to undertake this task, but Marshall ended up doing the writing because Schlesinger had his hands full dealing with the defense portfolio in the Office of Management and Budget (OMB), the successor to the Bureau of the Budget.

Marshall later called the comparison of US-USSR force postures as, "in effect, a first net assessment."[41] The one seemingly unambiguous insight that emerged from this early effort was that US military forces were "high-cost relative to Soviet forces."[42] What exactly this implied, however, was less clear. Although much of the evidence supported claims that US weapons generally cost more than their Soviet counterparts, American armaments often provided greater capabilities. This point suggests that comparisons of US and Soviet forces might not have been giving the US enough credit. Nonetheless, it seemed at the time that the Soviet Union was better at turning resources into weapons. This impression led Marshall to suggest that the United States might be "pricing itself out of the military competition with the Soviets, or at least severely handicapping itself."[43] What is more, this first assessment stressed the considerable importance of having better, more precise net assessments of where the United States' forces stood relative to those of the USSR. Accordingly, Marshall as well as others became convinced in the early 1970s that a national-level net assessment program was required. Crude metrics of the US-USSR balance had been acceptable when the United States was far ahead of the Soviet Union in offensive strategic-nuclear forces, naval forces, and military R&D. But by the early 1970s the Soviets had "caught up in almost all of these [areas]" and appeared to be on the brink "of passing us."[44] Hence the need to understand precisely the military position of United States vis-à-vis the Soviet Union—a competition that gave every sign of continuing for the foreseeable future. After all, the Cold War had not turned hot despite fears to the contrary and it appeared reasonable to anticipate that the superpower arms competition would basically remain a peacetime one.

Although the initial effort at comparing the overall US and USSR force postures highlighted the need for careful net assessments, Marshall's results in 1970 fell short of providing much in the way of definitive insights. It was evident to Marshall that comparing the number of weapons each side had in specific categories was grossly insufficient. Instead, it was necessary to employ "adequate means of assessing capabilities of one force to deal with another in specific contingencies"; in addition, much of the relevant intelligence data was skimpy or unavailable, especially in areas such as readiness and logistics.[45] As a result, the 1970 assessment included a four-page section discussing the nature of the net assessment problem. Rather than offering confident conclusions about the US position, Marshall instead offered the hypothesis "that the Soviets may be more efficient and effective in designing, procuring, and operating military forces" than the United States.[46] Later events would suggest that the concern about the United States "pricing itself out of many of the key military competitions" was overstated.[47] But in 1970 it seemed a definite possibility and it took considerable subsequent research and effort on ONA's part to place this initial judgment in its broader context.

In hindsight the analytic difficulties and data shortfalls encountered in the 1970 assessment for the Special Defense Panel could scarcely have surprised Marshall. In 1966 he had written a RAND paper entitled "The

Problems of Estimating Military Power." In introducing the conceptual problems of estimating relative military power he wrote:

> [M]ost attempts to explicitly measure military power are mere tabulations of forces of various sorts: the numbers of men under arms, the numbers of weapons of a given type, etc. This is itself an evasion of the problem of estimating military power, since it says nothing about the actual capabilities of the forces of one country to deal with another. For one thing, the geographical relationships of the countries and the availability of bases and logistic supply conditions are very significant to the outcome of any conflict between the forces described only in these terms. Merely adding up all U.S. forces and comparing them with Soviet forces, actual or potential, present or future, does not really tell one very much. One has to appeal to certain implicit notions as to how military engagements would in fact come out before such listings would have any significance.[48]

Marshall concluded that the "problems in constructing an adequate or useful measure of military power have not yet been faced"; defining "an adequate measure looks hard, and making estimates in real situations looks even harder."[49] Among other things, weighing relative military power faces the intractable problem of taking into account various nonquantifiable factors that affect outcomes in specific situations. This problem remains as stubbornly resistant to easy or mechanistic solutions today as it did back in 1966. Marshall's attempt in 1970 to assess the US-USSR military balance simply underscored the difficulty in measuring relative military power, whether in peacetime military competitions or in time of war.

IMPROVING FOREIGN INTELLIGENCE, NIXON'S BLUE RIBBON DEFENSE PANEL, AND NSC'S NET ASSESSMENT GROUP

Recall that Kissinger originally brought Marshall to the NSC to evaluate the flow and quality of foreign intelligence coming into the White

House. Both Nixon and Kissinger were dissatisfied with what they had been receiving, and Marshall agreed to review the situation and make suggestions on the processes by which intelligence flowed into the Oval Office. In December 1969 Marshall started interviewing representatives of those agencies responsible for providing intelligence to the White House as well as reviewing key documents such as the President's Daily Brief (PBD), which was regarded as CIA's premier deliverable to the president. Two fundamental questions soon emerged: how did intelligence managers decide what to send to the White House and how could those products be improved to better satisfy Nixon and Kissinger?

Marshall soon found out that Nixon no longer even read the President's Daily Brief.[50] Instead, as evidenced by his marginal comments, he paid greater attention to the competing intelligence summary generated by the NSC staff. Moreover, interviews revealed that CIA managers thought they were the best judges of the intelligence the President should receive and continued to provide what they considered relevant even though he was not reading the PBD. Marshall completed his report to Kissinger on the intelligence flowing into the Oval Office in May 1970. The report was more diagnostic than prescriptive, in part because of Marshall's uncertainty about what intelligence Kissinger, Larry Lynn, and others immediately concerned with specific national-security decisions and problems really needed.[51] As far as Marshall could tell, the Central Intelligence Agency was not withholding information from the White House, and the analyses of hard data and the factual reporting on Soviet forces appeared to be good. On the other hand, he found CIA's assumptions about Soviet behavior to be poor, including reliance on a "model of the Soviet government as a single unified actor pursuing an easily stated strategy."[52] This criticism reiterated the earlier concern over the rational-actor model of Soviet behavior that Marshall and Loftus had raised at RAND in the late 1950s. From their perspective the overreliance on this model of Moscow's decision-making limited understanding of past Soviet force posture decisions as well as the ability to better forecast the USSR's future choices. But regarding changes that might lead to intelligence that better satisfied the needs of Nixon, Kissinger, and other decision makers, Marshall's main suggestions were, first, better communication of White House needs to the intelligence community and, second, instituting new procedures to get non-standard products.[53]

In 1969 Nixon had established a Blue Ribbon Defense Panel headed by Gilbert H. Fitzhugh, the Chairman and Chief Executive Officer of Metropolitan Life Insurance, to examine defense organization and management. In 1970, as Marshall was completing his report on the quality-of-foreign-intelligence, staffers from the Fitzhugh Panel visited him. They wanted him to include in his report the recommendation that a net assessment activity be started on the National Security Council. While Marshall thought the idea had merit, he did not think it had much to do with the quality of intelligence being provided to the White House, so he did not include it.[54] But the idea of such activity did not end with Marshall's May 1970 report to Kissinger.

The Blue Ribbon Defense Panel delivered its report, *Defense for Peace*, to Nixon and Laird in July 1970. The Panel's 113 recommendations included establishing a net assessment group reporting directly to the Secretary of Defense on US and foreign military capabilities along with a long-range planning group to integrate assessments, technological projections, fiscal planning, and so forth.[55] Despite this recommendation Laird did not elect to create a net assessment activity in OSD in 1970. Later, after Marshall had moved to the Pentagon, Laird became curious about who among the Panel members had pushed this recommendation and what the underlying rationale had been. The member of the Blue Ribbon Panel who most strongly advocated establishing the Net Assessment Group in the OSD happened to be Rubin F. Mettler, the President and Chief Executive Officer of TRW. His motivation was based on the conviction that the SecDef needed a net assessment activity that could produce a comprehensive picture of the state of US-Soviet competition, where the competition was headed, and what the biggest issues were.[56] Mettler's view of what net assessment's aims should be was very close to the concept Marshall developed in 1972.

During 1970-1971 Marshall was drawn into other NSC projects. Having delivered his quality-of-foreign-intelligence report to Kissinger, Marshall agreed to oversee a follow-on study. The idea was to select an element of the USSR's ballistic missile program and do an in-depth, exemplar study. The heavy R-36 ICBM (designated the SS-9 by Western intelligence) was chosen, and over the next nine months Marshall supervised a CIA effort to lay out the design and bureaucratic history of the SS-9 and its antecedents.[57] This study was completed in late 1971. Together with the Special Defense Panel's initial attempt to assess the overall US-USSR military balance it was growing apparent that US-Soviet military competition would have to be parsed into a series of subbalances, starting with a comparison of US and USSR intercontinental nuclear forces. Also, the analytic metrics for assessing the strategic nuclear balance would be very different from those appropriate for assessing the military balance in Central Europe or the maritime competition.

While Marshall remained engaged in these projects, Nixon decided to restructure the foreign intelligence community. In late 1970 the President along with Kissinger and George P. Shultz, who headed OMB, called for a study of the Intelligence Community aimed at reorganizing it. The President intended to make changes and cut the intelligence budget by 25 percent.[58] Schlesinger was tasked to review the increases in the number and budgets of US intelligence agencies, identifying aspects that had not resulted in corresponding improvements in the intelligence produced.[59] Problems included the increasingly fragmented and disorganized distribution of intelligence functions; the community's domination by unproductively duplicative competition in collection; unplanned and unguided growth; and the high costs of the United States' growing reliance on technical collection systems such as reconnaissance satellites.[60] To address these problems, Schlesinger recommended that the intelligence community be reorganized as a first step toward making the quality of its products more commensurate with their costs. A decision was made to give the Director of Central Intelligence greater control over the Intelligence Community as well as responsibility for intelligence planning, review, coordination, evaluation, and production.[61] In addition, Schlesinger recommended establishing a National Security Council Intelligence Committee (NSCIC). The NSCIC would be chaired by Kissinger and represent the concerns of policy-level intelligence consumers.[62] The changes would be made by the President under his executive authority.[63]

In the wake of Schlesinger's study Kissinger asked Wayne Smith to begin developing the specific changes to the foreign intelligence community to satisfy the president. Smith, in turn, asked Marshall to be Kissinger's person on the effort. Schlesinger had a cell working for him in OMB that followed the intelligence community, and this cell did a good deal of the work in deciding on specifics. With the main changes having been decided upon, Marshall was asked in September 1971 to draft the final decision memorandum for Nixon along with letters on the reorganization to DCI Richard Helms at the CIA and Secretary Laird at the Defense Department. Once Marshall had finishing drafting these documents, Al Haig and Wayne Smith began brokering them within the administration to gain general acceptance. It was they, not Marshall, who added the paragraph to Nixon's November 1971 directive reorganizing foreign intelligence that established a Net Assessment Group (NAG) within the NSC. Once the NAG was added Haig and Smith started lobbying Marshall to head the new office, which he officially did in April 1972.[64]

MARSHALL'S CONCEPTION OF DIAGNOSTIC NET ASSESSMENT

The title of the organization notwithstanding, the NAG was initially focused on helping Kissinger manage the intelligence reorganization. In fact, the first assessor Marshall hired for the NAG, George E. "Chip" Pickett, was selected in part because of his background in military intelligence. What is more, the NAG's responsibility for producing assessments of US vis-à-vis foreign military capabilities did not sit well with Laird who felt that national net assessments fell within the purview of the Pentagon and not the National Security Council. His opposition had two immediate consequences. First, he established the position of the Director of Net Assessment in the Office of the Secretary of Defense in December 1971. But, as mentioned earlier, he did not appoint anyone to the position. Instead, his special assistant, William J. Baroody, Jr., assigned responsibility for net assessments to a long-range planning unit in Laird's Executive Secretariat under Colonel Donald S. Marshall. But when Colonel Marshall left the Executive Secretariat to work for Wikner, the net assessment activity in the Pentagon was orphaned.[65] Second, Kissinger was not inclined to contest whether the NSC or the Department of Defense (DoD) should oversee national net assessments with a defense secretary as politically powerful as Laird. As a result Kissinger delayed starting a national net assessment program until the spring of 1973, after Laird had been succeeded by Eliot L. Richardson in January.

The national net assessment program finally got underway on March 29, 1973, when Kissinger signed National Security Study Memorandum (NSSM) 178, "Program for National Net Assessment."[66] Marshall then convened an ad hoc group to develop guidelines and procedures for conducting national net assessments.[67] Kissinger approved the group's recommendations on June 28, 1973, in National Security Decision Memorandum (NSDM) 224, "National Net Assessment Process, NSSM 178."[68] And on September 1, 1973, Kissinger signed NSSM 186, which directed that the first national net assessment compare the costs and capabilities of US and Soviet ground forces and be run by the Department of Defense.[69]

The delay in starting national net assessments frustrated Marshall but gave him time to develop his own conception of net assessment. In April 1972 Marshall sent Air Force Colonel Harold Hitchens a draft paper in which he attempted to outline the net assessment enterprise as he conceived it. In his cover note he highlighted two emerging themes about the nature and scope of such assessments. First, although the notion of net assessment was not well defined, current usage envisioned it as "a comparison of U.S. forces, programs, [and] capabilities (perhaps plus Allies), with those of potential opponents"; and, second, net assessments, in contrast to other analyses, would be "the most comprehensive, and in principle concern themselves with actual outcomes of combat or of competitions."[70] In addition, Marshall's draft went on to explain that the aim of national net assessments should be to provide even-handed diagnoses of emerging problems and opportunities in the US-Soviet competition rather than recommend specific actions or solutions.[71]

In August 1972, Marshall finalized the draft paper he had sent Hitchens. It contained the following conception of diagnostic net assessment:

> [I]t is a careful comparison of U.S. weapon systems, forces, and policies in relation to those of other countries. It is comprehensive, including description of the forces, operational doctrines and practices, training regime[s], logistics, known or conjectured effectiveness in various environments, design practices and their effect on equipment costs and performance, and procurement practices and their influence on cost and lead times. The use of net assessment is intended to be diagnostic. It will highlight efficiency and inefficiency in the way we and others do things, and areas of comparative advantage with respect to our rivals. It is not intended to provide recommendations as to force levels or force structures as an output.[72]

Marshall's two-and-a-half page memo went on to observe that net assessment in his sense "is not an easy task" and would require "sustained hard intellectual effort" for a number of reasons, including the virtual "non-existence" of appropriate analytic methods, the fact that data problems "abound" even regarding US forces, and the low priority the intelligence community had given to some aspects of Soviet forces important to good net assessments.[73]

The NSSM 186 (Phase I) Assessment and Moving to DoD

The NSSM 186 assessment of US and Soviet ground forces was overseen by Marshall but not actually done by him or his small NAG staff. Instead, NSSM 186 was conducted by an interagency working group headed by Robert A. Stone from the Office of the Assistant Secretary of Defense, Program Analysis and Evaluation (PA&E).[74] Officers and analysts from the Joint Staff, DDR&E, the US Army, and the Marine Corps were brought in to assess American ground forces; Defense Intelligence Agency (DIA) and CIA experts were tasked to evaluate Soviet forces.[75] In addition, Patrick J. Parker, the Deputy Assistant Secretary of Defense for Intelligence Assessment, chaired NSSM 186's steering group.[76] By the time this assessment was completed in April 1974, Marshall, his two net assessors ("Chip" Pickett and Robin B. Pirie), along with two secretaries (Jo Hunerwadel and Lexi Crow), had moved to the Pentagon. Again, their move was engineered by Schlesinger who replaced Richardson as SecDef in mid-1973 and pressed Marshall to move the net assessment function to OSD. With Kissinger's acquiescence the transfer took place in October 1973, the same month as the Yom Kippur War.[77]

It is difficult to overstate the significance of transferring the net assessment function from the National Security Council to the Department of Defense. Previously, net assessments were conducted by the department or agency with the primary interest and responsibility for the area of study with other participants included on working groups as required.[78] The problem that emerged during the NSSM 186 assessment in 1973–1974 concerned the inclination of some participants to protect the vested interests of their organizations rather than conduct the sort of no-holds-barred analysis Marshall desired. When Marshall and Schlesinger read the ground-forces assessment in April 1974 they discovered it amounted to a lowest-common-denominator analysis, lacking any judgments that might ruffle bureaucratic feathers. The NSSM 186 report was basically a descriptive account of the opposing ground forces and argued that no conclusions could be drawn from the asymmetries between them, especially regarding whether the United States or the USSR was more efficient or successful in converting resources into ground combat power and capabilities. Any substantive judgments on the overall military balance required taking factors into account such as contributions of US mobility and the tactical air forces of the US and their European allies.[79] Furthermore, because the entire Army and Marine Corps would not be fighting the entire Soviet Army in any plausible scenario, the study proffered no context for thinking about possible combat outcomes against meaningful objectives. At the same time the data and intelligence gaps proved to be worse than expected. In the event, NSSM 186 was not a net assessment. In fact, in some areas NSSM 186 defied common sense. For instance, DIA experts on the Russian military insisted that the semi-annual influx of raw conscripts into the Soviet army did not affect readiness.[80]

Marshall and Schlesinger's disappointment over the NSSM 186 study reinforced their desire to establish in OSD a radically different approach to doing net assessments than had been envisioned for the NSC's NAG.[81] Instead of interagency working groups, future net assessments would be researched and written by one or two members of Marshall's staff under his supervision. The assessments would be done specifically for the Secretary of Defense to help him with the long-term strategic management issues facing the Defense Department in the most important military competitions. ONA's assessments would endeavor to highlight one or two of the most pressing emerging problems or attractive opportunities for the United States to compete more effectively and would do so early enough for the SecDef to still have time to make decisions about them. There would be no set schedule for producing net assessments and, perhaps most significantly, ONA's balances would not be coordinated or vetted by any other part of the Pentagon bureaucracy before going to the SecDef. Finally, ONA would have a research budget to enable the office to draw upon individuals and organizations outside the US government, including outside the US intelligence community.

With a few limited exceptions during certain periods, these are broadly the guidelines under which ONA has operated to this day.[82] While originally laid down by Schlesinger, these guidelines were later accepted by both Donald Rumsfeld and Harold Brown between 1975 and 1980.[83] Their acceptance of these unusual bureaucratic arrangements was pivotal to Marshall's net assessment enterprise becoming an enduring Pentagon institution. Looking back, Marshall was, and remained, convinced that net assessment would not have evolved the way it did after 1973 without the fortuitous move to the Pentagon.[84]

ONA IN THE LATE 1970s AND 1980s

The first order of business once Marshall arrived at the Pentagon was to begin developing a capability to produce the kinds of careful comparisons of US (and allied) forces with those of competitors and adversaries he had envisioned back in 1971 and 1972. Under Schlesinger, ONA's assessments were not the long, highly classified balances that Marshall's office began forwarding to Secretary Brown in early 1977 after Brown had succeeded Rumsfeld. The data required to assess long-term trends took years to gather, particularly on NATO forces.[85] Moreover, in the 1960s at RAND Schlesinger and Marshall had become close personally and intellectually. Schlesinger realized that Marshall was so bright that he could see patterns and implications without having the underlying data —that is, the detailed, comprehensive information most people required to reach the same conclusions.[86] So during Schlesinger's time as SecDef lengthy net assessments were unnecessary. Instead, Marshall regularly visited Schlesinger in his Pentagon office and conveyed the state of various balances with a graph here, a table there, and various other bits and pieces of information.[87] The two men also had private time together when the Marshalls travelled with the Schlesingers. That relationship enabled Marshall to convey net assessments to Schlesinger in an informal and unstructured manner.

Things changed in the autumn of 1975, around Halloween, when President Gerald R. Ford replaced Schlesinger with Rumsfeld. In the aftermath of what the press dubbed the "Halloween Massacre" Marshall anticipated going back to California and RAND. Instead, Rumsfeld made it clear that he wanted net assessment to continue under the guidelines established by Schlesinger. Realizing that a simple graph or table would no longer suffice to convey the state of various US-USSR balances, Marshall began pushing his small staff to prepare more comprehensive assessments.

The first two of these more fulsome balances were completed in early 1977 after Harold Brown had succeeded Rumsfeld. The first, in February, was a US-Soviet Anti-Submarine Warfare (ASW) balance; the other, in March, a US-Soviet strategic-nuclear assessment. Marshall forwarded five more assessments to Brown in 1978, including the NATO-Warsaw Pact, military investment, and maritime balances. Of these seven assessments only the European balance written by Lieutenant Colonel Peter R. Bankson has been declassified. Since almost all of ONA's assessments right down to the present day remain classified, it is difficult to provide more than broad impressions of their contents and conclusions.

Figure 1a. The Structure of ONA's Early Balances.

Net Assessment of Soviet Military Balance for Special Defense Panel (1970)
>   A. Trends in the Role and Use of Military Force
>   B. Facts and Trends in the Current Military Balance
>   I. The Nature of the Net Assessment Problem
>   II. Ground Forces
>   III. Naval Forces
>   IV. Tactical Air Forces
>   V. Air Defense
>   VI. Strategic Offensive Forces
>   VII. Perceived Similarities and Differences in the Defense Planning Process
>   VIII. Conclusions and Recommendations

General Structure of Cold War Net Assessments (1976)
>   I. Basic Assessment
>   II. Key Asymmetries
>   III. Major Uncertainties
>   IV. Emerging Problems and Opportunities

Figure 1b. The Structure of ONA's Early Balances (Cont.).

"The Military Balance in Europe" (1978)

    I. Introduction

    II. Basic Assessment

    III. Context of the Balance

        • *how war comes*

        • *technological modernization*

        • *the influence of the strategic balance*

        • *theater nuclear forces*

        • *conventional forces—Central Region*

        • *the role of aviation and air defense forces*

        • *command, control and communications (C3)*

        • *counter C3*

        • *force deployment*

        • *sustainability*

        • *chemical operations*

        • *NATO flanks*

        • *major uncertainties*

    IV. Key Issues

        • *thinking about how war might come*

        • *countering soviet emphasis on radio-electronic combat*

        • *focusing on deterrence*

Nevertheless, Figure 1 provides some insight into the general structure of net assessments during this period as well as the wide range of factors and forces they attempted to take into account. As the table of contents for ONA's 1978 NATO-Warsaw Pact balance indicates, the assessment highlighted three issues for Secretary Brown's attention. In this instance all three were essentially problems rather than opportunities that the United States or NATO might be able to exploit to advantage. The first, about how war might come in Europe, raised the need to develop a richer set of scenarios that would force the alliance to think through crisis management, enhance deterrence in periods of increased tension, make the transition from peacetime to wartime if deterrence failed, and speed up mobilization.[88] The second addressed the realization that Soviet radio electronic combat (REC) doctrine viewed command, control and communications (C3) as being far more critical to combat effectiveness than did NATO doctrine. The Soviets had singled out C3 as an increasingly pivotal aspect of war, studied it in a comprehensive way that their American counterparts had not, made extensive preparations to disrupt or destroy NATO C3 down to the battalion level, and had hardened their own C3 far more extensively than had NATO or US forces in Europe. The American approach to C3 was fragmented, ad hoc, tactical rather than strategic, and focused on data processing and sensors.[89] The third issue this assessment highlighted was that while deterrence of war in Europe depended on such things as Soviet perceptions of the correlation of forces between NATO and the Warsaw Pact, we had limited understanding of how the Soviets actually assessed the balance of forces in Europe.[90]

This last problem, of course, also affected the even more critical issue of deterring a general nuclear war between the United States and the Soviet Union. As Marshall wrote in 1982:

> Since the major American objective is deterrence of the Soviet Union from a wide range of activities, a major component of any assessment of the adequacy of the strategic [nuclear] balance should be our best approximation to a Soviet-style assessment of the strategic balance. But this should not be the standard U.S. calculations done with slightly different assumptions about missile accuracies, silo hardness, etc. Rather it should be, to the extent possible, an assessment structured as the Soviets would structure it, using those scenarios they see as the most likely and their criteria and ways of measuring outcomes. This is not just a point of logical nicety since there is every reason to believe that the Soviet assessments are likely to be structured much differently from their U.S. counterparts. The Soviet calculations are likely

to make different assumptions about scenarios and objectives, focus attention upon different variables, include both long-range and theater forces (conventional as well as nuclear), and may at the technical assessment level perform different calculations, use different measures of effectiveness, and perhaps use different assessment processes and methods.[91]

By the time these words appeared in *Policy Sciences*, better understanding of Soviet assessments had become one of the two or three most important lines of supporting research for ONA's balances.[92] Because none of ONA's assessments of the US-Soviet strategic-nuclear balance have been declassified, it is difficult to say much about their conclusions. However, by the time the joint SecDef/DCI assessment of US and Soviet intercontinental nuclear forces was completed in late 1983, Marshall believed that considerable progress had been made in understanding Soviet assessments. Indeed, better insight into Soviet assessments appears to have been one of the main reasons both ONA and the CIA judged US strategic-nuclear forces in the early 1980s to be adequate to deter a Soviet nuclear attack on the US homeland. In this area at least, ONA's judgment about the adequacy of the balance aligned with the CIA's. National Intelligence Estimate (NIE) 11-3/8-83, *Soviet Capabilities for Strategic Nuclear Conflict, 1983-93*, focused on the USSR's strategy, plans, operations, and capabilities as the CIA believed Soviet leaders perceive them."[93] Despite the intelligence gaps, uncertainties, and ongoing modernization of Soviet nuclear forces, NIE 11-3/8-83 concluded that "The Soviets see little likelihood that the United States would initiate a surprise nuclear attack from a normal peacetime posture; we believe it is unlikely that the Soviets would mount such an attack themselves."[94] NIE 11-3/8-82, the previous February, offered a similar judgment: "Soviet leaders have stated that nuclear war with the United States would be a catastrophe that must be avoided if possible and that they do not regard such a conflict as inevitable".[95]

These judgments about Soviet attitudes regarding nuclear war appear to have been accurate. Interviews with former high-ranking Soviet general staff officers in the early 1990s revealed that while Soviet leaders thought nuclear forces had political and deterrent value, by the early 1970s they had concluded that intercontinental nuclear capabilities had no military utility and their use should be avoided.[96] Thus, despite the USSR's achievement of rough nuclear parity in the early 1970s, ONA concluded that there was "an adequate balance in the size and capabilities of US and Soviet strategic forces," a judgment which remained Marshall's view during the rest of the Cold War.[97]

THE REAGAN YEARS

When Ronald W. Reagan succeeded Jimmy Carter as president in 1981, Caspar W. Weinberger succeeded Harold Brown as the Secretary of Defense. The new administration's outlook led quickly to the perception in ONA that the new defense secretary neither needed nor valued the kinds of careful net assessments the office had produced for Secretary Brown. Under Brown, ONA had not only produced ten mature net assessments in a three-year period but Marshall and his deputy, Commander James Roche, had been the DoD representatives to the Comprehensive Net Assessment that Carter had initiated in 1977 on the NSC under Zbigniew Brzezinski. Weinberger shared Reagan's view that the United States had fallen behind the Soviet Union in key areas of military competition and the first order of business for the Pentagon was building up US forces. Because net assessments had been diagnostic rather than prescriptive, ONA's products had little to offer Weinberger in his endeavor to begin catching up with the Soviet Union by substantially increasing defense spending.

Reagan saw the Cold War as fundamentally a struggle of competing ideas and economic systems. He regarded the Soviet system as politically illegitimate and economically flawed, and he believed that representative democracy and free markets could defeat the USSR.[98] Privately, he saw the United States as having fallen dangerously behind the Soviet Union, especially in intercontinental nuclear forces. Armed with the political mandate of a landslide election victory in 1980, Reagan was able to win Congress' support for major increases in defense spending. From fiscal year (FY) 1980 to FY 1985, US defense spending grew some fifty percent, and Weinberger's overriding priority was to figure out how the Defense Department could absorb the additional funding. As a start National Security Decision Directive 12, "Strategic Forces Modernization Program," called for making US strategic C3 more survivable, modernizing the bomber force with the B-1 and B-2, developing a more accurate D-5 submarine launched ballistic missile (SLBM), beginning research on advanced air and space defenses, and fielding 100 operational MX land-based ICBMs.[99]

Another development early in the Reagan administration that affected ONA was the desire of Weinberger and the new DCI, William Casey, to get the Defense Department and the CIA working together. Under Brown, DCI Stansfield Turner had suggested getting the CIA into the net assessment business. Brown had rebuffed this suggestion, including categorically rejecting Turner's request to acquire Pentagon data on US forces. Not surprisingly Brown's response led to tension and bruised feelings between the CIA and the Defense Department toward the end of the Carter administration.

Following a 1981 meeting between Weinberger and Casey steps were taken to remedy this situation. Weinberger and Casey agreed that "net assessments, when undertaken, would be published under the joint auspices of the Secretary of Defense and the Director of Central Intelligence," and DoD would also provide a freer flow of US force data to the intelligence community.[100] The first collaborative SecDef/DCI net assessment was to be on US and Soviet strategic-nuclear forces and was to be published after the next version of NIE 11-3/8-83, *Soviet Capabilities for Strategic Nuclear Conflict, 1982-92*, which appeared in February 1983.

Marshall oversaw the preparation of the SecDef/DCI net assessment for the Defense Department. Henry S. Rowen, chairman of the National Intelligence Council and former president of the RAND Corporation, directed the effort for the Central Intelligence Agency. The result was a two-volume assessment completed in November 1983. Volume 1 was a short executive summary largely drafted by US Navy captain Charles Pease in ONA and Lawrence Gershwin, who was the national intelligence officer for Soviet strategic forces at CIA. Volume 1 contained the key judgments about the US-Soviet competition in nuclear forces and, due to its sensitivity and classification, received very limited distribution. Volume 2, which ran over 350 pages, contained detailed information on both sides' forces and capabilities for intercontinental nuclear war. Though also highly classified, Volume 2 was given wider distribution than Volume 1.

In hindsight, Marshall deemed the 1983 SecDef/DCI assessment of strategic nuclear forces to have been the "most satisfactory assessment" of this balance ONA ever produced.[101] In large part, this success could be attributed to progress made since the first ONA nuclear assessment in 1977 on understanding Soviet assessments of the competition. Given this understanding, Marshall's view of the US-Soviet competition in nuclear arms during the 1980s does not appear to have been nearly as pessimistic as Reagan's was when he became president. Granted, the administration had not found a solution to the growing vulnerability of US land-based ICBMs. But even in the late 1980s, Marshall remained convinced that Soviet leaders were not at all inclined to risk all-out war, either by the first use of nuclear weapons or a conventional attack on Western Europe.[102] As a result, US intercontinental nuclear forces were considered to be adequate in deterring a nuclear war with the USSR.

After the SecDef/DCI assessment of strategic forces was completed, Marshall and Rowen considered working on a second joint balance. But in light of the heavy burden the nuclear assessment had imposed on the CIA's analysts, Rowen demurred. On the CIA's side many of the same analysts who had supported the SecDef/DCI assessment had also been tasked during the same period to develop NIE 11-3/8 on Soviet capabilities for strategic nuclear conflict. Rowen therefore had no appetite for embarking on a second joint net assessment. Neither Weinberger nor Casey was inclined to force the issue. That ended the Reagan administration's early inclination to have net assessments done jointly by the DoD and the CIA. For the balance of the rest of Reagan's presidency, ONA net assessments defaulted to what they had been under Schlesinger, Rumsfeld, and Brown: a purely DoD enterprise conducted by Marshall and his small ONA staff and written for the personal use of the defense secretary.

Another change that occurred during Reagan's second term was subordinating ONA to the Under Secretary of Defense for Policy, Fred Charles Iklé. Iklé had been a colleague of Marshall's at RAND and was the Under Secretary of Defense for Policy from 1981 to 1988. Reflecting Weinberger's lack of interest in the kinds of careful net assessments ONA had produced under Harold Brown, Iklé's approach was to utilize Marshall's office to conduct various special projects. Laird's 1971 directive establishing the office had the Director of Net Assessment reporting solely to the Secretary of Defense. In September 1985, the directive was revised to make Marshall the principal advisor on net assessment matters to both Iklé and Weinberger.[103] This allowed Marshall to conduct assessments as he had previously done, but fewer net assessments were completed during the Reagan years than had been produced during the Carter years.

COMPETITIVE STRATEGIES

By the beginning of the second Reagan administration Weinberger had become sensitive to widespread criticism of his defense strategy, which appeared to be little more than requests for ever larger defense budgets. In response, Weinberger turned to Graham T. Allison at Harvard University's Kennedy School of Government to be his special advisor on strategy. As of the summer of 1985 Allison was dividing his time between Harvard and the Pentagon. When in Washington he occupied an office near the Secretary. Having worked closely with Marshall at RAND in the 1960s, it was natural for Allison to turn to his former mentor for ideas to help bolster Weinberger's credibility as a strategist. Marshall immediately offered an idea he had suggested to Iklé four years earlier, namely, cost-imposing or *competitive* strategies.[104] It was not a complicated concept and arose from a question Marshall had raised earlier: What sort of strategies should the United States adopt to be more effective in the continuing peacetime competition with the Soviets?[105] Marshall recommended developing strategies that capitalized on enduring US strengths while exploiting the persistent weaknesses and vulnerabilities of the USSR.[106]

Weinberger embraced the idea. In his February 1986 annual report to Congress he announced that competitive strategies would serve as a major theme of the Defense Department for the balance of the Reagan administration.[107] When Frank Carlucci replaced Weinberger in 1987 he renewed the effort to institutionalize competitive strategies in the Pentagon.[108] In the meantime, however, the military services and Joint Staff gradually undermined the competitive strategies effort. To the extent such strategies were possible, they believed that whatever could be done was already being done. Behind this attitude was the fear that competitive strategies could be used by the SecDef to alter the preferred force postures and acquisition programs of the military services. Consequently, even before Richard Cheney succeeded Carlucci as SecDef in 1989, the opposition from the services and the Joint Staff managed to neuter competitive strategies, and the administration of George H. W. Bush did not choose to pursue the initiative.

THE SOVIET DEFENSE BURDEN

Prior to being appointed the Secretary of Defense in July 1973, Schlesinger had served as the Director of Central Intelligence for five months. During those months he and Marshall regularly got together to discuss intelligence issues. Perhaps the most consequential matter was CIA estimates of the burden that Moscow's military spending imposed on the Soviet economy. At the time, the intelligence agency's economists estimated that Soviet military spending was consuming only 6 to 7 percent of the USSR's gross national product (GNP).[109] But, as mentioned earlier, CIA estimates of the dollar costs of Soviet military programs indicated that Moscow also was outspending Washington in absolute terms (see Figure 2). At the same time CIA analysts also insisted that Soviet GNP amounted to around 55 percent of US GNP.

Figure 2. US-USSR Military Spending, 1964–1976.

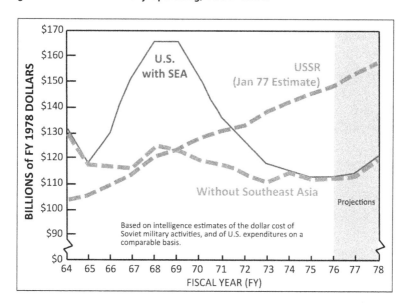

Source: Donald H. Rumsfeld, "Annual Department of Defense Report for Fiscal Year 1978" (Washington, DC: Office of the Secretary of Defense, January 17, 1977), 3.

Schlesinger and Marshall simply could not reconcile CIA's estimates of Soviet military spending and the size of the Soviet economy with the Agency's estimate of the USSR's military burden. If the Soviet economy was around half the size of the American economy and the Soviets were outspending the US military in absolute terms, then the USSR's military burden had to be much higher than the official CIA estimate of 6 to 7 percent. As DCI Schlesinger had asked CIA's economists to reexamine their estimates of the USSR's military burden, but they were not immediately inclined to do so.

Consequently, when Marshall moved to the Pentagon in October 1973, one of the first assignments Schlesinger gave him was to continue pressing the CIA on the burden issue. The resulting burden paper by Edward Proctor was forwarded to Schlesinger in April 1975. To the frustration of Schlesinger and Marshall its central conclusion was that the USSR's military burden was "less than 8 percent of GNP."[110] In other words, the CIA's economists had not appreciably revised their burden estimates since Schlesinger's brief tour as DCI in 1973. By the time Proctor's paper reached the Pentagon Marshall had privately concluded that Soviet military activities likely absorbed 10 to 20 percent of GNP rather than the 6 to 8 percent reported in past CIA analyses.[111] Thus began a controversy between ONA and CIA that continued through the Cold War's end.

In May 1976 new estimates of Soviet defense spending in rubles (rather than dollars) did lead CIA to increase its estimate of Moscow's defense burden to the lower end of Marshall's 1975 estimate. The paper's main finding was that since 1970 "*defense requirements had been absorbing 11-13 percent of [Soviet] GNP (vice less than 8 percent), depending on whether defense was defined narrowly (U.S. definition) or broadly (Soviet definition)* [emphasis in the original].[112] This "bombshell," as CIA analysts Noel E. Firth and James H. Noren called it, generated mistrust of CIA's estimates of Soviet defense spending even among senior CIA managers, including Robert Gates.[113] Although official CIA estimates of the USSR's military burden never exceeded 14–16 percent through 1990, Gates later wrote that he judged the burden to have been "between 25 and 40 percent."[114]

From ONA's standpoint, most of the disagreement from the early 1970s to the 1980s with the CIA estimates of the ratio between Soviet military spending and the USSR's GNP concerned what should be included in the numerator. As Marshall wrote in a prepared statement for the Joint Economic Committee in 1987, there appeared to be at least three distinct tranches to Soviet military spending. The first included men, equipment, research and development, military portions of the space program, atomic weapons, etc., which were visible to intelligence sources such as satellite reconnaissance.[115] But there were two other tranches: one included "civil defense, industrial mobilization preparations, [and] dual use investments" such as ensuring that Aeroflot airliners and Moscow's commercial fishing fleet could transport military equipment in wartime; the other was the cost of maintaining the USSR's external empire in Eastern Europe and elsewhere.[116] At this juncture Marshall's guess was that these three tranches had amounted to between 20 and 30 percent of Soviet GNP over the prior ten years.[117]

This was not the end of the story, however. There was also a problem with the denominator. As early as 1979, the émigré Soviet economist Igor Birman had alerted Marshall to the likelihood that CIA was substantially overestimating the size of the USSR's GNP. If Birman was right, then the denominator in CIA burden estimates was too large. In addition, Marshall discovered in 2001 that there was a fourth spending tranche that had been invisible to US intelligence. At a meeting in Paris with Colonel Vitaly Shlykov, who had formerly served in the planning section of the Soviet General Staff, the Russian revealed that Moscow had produced and maintained "gigantic war reserve stocks" based on exaggerated estimates of likely US war production in the event of a mobilization similar to World War II.[118] Taking into account Shlykov's fourth tranche and reducing Soviet GNP to around 25 per cent of the US economy, Marshall later estimated that Soviet military spending during the last decades of the Cold War had probably been somewhere in the range of between 35 and 50 percent of the USSR's GNP.[119] In sum, ONA's successive estimates of the USSR's military burden were much closer to the truth than the Central Intelligence Agency's from the early 1970s to the Cold War's end.

The disagreement between ONA and CIA over the magnitude of the burden imposed on the Soviet economy by military expenditures and programs goes to the heart of diagnostic net assessment as Marshall developed and practiced it from 1973 to 1991. Marshall's longevity enabled him to continue pushing the intelligence community on the burden issue over nearly two decades. His budget for outside research allowed him to fund studies on this issue outside the government by a number of scholars, including émigrés such as Birman and Western researchers such as Marshall's former RAND colleagues Henry Rowen and Charles Wolf. Indeed, most of the "alternative" research outside the US intelligence community on Soviet military spending during the second half of the Cold War was funded by ONA. The Office of Net Assessment, therefore, was able to provide an independent voice on an issue fundamental to US Cold War strategy unencumbered by the institutional positions of government bureaucracies. ONA's analytic independence and ability to tailor its products to the long-term strategic management needs of defense secretaries constituted the office's competitive advantage. As Harold Brown later recalled, during his tenure as defense secretary ONA's studies and reports were different from those sent to him by other parts of the Pentagon.

> They started from a different premise: that is, stand back, we're in this competition which goes beyond the military, but we have this competitor, [and] what he does is going to depend on what we do. [And] what we do is going to depend on what he does. [So] what are our fundamental advantages, disadvantages, and how you adopt strategies and take steps that rest on your competitive advantage?[120]

Marshall's assessments, Brown emphasized, always included the political advantages the United States might have as well as the military ones, and highlighted both sides' strengths and weaknesses by integrating qualitative factors along with quantitative data.

* * *

Net assessment became a recurring US government activity with Truman's founding of the NSC's Special Evaluation Subcommittee in January 1953. Renamed the Net Evaluation Subcommittee under Eisenhower, annual assessments of the likely results of a general nuclear war with the USSR continued until McNamara disestablished the NESC in 1965. Within a few years, however, calls to reestablish a net assessment function within the NSC or the Defense Department emerged, eventually leading to Nixon's creation of the NSC's Net Assessment Group in 1971. Andrew Marshall, who had been a consultant to the NSC, was asked to head the NAG, which led to him entering government service. With the first national net assessment underway Kissinger acquiesced to Schlesinger's request to transfer both Marshall, his small staff, and the NAG's net assessment function to the Pentagon in October 1973, where it remains to this day. With Schlesinger's support Marshall then began developing diagnostic net assessment as a new form of analysis intended to provide defense secretaries and other senior DoD managers with early warning of emerging strategic problems and opportunities. During the 1970s and 1980s, ONA's balances sought to provide careful assessments of where the United States and its allies stood relative to the USSR and its allies in the most important areas of military competition: namely the strategic-nuclear, European, maritime and investment balances.

Even before the Cold War ended, however, Marshall's focus began to shift to the prospect of a revolution in military affairs brought about by the integration of precision conventional weapons and wide-area sensors with computerized battle networks. During the 1990s much of ONA's analysis and efforts focused on getting the military services to begin thinking about the long-term implications of a mature precision-strike regime. Arguably the analytic framework for diagnostic net assessment that Marshall developed in the early 1970s proved adaptable to this very different issue about future war.

Notes

1. Willard C. Matthias, *America's Strategic Blunders: Intelligence Analysis and National Security Policy, 1936–1991* (University Park: Pennsylvania State University, 2001), 111. The SESC was chaired by Lieutenant General Ida Edwards, USAF (Ret.) with Matthias as his staff assistant.
2. Melvin R. Laird, DOD Directive 5105.39, "Director of Net Assessment," December 6, 1971.
3. Richard M. Nixon, "Organization and Management of the US Foreign Intelligence Community," November 5, 1971, 6 (released October 31, 2002).
4. James R. Schlesinger, "Net Assessment," memorandum, October 13, 1973.
5. US Department of Defense, Directive 5105.39, "Director of Net Assessment" (Washington, DC: Office of the Secretary of Defense, December 6, 1971).
6. Harry S. Truman, "Statement by the President on the Hydrogen Bomb," in *The American Atom: A Documentary History of Nuclear Policies from the Discovery of Fission to the Present*, ed. Philip L. Cantelon, Richard G. Hewlett, and Robert C. Williams (Philadelphia: University of Pennsylvania Press, 1984), 127.
7. Bernard Brodie, Charles Hitch, and Ernst Plesset, "Implications of Large-Yield Nuclear Weapons," R-237 (Santa Monica, CA: RAND Corporation, July 10, 1952), iii, 1, 2, 17.
8. James S. Lay, "Directive for a Net Capabilities Evaluation Subcommittee" (Washington, DC: National Security Council, June 23, 1954; declassified February 1987).
9. William Z. Slany, Lisle A. Rose, and Neal H. Petersen, eds., *Foreign Relations of the United States, 1952–1954*, vol. 2, part 1, *National Security Affairs* (Washington, DC: US Government Printing Office, 1984), 335.
10. Steven J. Zaloga, *The Kremlin's Nuclear Sword: The Rise and Fall of Russia's Strategic Nuclear Forces, 1945–2000* (Washington, DC: Smithsonian Institution Press, 2002), 15–16. On a round-trip mission from northern bases in the eastern Soviet Union, the Tu-4 could not even reach the State of Washington.
11. Pavel Podvig, Oleg Bukharin, Timur Kadyshev, Eugene Miasnikov, Igor Sutyagin, Maxim Tarasenko, and Boris Zhelezov, eds., *Russian Strategic Nuclear Forces* (Cambridge, MA: MIT Press, 2001), 350, 375–377, 382; and

Zaloga, *Nuclear Sword*, 26, 28. The M-4 (Bison A) was used to deceive Western military attachés in 1955 about Russian heavy bomber production. The M-4 was later redesigned to provide the necessary range to reach the Continental United States on two-way missions.

12. Slany, Rose, and Petersen, eds., *Foreign Relations of the United States, 1952–1954*, vol. 2, part 1, *National Security Affairs*, 332–333.

13. Robert R. Bowie, "Summary Evaluation of the Net Capability of the USSR to Inflict Direct Damage on the United States up to July 1, 1955," memorandum for the Secretary of State, NSC 140/1 (Washington, DC: National Security Council, June 2, 1953; declassified March 1976), 1.

14. Ibid., 2.

15. David S. Peterson, *Foreign Relations of the United States, 1964–1968*, vol. 10, *National Security Policy* (Washington, DC: US Government Printing Office, 2002), 202. Until recently only a few SESC/NESC reports were available. In July 2014, however, the National Security Archive at The George Washington University published the majority of them.

16. Peterson, *Foreign Relations*, vol. 10, 202.

17. McGeorge Bundy, "Discontinuance of the Net Evaluation Subcommittee of the National Security Council," National Security Action Memorandum 327 (Washington, DC: National Security Council, March 18, 1965).

18. Leon W. Johnson, memorandum to Robin B. Foster, Stanford Research Institute (December 9, 1968), 2–3.

19. Stephen E. Ambrose with Richard H. Immerman, *Ike's Spies: Eisenhower and the Espionage Establishment* (New York: Doubleday, 1981), 253.

20. Ray S. Cline, *Secrets, Spies and Scholars: Blueprint of the Essential CIA* (Washington, DC: Acropolis Books, 1976), 141.

21. Ambrose, *Ike's Spies*, 234.

22. Cline, *Secrets*, 142.

23. US, Executive Office of the President, National Security Council, NSC 140/1, "Report to National Security Council by the Special Evaluation Subcommittee of the National Security Council" (Edwards Report) (Washington, DC: The White House, May 18, 1953).

24. Cline, *Secrets*, 143.

25. Paul K. Davis, "The Role of Uncertainty in Assessing the NATO-Pact Central Region Balance," N-2839-RC (Santa Monica, CA: RAND Corporation, 1988), v, vii, 9, 14.

26. Ibid., v.

27. Marc Trachtenberg, *History and Strategy* (Princeton, NJ: Princeton University Press, 1991), 29.

28. At the height of the Cuban Missile Crisis in 1962, the Strategic Air Command had 66 B-52s armed with nuclear weapons operating on 24-hour airborne alert missions. Bernard C. Nalty, "The Air Force Role in Five Crises, 195–1968: Lebanon, Taiwan, Congo, Cuba, Dominican Republic" (Washington, DC: USAF Historical Division Liaison Office, June 1968), 43.

29. Ibid., 30.

30. Loftus pointed out that if American leaders were reluctant to give the military with full control of nuclear weapons, then Soviet leaders were even less likely to do so based on its sensitivity to possibilities of dissident groups obtaining nuclear weapons and using them against the regime. Joseph E. Loftus, "Ten Minutes on the Next Ten Years," D(L) 2726 (Santa Monica, CA: RAND Corporation, February 14, 1955), 2–4.

31. Andrew W. Marshall, "Net Assessment in the Department of Defense," memorandum for record (September 21, 1976), 2.

32. Andrew W. Marshall, "Comments on the US/Soviet Navy Net Assessment," memorandum for Rear Admiral Harry D. Train II, USN (February 7, 1974), 1.

33. James R. Schlesinger, keynote address, Kennan Institute and Woodrow Wilson Center conference, March 27–28, 2002, in Blair A. Ruble, *U.S. Assessments of the Soviet and Post-Soviet Russian Economy: Lessons Learned and Not Learned* (Washington, DC: Woodrow Wilson Center for International Scholars, November 2002), Occasional Paper #243, p. 117.

34. Noel E. Firth and James H. Noren, *Soviet Defense Spending: A History of Estimates, 1950–1990* (College Station, TX: Texas A&M Press, 1998), 54–55. In Fiscal Year (FY) 1972, US spending on national defense was 6.7 percent of gross domestic product (GDP), and fell to 5.9 percent in FY 1973 as the United States withdrew from Vietnam (Office of the Under Secretary of Defense (Comptroller), "National Defense Budget Estimates for FY 2013," March 2012, 265).

35. Andrew W. Marshall, "Comparisons, R&D Strategy, and Policy Issues," WN-7630-DDRE (Santa Monica, CA: RAND Corporation, October 1971; declassified July 2005), iii.

36. Ibid., vii.

37. Ibid., 26.

38. Ibid., 3, 28.

39. Andrew W. Marshall, "1969–1975," interview, transcribed by Kurt Guthe, December 14, 1993, 5–9 and 5–10. The page reference 5–9 refers

to the ninth page in the fifth of the eleven interviews Guthe did with Marshall.

40. Ibid., 5–14.

41. Ibid.

42. Andrew W. Marshall, "Net Assessment of US and Soviet Force Posture: Summary, Conclusions and Recommendations" (September 1970; declassified March 2004), 1–2.

43. Ibid., 2.

44. Ibid., 2.

45. Ibid., 1.

46. Andrew W. Marshall, "Net Assessment of US and Soviet Force Posture" (September 1970; declassified March 2004), 3.

47. Ibid., 23.

48. Andrew W. Marshall, "The Problems of Estimating Military Power," P-3417 (Santa Monica, CA: RAND Corporation, August 1966), 2.

49. Ibid., 9.

50. Marshall, "1969–1975," interview, 5–11 and 5–12.

51. Andrew W. Marshall, "Intelligence Inputs for Major Issues: A Substantive Evaluation and Proposal for Improvement," memorandum for Henry A. Kissinger (Washington, DC: National Security Council, May 1, 1970), 3.

52. Ibid., 2; and Marshall, "1969–1975," interview, 5–12.

53. Marshall, "Early 1950s," interview, September 16, 1993," 4–5; Marshall, "1981–1984," interview, July 26, 1994, 7–9.

54. Marshall, "1969–1975," interview, December 14, 1993, 5–14 and 5–15.

55. Blue Ribbon Defense Panel, Defense for Peace: Report to the President and the Secretary of Defense on the Department of Defense (Washington, DC: July 1, 1970), 7, 59, 212–216.

56. Marshall, "1969–1975," interview, December 14, 1993, 5–15.

57. Marshall, "1969–1975," interview, 5–13 to 5–14. The R-36 (SS-9) has been called as the "red Titan" with a throw-weight of over five tons. See Zaloga, Nuclear Sword, 109, 111–112.

58. Marshall, "1969–75," interview, 5–16.

59. James R. Schlesinger, "A Review of the Intelligence Community" (March 10, 1971), 1. The Director of Central Intelligence at the outset of the Nixon administration was Richard M. Helms. On Schlesinger's intelligence review from a CIA perspective, see Douglas F. Garthoff, Directors of Central Intelligence as Leaders of the US Intelligence Community, 1946–2005 (Washington, DC: Central Intelligence Agency, 2005), 65–69.

60. Schlesinger, "Intelligence Community," 5, 8, 9, 10. The literature survey on the Intelligence Community dating to 1960 concluded that its cumulative impact was more negative than its achievements. See "An Historical Review of Studies of the Intelligence Community for the Commission on the Organization of the Government for the Conduct of Foreign Policy" (Washington, DC: Central Intelligence Agency, December 1974).

61. Schlesinger, "Intelligence Community," 29–30.

62. Ibid., 31–33; and Richard M. Nixon, "Organization and Management of the US Foreign Intelligence Community," memorandum (Washington, DC: The White House, November 5, 1971), 4–5.

63. "Comments on 'A Review of the Intelligence Community'" (n.d.), 2–3.

64. Ibid.; and Nixon, "Organization and Management," 6. Marshall became the unofficial NAG director in early 1972 but did not become a government employee until leaving RAND in April.

65. Phillip A. Karber, "Military Balancing and Strategic Development: The Path Toward a National Net Assessment" (Washington, DC: Institute for Law, Science and Global Security, Georgetown University (October 31, 2010), 88–89.

66. Executive Office of the President, National Security Study Memorandum 178, "Program for National Net Assessment" (Washington, DC: The White House, March 29, 1973).

67. The first meeting of the ad hoc group took place on April 13, 1973. The main representative of the Pentagon was the Assistant Secretary of Defense for Intelligence, Albert C. Hall.

68. US, Executive Office of the President, National Security Council, National Security Study Memorandum 224, "National Net Assessment Process, NSSM 178" (Washington, DC: The White House, June 28, 1973).

69. Executive Office of the President, National Security Study Memorandum 186, "National Net Assessment of the Comparative Costs and Capabilities of US and Soviet Military Establishments" (Washington, DC: The White House, September 1, 1973).

70. Andrew W. Marshall, note to Harold L. Hitchens, Headquarters, US Air Force (AF/XODCC), April 26, 1972.

71. Andrew W. Marshall, "The Nature and Scope of National Net Assessment," memorandum (Washington, DC: National Security Council, March 26, 1972), 2. RAND's development of systems analysis sought to apply operations research techniques to higher-level "decision-making particularly with regard to the choice of weapons systems and the allocation of resources among alternative forces and programs" (Charles

J. Hitch, "Decision-Making in the Department of Defense," H. Rowan Gaither Lectures in Systems Sciences, University of California, Berkeley, April 5–9, 1965, 3.

72. Andrew W. Marshall, "The Nature and Scope of Net Assessments," memorandum (Washington, DC: National Security Council, August 16, 1972), 1.

73. Ibid., 2.

74. Marshall, "1969–1975," interview, December 14, 1993, 5–30.

75. "Study Outline for National Net Assessment of US and Soviet Ground Forces (NSSM-186)" (n.d.), 1.

76. The steering group included the Secretaries of the Army and the Navy, the CIA and DIA directors, the Director of Defense Research and Engineering, the Assistant Secretary of Defense for Program Analysis and Evaluation (PA&E), the Chairman of the Joint Chiefs of Staff, and Marshall.

77. Responsibility for net assessments was transferred to the Secretary of Defense when the NAG moved to the Pentagon. Henry A. Kissinger, "National Net Assessment Process," National Security Decision Memorandum 239 (Washington, DC: National Security Council, November 27, 1973).

78. Andrew W. Marshall, "Proposed Procedures for National Net Assessment," memorandum for Ad Hoc Net Assessment Group (Washington, DC: National Security Council, April 9, 1973), 1, 3.

79. Phase 2 of NSSM 186 focused on NATO and Warsaw Pact air power.

80. Marshall later discussed the impact of conscripts on readiness in the Soviet Army with Lieutenant General Daniel O. Graham, USA, who headed the Defense Intelligence Agency. Graham told Marshall that the DIA position on the issue was nonsense. Marshall, "Themes," interview, September 24, 1993, 10–6.

81. Marshall, "1973–1980," interview, April 8, 1994, 6–8 and 6–9.

82. For example, when DOD Directive 5105.39, "Director of Net Assessment" (December 1971), was revised in 1985, Marshall was subordinated to the Under Secretary of Defense for Policy rather than to the Secretary. But when DOD Directive 5111.11 replaced DOD Directive 5105.39 (September 1985), Marshall again reported to the Secretary.

83. Andrew W. Marshall, "The Formative Period of the Office of Net Assessment," memorandum for Andrew D. May and Barry D. Watts (Washington, DC: Office of the Secretary of Defense, September 3, 2002), 5.

84. At a meeting with Schlesinger on October 3, 1973, Marshall agreed to move to the Pentagon and establish a major assessment program. Andrew W. Marshall, "Departure Planning," memorandum for Brent Scowcroft (Washington, DC: National Security Council, October 3, 1973).

85. The ground forces study in 1973–1974 under NSSM 186 was followed by the phase 2 study, which examined US-USSR tactical air forces. NSSM 186 was directed from 1974 to 1988 by Phillip A. Karber of BDM Corporation and became a long-term ONA contract effort known as Project 186 to support the military balance in Europe. Karber received guidance for phase 2 from Schlesinger who wanted trend data illustrating past developments as the basis to project the future posture of the Warsaw Pact, more qualitative facets of the balance, and comparisons in an operational context. Diego Ruiz Palmer, "Beyond Metrics: Assessing the Balance of Force in Europe, 1975–1990," unpublished paper for a conference in 2008 on net assessment.

86. Interview with Schlesinger, "Interviews and Materials on the Intellectual History of Diagnostic Net Assessment," ed. Barry D. Watts (Washington, DC: Center for Strategic and Budgetary Assessments, July 1, 2006), 110.

87. Ibid., 109.

88. Office of the Secretary of Defense (Net Assessment), "The Military Balance in Europe: A Net Assessment" (March 1978), 104.

89. See Gerry Dunne, "Cold War Net Assessment of US and USSR Military Command, Control and Communications (C3)," unpublished paper for ONA conference on "Net Assessment: Past, Present and Future," March 28–29, 2008. Commander Dunne finished the US-USSR C3 balance in 1978 but it remains classified. With Marshall's concurrence, his conference paper from 2008 summarized the main findings of that assessment.

90. Office of the Secretary of Defense (Net Assessment), "Military Balance in Europe," 108–109.

91. Andrew W. Marshall, "A Program to Improve Analytic Methods Related to Strategic Forces," *Policy Sciences* 15 (November 1982), 48.

92. Other long-term research to support ONA's Cold War balances included the future security environment and the military burden on the Soviet economy. The best account of the former is contained in Andrew W. Marshall and Charles Wolf, Jr., *The Future Security Environment: Report of the Future Security Environment Working Group, submitted to the Commission on Integrated Long-Term Strategy* (Washington, DC: The Pentagon, October 1988). This research led to the realization that military pro-

grams consumed at least twice as much of the Soviet GNP as the CIA estimated.

93. United States, Central Intelligence Agency, "Soviet Capabilities for Strategic Nuclear Conflict, 1983–93," vol. 1, "Key Judgments and Summary," NIE 11-3/8-83 (Washington, DC: Director of Central Intelligence, March 1984), 13.

94. Ibid., 13.

95. CIA, *Soviet Capabilities for Strategic Nuclear Conflict, 1982–92*, Vol. I, *Key Judgments and Summary*, NIE 11-3/8-82, February 1983, 5.

96. John G. Hines and Daniel Calingaert, "Soviet Strategic Intentions, 1973–1985: A Preliminary Review of US Interpretations," WD-6305-NA (Santa Monica, CA: RAND Corporation, December 1992), 5. See, for example, Hines' interviews with Andrian A. Danilevich and Vitalii Nikolaevich Tsygicko in John G. Hines, Ellis M. Mishulovich, and John F. Shull, *Soviet Intentions 1965–1985*, vol. 2, *Soviet Post-Cold War Testimonial Evidence* (McLean, VA: BDM Federal, September 22, 1995), 19, 22–25, 137–138.

97. Andrew W. Marshall and James G. Roche, "Strategy for Competing with the Soviets in the Military Sector of the Continuing Political-Military Competition" (Washington, DC: Office of Net Assessment, July 26, 1976), A-2.

98. James Mann, *The Rebellion of Ronald Reagan: A History of the End of the Cold War* (New York: Viking, 2009), 23–24.

99. Executive Office of the President, National Security Decision Directive 12, "Strategic Forces Modernization Program" (Washington, DC: The White House, October 1, 1981), 1–2.

100. Frank C. Carlucci, "Preparation of Net Assessments and the Provisions of US Force Data to the CIA," memorandum (Washington, DC: Office of the Secretary of Defense, June 12, 1981).

101. Marshall, "1981–1984," interview, July 26, 1994, 7–21.

102. Marshal Sergei Akhromeyev, who headed the Soviet General Staff from 1984 to 1988, stated in 1991 that "At no time did the USSR ever intend to make first use of nuclear weapons. In a military sense, the side that attacked preemptively would win, but in practical terms neither side would win. Even to the Soviet General Staff it was clear that nuclear weapons were not really military weapons but were political tools." Hines, Mishulovich, and Shull, *Soviet Intentions 1965–1985*, vol. 2, *Soviet Post-Cold War Testimonial Evidence*, 5–6.

103. US Department of Defense, Directive 5105.29, "Director of Net Assessment," September 27, 1985, 1. A revised directive issued in August 2001

described the Director of Net Assessment as principal staff assistant and exclusive advisor on net assessment to the Secretary of Defense.

104. David J. Andre, "New Competitive Strategies Tools and Methodologies," vol. 1, "Review of the Department of Defense Competitive Strategies Initiative, 1986–1990," SAIC-90/1506 (McLean, VA: Science Application International Corporation, November 1990), 2.

105. Andrew W. Marshall, "Competitive Strategies—History and Background" (March 3, 1988), unpublished paper for a conference on competitive strategies, 1.

106. Ibid., 2.

107. Caspar W. Weinberger, *Annual Report to the Congress, Fiscal Year 1986* (Washington, DC: US Government Printing Office, February 5, 1986), 87.

108. Andre, "Competitive Strategies," 9.

109. Noel E. Firth and James H. Noren, *Soviet Defense Spending: A History of CIA Estimates, 1950–1990* (College Station: Texas A&M University Press, 1998), 54.

110. Ibid., 55.

111. Andrew W. Marshall, letter to Richard Kaufman of the Joint Economic Committee, September 18, 1975, 1.

112. Firth and Noren, *Defense Spending*, 59.

113. Ibid., 59, 70.

114. Ibid., 130–31; Robert M. Gates, *From the Shadows: The Ultimate Insider's Story of Presidents and How They Won the Cold War* (New York: Simon and Schuster, 1996), 318.

115. Andrew W. Marshall, "Commentary," in Joint Economic Committee, Congress of the United Sates, *Gorbachev's Economic Plans*, vol. I, *Study Papers* (Washington, DC: US Government Printing Office, 1987), 482.

116. Ibid., 482–83.

117. Ibid., 484.

118. Andrew W. Marshall, letter to Thomas C. Reed, September 27, 2001, 3.

119. Ibid., 2.

120. Interview with Harold Brown (January 27, 2006), 5, transcribed by Barry D. Watts.

CHAPTER 3

NET ASSESSMENT AFTER THE COLD WAR

Barry D. Watts and Andrew D. May

In the wake of the unexpected collapse of the Soviet Union in 1991, the rivalry between Moscow and Washington that had dominated international relations since the late 1940s came to an end. US national security was no longer focused on long-term competition with a single near-peer rival. Almost overnight the prospects of a large-scale nuclear exchange between the United States and the former Soviet Union, or a conventional invasion of Western Europe by the Warsaw Pact, all but vanished. The United States abruptly found itself in a remarkably favorable geostrategic situation with substantial margins of military and economic advantage. Liberal democracy and free markets were triumphant. So much so that Francis Fukuyama famously wondered if history had reached the end point of mankind's ideological evolution and the universalization of Western liberal democracy as the final form of human government.[1] In the Pentagon the Office of Net Assessment (ONA) was confronted with a vastly different international security environment than it had faced during the long Cold War.

FORECASTING THE FUTURE SECURITY ENVIRONMENT

As early as 1987 Andrew W. Marshall had cautioned Under Secretary of Defense for Policy Fred C. Iklé that in twenty or thirty years the world was going to be very different from what it was in the early 1990s. At the time Iklé co-chaired the Commission on Integrated Long-Term Strategy (CILTS) with Albert J. Wohlstetter. CILTS' remit was to propose adjustments to US strategy in response to foreseeable changes in the international security environment. In structural terms, Marshall told Iklé that political-military competition would shift from a contest between two dominant players to a multiplayer game with at least four medium-size players in addition to the United States. He called attention to a number of possible developments any or all of which could bring about this change: the emergence of China as the dominant military power in Asia and the Pacific; the growth of Japan into an economic powerhouse; the likelihood that Russia would retain military parity with the United States, especially in nuclear arms; the maturation of the then-emerging revolution in military affairs (RMA) based on precision weapons, wide-area surveillance, and battle networks; and the possibility that Washington would need to do more to protect American security interests in the Western Hemisphere.[2]

Three decades on Marshall's 1987 assessment of the evolving post-Cold War security environment seems prescient even if incomplete. Forecasting the shift from a two- to a multiplayer competition has been borne out by the economic and military rise of China; renewed competition with Russia in Ukraine, Syria, and most recently Venezuela; North Korea's development of nuclear weapons; and Iran's implacable hostility toward the United States, sponsorship of terrorism, and regional ambitions. What Marshall's memo to Iklé failed to anticipate was the impact that terrorist organizations such as al Qaeda and, later, the Islamic State would exert on the United States and its allies, especially in Afghanistan, Iraq, and Syria. The main opponents to the United States today include not only an increasingly assertive China and a revanchist Russia, but Iran, North Korea, and, among the many terrorist organizations, al Qaeda, the Taliban, and the remnants of the Islamic State. Refugees from the civil wars in Libya and Syria have added further complexities to the international security environment by destabilizing Europe. In sum the security challenges now confronting the United States are more complex and diverse than the threats posed by the Soviet Union during the Cold War. Simply trying to prioritize so diverse an array of national-security challenges in terms of their urgency, severity, and likely longevity would be a daunting task for any net assessment program. The current security environment, therefore, raises the obvious question: What assessments should ONA be undertaking in the third decade of the 21st century?

THE LOGIC OF ONA'S PRINCIPAL COLD WAR BALANCES

During the Cold War the question of what balances to undertake was easy to answer. The underlying logic was as follows. First, since there was only one competitor posing an existential threat to the United States—namely the Union of Soviet Socialist Republics (USSR)—the net assessment program should focus on how US military forces and capabilities stacked up against those of the USSR. Second, Marshall's attempt in 1970 to capture the overall US-Soviet political-military competition in a single, comprehensive net assessment proved to be a bridge too far. The competition needed to be parsed into its major components. Marshall and defense secretary James R. Schlesinger instinctively agreed that ONA should focus on three major sub-competitions: the balance of US and USSR intercontinental or strategic nuclear forces; the balance between North Atlantic Treaty Organization (NATO) and Warsaw Pact (WP) forces in central Europe; and the US-USSR maritime balance. To these three principal net assessments they added a fourth: the two sides' investments in military programs.

There were clear reasons for each of these choices. By the mid-1950s when the Soviets started fielding long-range bombers capable of striking the continental United States with atomic weapons, nuclear deterrence became the overriding objective of American strategy. Because a NATO-Warsaw Pact conflict was the most plausible trigger for escalation to general nuclear war, the adequacy of the European balance was linked to the strategic-nuclear balance. Next, the US-Soviet maritime competition was a surrogate for overseas power projection, particularly for the reinforcement of NATO in the event of a conventional war in Europe. Finally, the military investment balance provided not only a sense of how the competition might evolve in the future but also of the two superpowers' ability to hold up their ends of the competition in the long run.

With the demise of the Soviet Union, however, the compelling logic underpinning Marshall's choices of ONA's principal net assessments abruptly vanished. Without the USSR against what country's military would comparisons with US forces and capabilities make sense? Also, what net assessments would support the long-term strategic management needs of the secretary of defense? In the 1990s the US military appeared to be so dominant that the very need for careful net assessments was open to question. There simply was no longer a near-peer adversary against which to measure the adequacy of US forces.

Marshall's initial response to this situation was to focus on the implications of an emerging revolution in military affairs (RMA). This late twentieth-century RMA stemmed from a number of developments including the success of laser-guided bombs toward the end of the Vietnam War[3] and the potential of "near zero miss" conventional munitions to provide alternatives to massive nuclear retaliation in a variety of situations. The final report of the Long-Range Research and Development Planning Program (LRRDPP) in 1975 concluded that "near zero miss" munitions were technically possible, promised to be militarily effective against targets requiring pinpoint accuracy, and, if married with wide-area sensors and battle networks, could revolutionize warfare.[4] Over the next decade the Pentagon developed the technical wherewithal—including the stealthy F-117 and the Pave Mover MTI (moving target indicator) radar —needed to begin moving toward a mature precision-strike regime. The success of these developments not only underpinned defense secretary William J. Perry's offset strategy, which exploited precision strike to compensate for the quantitative advantages of the Warsaw Pact in main battle tanks, artillery, and other ground combat weaponry, but was also evident in course and outcome of the 1991 Persian Gulf War (Operation Desert Storm).[5]

ONA's RMA Period, 1989-1996

By the late 1980s Marshall recognized the need to move beyond the Soviet-oriented net assessments that ONA had done since the 1970s.[6] When Lieutenant Colonel Andrew F. Krepinevich, Jr., USA, was assigned to ONA's small staff in 1989, he thought he would be asked to update the most recent version of the NATO-WP balance that Lieutenant Colonel Jeffrey S. McKitrick, USA, had written. But Marshall instead directed Krepinevich to turn to the question of whether Soviet theorists were right in predicting the emergence of a military-technical revolution (MTR) stemming from the technological advances that had been foreseen by the LRRDPP.

Looking back over the 20th century, Soviet theoreticians had identified two prior periods of technology-driven revolutionary change in how wars were fought. The first MTR arose with the introduction of aircraft, chemical weapons, and motorization during World War I; the second was sparked by the advent of nuclear weapons, ballistic missiles, and early computers during World War II.[7] By the late 1970s, the Soviet military anticipated a third twentieth century MTR. In 1984, Marshal N. V. Ogarkov, the Chief of the Soviet General Staff, publicly asserted that automated reconnaissance-strike complexes featuring long-range, high-accuracy guided munitions together with advances in computerized control systems would intensify the destructive power of conventional weapons and bring them closer to nuclear weapons in their effectiveness on the battlefield.[8] Marshall believed that the Soviets were right. The LRRDPP had, of course, reached similar conclusions in 1975 to Ogarkov's in 1984. And the 1988 examination of long-term US strategy by Iklé and Wohlstetter in *Discriminate Deterrence* had stated that further exploitation of microelectronics, sensors, information processing and directed energy would lead to "revolutionary changes in the nature of war."[9] Additional signs that the US military might be on the cusp of far-reaching changes in war's conduct emerged from Desert Storm in early 1991. The ease with which the US-led coalition defeated the Iraqis and liberated Kuwait owed much to precision munitions (especially laser-guided bombs and Toma-hawk cruise missiles), stealthy F-117s, M-1 tanks that were far superior to Iraq's Soviet-supplied T-72s, the MTI radar of the Joint Surveillance and Target Attack Radar System (JSTARS), satellite reconnaissance, and a partially filled Global Positioning System constellation.[10]

Marshall had several reasons for focusing ONA on the prospect of another MTR. The most obvious ones were the Cold War's end and the absence of a near-peer competitor. But beyond these realities he wanted to encourage American defense officials—especially the mid-level officers who would eventually have to cope with the RMA as it matured—to decide whether they thought Soviet theorists were correct in their belief that "technological developments would lead to major changes in warfare" over the next couple decades.[11] Was a period of major change dawning in war's conduct comparable in their impact to *blitzkrieg* or carrier aviation during the interwar years 1918–1939? If it was, the Pentagon would be confronted with strategic management issues such as identification of appropriate innovations in precision weaponry and encouraging experimentation to develop appropriate operational concepts and organizations for their employment.

ONA released Krepinevich's MTR assessment in July 1992. Unlike the balances developed during the Cold War, this assessment was not only unclassified from the outset but was also developed with the active participation of military officers, civilian defense officials, and intelligence experts from across the national-security community. ONA's offices, located on the A-Ring of the Pentagon, were a sensitive compartmented intelligence facility or SCIF. Marshall's Cold War balances had been prepared behind closed doors of this SCIF by staff members drawing on highly classified information. For example, the first net assessment of the US-USSR strategic nuclear balance by Lieutenant Colonel Frederick W. Giessler, USAF, and Peter J. Sharfman in 1977 was classified above TOP SECRET and has never been declassified. Similarly, the anti-submarine warfare balance completed in 1978 by then Commander James G. Roche, USN, was deemed so sensitive by the Navy that when William Perry, the Under Secretary of Defense for Research and Engineering, asked to see it he was denied access. Thus, involving people outside ONA to discuss and comment on working versions of the MTR assessment through questionnaires and meetings was a radical departure from the way ONA's Cold War balances had been written.

Another difference between Cold War balances and the MTR assessment involved the time horizon. The key Cold War assessments typically used trends to suggest where the United States would stand relative to the competition in a given area during the next five-to-seven years. The MTR's time horizon, like *Discriminant Deterrence*'s, endeavored to make projections twenty years or more into the future. This more distant time horizon marked a subtle shift toward ONA's balances trying to look decades into the future rather just a few years.

Research on the interwar years suggested that major military revolutions integrated four main elements: new or advanced technologies, the application of these technologies to new military systems, innovative operational concepts, and organizational adaptations. ONA's MTR assessment used this same four-element framework, all of whose elements had been evident in the German advance into France and the Low Countries in 1940. Starting on May 10, five *Panzer* divisions of Army Group A transited the rugged terrain and dense forests of the Ardennes, crossed the Meuse River, and drove to Dunkirk in only fourteen days, shattering both French and British forces. During the interwar years, aircraft and tank technologies had matured enough to enable the mechanization of the German concept of maneuver warfare (*Bewegungskrieg*). The underlying operational concept was the idea that fast-moving armor and motorized infantry formations with air support could break through defenses and penetrate deep into rear areas to dislocate and unbalance the enemy. The *Panzer* division with radios in every tank provided the organizational structure for this concept. The result was a highly mobile form of mechanized, combined-arms warfare commonly known as *blitzkrieg* (lightning war). *Blitzkrieg* exemplifies Mike Vickers and Bob Martinage's later characterization of military revolutions as "periods of discontinuous change that render obsolete or subordinate existing means for conducting war."[12]

Once the MTR assessment was completed in July 1992, Marshall distributed it to the top leadership of the Pentagon, starting with Under Secretary of Defense for Policy, Paul D. Wolfowitz. Marshall expected the assessment to generate "a lot of resistance and flak" but was pleasantly surprised at the degree to which people tended to agree that a period of revolutionary change in the conduct of warfare was underway.[13] To spread the assessment's findings more widely, Marshall asked Krepinevich to begin briefing them in national security venues outside Washington. Venues at which Krepinevich did so in the fall included the John M. Olin Institute for Strategic Studies at Harvard University, the Naval Postgraduate School in Monterey, California, and the Los Alamos National Laboratory in New Mexico. While much of the resulting discussions focused on how the US military might best exploit the emerging MTR, one useful piece of feedback occurred when Krepinevich briefed the Naval War College. There the subject of his presentation was introduced as the military-*technological* revolution. But as the assessment had stressed, the most difficult and important components of the MTR were not new technologies or their applications, but how to develop appropriate operational concepts for new military systems and how best to organize forces to employ them.[14] The upshot was that by the summer of 1993 Marshall advised that the term "military-technical revolution" should be avoided and, instead, replaced with "revolution in military affairs."[15]

The MTR assessment not only triggered debate in the US defense establishment but also eventually spread the debate about war's future overseas making the MTR assessment the best known of all ONA's military balances. In keeping with Marshall's desire to motivate the American military to begin thinking about the best response to the RMA, ONA devoted much of the 1990s to sponsoring RMA meetings, roundtables, workshops, and wargames. One particularly noteworthy event in late 1992 involved a high-level meeting in Annapolis between business leaders and senior military officers. Attendees from industry included James C. McGroddy (IBM), Richard T. Roca (AT&T), Ivan E. Sutherland (Sun Microsystems), and Robert J. Spinrad (Xerox). Department of Defense (DoD) participants included the Air Force chief of staff General Merrill McPeak; future Marine Corps commandant General Charles Krulak; General Dennis Reimer, who would succeed General Gordon Sullivan as Army chief of staff in 1995; and Vice Admiral William Owens, who became a vocal proponent of the RMA as vice chairman of the Joint Chiefs of Staff.[16] Marshall's conclusion from this meeting was that the industry executives had given the military leaders a very different way of looking at the challenges of innovation along with some stern warnings based on their own experiences as to how even the most dominant organizations could be brought low in a period of dynamic technological change.[17]

In September 1993, then Deputy Secretary of Defense Perry established a DoD-wide project on the RMA to assess whether the US military would be faced with revolutionary changes over the next two decades that would require substantive changes in American weapon systems, operational concepts, or organizations.[18] By early 1996 Admiral Owens was advocating his concept of an all-seeing US system-of-systems as the proper response to harnessing the RMA.[19] By then scores of RMA wargames, workshops, and roundtables had been conducted, and Marshall had joined General Sullivan, the chief of staff of the US Army, in a series of dominant maneuver workshops and wargames to develop the Army's response to the RMA.[20] Of note, while Marshall consistently advocated conducting field experiments, only the Marine Corps conducted one: Hunter Warrior in 1997, which explored using light forces inserted by air and supported by long-range precision fires to combat heavy armored formations.[21]

Exploring the prospective implications of the emerging RMA became, for several years, the overarching activity of ONA's staff. Much of the research Marshall funded during this period sought to better understand how militaries had responded to fundamental changes in warfare in the past. Were there lessons that DoD could apply to its present situation? For a variety of reasons Marshall believed that the changes in warfighting that took place between the two world wars were the most fruitful to explore, and he sponsored a series of books on this period by historians Williamson Murray and Alan Millet on interwar military transformation. Marshall was especially drawn to the development of naval aviation during the interwar years by the United States, Japan, and Britain. Drawing on ONA-funded research by Thomas C. Hone and Mark D. Mandeles, Commander Jan M. van Tol, USN, in Marshall's office published two articles on the American development of carrier aviation during 1918–1939.[22] Marshall's research funds also paid for Wick Murray and Allan Millett's 1996 *Military Innovation and the Interwar Period.*[23]

Of all the methods used by Marshall and his staff to assess the scale, scope, and character of the emerging RMA, wargaming arguably became the most prominent. Building on the MTR/RMA games of the 1990s, ONA initiated a series of 20XX wargames to examine a broad set of possible future contingencies and adversaries including China. The 20XX games explored technological advances in unmanned systems, ubiquitous sensors, precision strike, undersea warfare, conflict in space, and miniaturization.[24] These and other ONA-sponsored games aimed at helping Pentagon leaders to think about the possible character of future warfare and consider the degree to which existing forces, organizational arrangements, and operational concepts were suitable for this emerging environment. Wargames were also used to help test and refine proposed operational concepts including many that were developed by Vickers, Martinage, and others as outgrowths of the 20XX series.

Much of the RMA wargaming and analysis during this period was based on the premise that long-range precision strike appeared likely to become, as Marshall put it in 1993, the dominant operational approach of major powers like the United States.[25] But Marshall also offered a second idea on how war's conduct might change. The "information dimension or aspect of warfare," he wrote, "may become increasingly central to the outcome of battles and engagements, and therefore the strategy and tactics of establishing information superiority over an adversary will become a major focus of the operational art."[26] While he made this point over two decades before the Russians exploited cyber and social media to undermine public confidence in American political institutions during the 2016 presidential election, the rise of cyberwar not only confirms Marshall's suspicion about the increasing importance of information in force-on-force combat but also extends information's use as a weapon far beyond battles and engagements. Indeed, as the Russians have demonstrated, such nonviolent means can "be more potent sources of national power and influence than the overt violence of Clausewitzian war."[27]

THE RMA ABROAD

One question that arose from ONA's various efforts to get the American military thinking about the RMA was how military leaders in other nations might respond to the prospect of a maturing precision-strike regime. In the early 1990s ONA sponsored a small team of analysts at the Science Applications International Corporation (SAIC) to track the articles on future warfare written in military journals and other semi-official periodicals in a number of different countries.[28] Starting with an initial set of approximately 20-30 countries and then focusing on a subset of about 8-10, the SAIC team found that few foreign militaries were writing about future warfare or the RMA with rigor or originality. There were a few nations—notably Sweden and Israel—that had become home to small cadres of officers who were beginning to think seriously about the changing character of warfare. Building on these findings ONA began a series of meetings with the Swedish and Israeli militaries to exchange views on the emerging RMA.[29]

The most striking foreign writings about the RMA, however, were coming out of China. As SAIC analysts began digging into what Chinese officers were writing about military transformation, they quickly discovered that the Chinese were among the most thoughtful and attentive observers and commentators on the changing character of war. Furthermore, People's Liberation Army (PLA) officers clearly regarded the American military as the benchmark against which their own military should be measured. They also wrote, very openly, about an anticipated conflict between China and the United States. Although Marshall and Wolf had identified the probable rise of the Chinese economy in their work on the future security environment for the CILTS report, the breadth, magnitude, and forthright ambitions of the Chinese military were surprising and led Marshall to begin tracking PLA thought and activities more closely.[30]

WATCHING THE DRAGON

Close study of the People's Republic of China (PRC) became one of the main thrusts of ONA's research program by the early 2000s. Research on the PRC began with ONA funding a small cadre of analysts to track PLA thinking about future war. One of the earliest contributors to this line of inquiry was Michael Pillsbury. His 1997 compendium of translated PLA articles, *Chinese Views of Future Warfare*, was published by the National Defense University. Sponsored by ONA and the Atlantic Council, this compendium opened with eleven articles on Deng Xiaoping's strategic thought.[31] These articles alone went far to confirm Marshall's recurring caution about assuming that a foreign country's strategic and military assessments would be a mirror image of our own. During the Cold War Marshall had found that Soviet assessments "make different assumptions about scenarios and objectives . . . perform different calculations, use different measures of effectiveness, and perhaps use different assessment processes and methods."[32] As different as Soviet assessments proved to be compared to those of the West, Chinese assessments were even more alien.

Pillsbury was by no means the only researcher Marshall supported or encouraged in his quest to better understand Chinese assessments. Among the many others Marshall supported until his retirement in 2015 were John Battilega at SAIC, Aaron Friedberg at Princeton, and Laurent Murawiec at the Hudson Institute. Working independently but under Marshall's direction, these researchers began to develop a picture of Chinese geostrategic ambitions that did not fit comfortably with prevailing hopes that China might somehow be brought into the US-led world order. The China analysts working for ONA—a group that over time came also to include Jacqueline Deal, Christopher Ford, Stephen Rosen, and Arthur Waldron—described a China with an appetite to exert far greater influence and a PLA attuned to the changing character of warfare. The goal of Battilega's group, for example, was to follow, translate, and evaluate writings in Chinese military journals and other open-source publications in a systematic effort to understand the Chinese perspective on future war and the kind of conflict with the United States that occupied PLA officers. Marshall directed others, including Thomas Welch and Daniel DeMots in his office, along with contractors John Milam and Mark Herman, to concentrate on China's responses to American precision-strike weaponry.[33]

One of the more significant insights that surfaced from this body of research was the realization that the PLA was aggressively pursuing what became known in the West as anti-access/area-denial (A2/AD) capabilities. The premise behind this insight was that any serious adversary would surely seek ways to blunt or degrade US capabilities to conduct precision strikes from forward deployed naval forces such as carrier battle groups or by long-range air forces and forward based land forces. The systematic collection of information on PLA programs by ONA uncovered unambiguous evidence that this was precisely what the Chinese military was seeking to do. In fact, China's burgeoning A2/AD capabilities were part of a more comprehensive set of initiatives begun after the 1991 Persian Gulf War to prepare the Chinese military for "local wars under modern high-tech" and, since 2002, under what their theorists termed "informationalized" conditions.[34] By mid-2000s, it became evident that China was investing heavily in advanced precision weapons and battle networks aimed at denying US forces access to the western Pacific as far east as Guam. Ballistic missiles such as the Dongfeng (DF)-21D and DF-26—both advertised by the PLA as "carrier killers"—were designed, if war came, to impose severe costs on US bases and naval forces as far east from China's coastline as the second island chain that runs from southern Japan through Guam and Palau to eastern Indonesia and Australia. While this conclusion seemed relatively unassailable, it is important to note the difficulties of understanding Chinese military thought. For example, the US military does not have terms or overarching concepts corresponding to the Chinese notions of "informationized operations" (*xinxi hua zuozhan*) and "informationized war" (*xinxihua zhanzheng*).[35] Thus, Chinese thinking is harder to grasp than Soviet thinking was during the Cold War.

Although the PLA was the most worrisome developer of A2/AD capabilities, China was not the only prospective competitor to do so. Indeed, Marshall concluded that as long as the United States used precision strike to bolster overseas power projection, adversaries would pursue countermeasures. In the early 2000s a series of studies and wargames examined this growing problem. Subsequently, in 2002, Colonel Jerry B. Warner, USA, prepared a detailed analysis of how prospective US adversaries could exploit precision strike to field robust A2/AD capabilities. This study remains classified but was the most thorough analysis of how the same precision-strike capabilities that the US exploited for offensive power projection could be harnessed to the defensive mission of creating keep-out zones US forces would be hesitant to enter. To cite a recent example of this alarming trend, the DF-26, which has the range to reach American bases on Guam, was both deployed and, according to Chinese media, successfully tested as a carrier killer in January 2019.[36] The growing problem of proliferating A2/AD keep-out zones will undoubtedly be one that ONA will continue to track in the years and decades ahead.

From the late 1990s to 2015 Marshall instigated a steady and growing stream of wargames, studies, and translation efforts aimed at better understanding Chinese assessments. Over time research on China gradually supplanted the RMA as the centerpiece of ONA's research program. And while American appreciation of Chinese assessments probably still falls short of what it should be, much of the progress to date has been due to Marshall's willingness to fund research he judged to be important to US national security, whether it was appreciated elsewhere in the Pentagon or not. Especially in the long term China is a far more formidable competitor than the Soviet Union was. During the Cold War the Soviets never opened their economy to the world as Deng Xiaoping did China's in 1978. Whereas at the Cold War's end Soviet GDP was probably no more than 25 percent of US GDP, the International Monetary Fund forecasts that by 2020 China's GDP ($15.5 trillion in current prices) will be almost 70 percent of US GDP ($22.3 trillion) and the PRC will have four times the American population.[37] Such comparisons argue that China will be a tough competitor, one requiring far more strategic competence than the United States has exhibited in recent decades.

Post–Cold War Diagnostic Net Assessment

Starting in 1996 Marshall began thinking about refocusing ONA on a portfolio of more traditional net assessments. He believed ONA had expended enough time and energy on helping the US military services to begin thinking about how best to respond to the RMA. But deciding on a future portfolio of net assessments ONA should undertake proved to be no easy task. Recall that during the Cold War there had been a straightforward logic behind ONA's strategic, European, maritime, and investment balances. The preeminent US goal of deterring general nuclear war had enabled Marshall and Schlesinger to decide quickly on these four key balances. But there was no obvious, comparable logic for net assessment in the early 21st century. In fact, during the late 1990s and early 2000s Marshall's judgment was that the US military was so dominant that net assessments would not need much work or data collection to highlight the most important emerging strategic problems and opportunities. Not surprisingly few net assessments were attempted, much less completed, during this period. From the mid-1990s to 2001, ONA produced only one net assessment, an undersea analysis in 1998 that examined threats to US undersea infrastructure on the continental shelves.

In 1996 Marshall convened former members of his staff to explore the future character of ONA, the nature of the net assessment process, and the likely topics to be addressed as net assessments. What were the right roads for ONA to take and what was the best way to pursue them? Although no real progress was made in answering these questions at the 1996 meeting, Marshall thought that answers were likely to become clear enough over the next eighteen months to facilitate a return to more traditional assessments, if not to suggest the key balance areas to pursue.

This judgment proved optimistic and in 1999 Marshall convened a two-day offsite to consider how ONA ought to structure its net assessment program. Once again, progress was minimal—so much so in Marshall's view that he ended the offsite early on the second day.[38] But the problem of developing an underlying logic for future net assessments did not go away.

In May 2000 Marshall returned to it. This time he proposed two ideas for clarifying the character of future net assessments. The first sprang from ONA's longstanding goal of assisting senior officials in coping with the long-term strategic management challenges facing the Defense Department. Here Marshall suggested stepping back from concentrating on the character of future net assessments and, instead, reviewing what ONA could do to help top DoD managers to think about directions in which US military programs and forces might evolve so as to retain substantial advantages over prospective adversaries. One possibility that seemed to warrant attention was that other states, or even non-state actors, could take available precision-strike technology and use it in some very destructive and innovative ways. Another possibility was that the net assessment program should focus on sustaining long-term advantages in DoD's core competencies.

Marshall's second idea was based on the assumption that if the United States had an adequately formulated strategy, then a program of net assessments could be structured around the strategy. The practical problem, however, was that past administrations had seldom managed to articulate comprehensive national-security or defense strategies, instead simply listing desirable objectives. Indeed, the aptitude of the national security community "to craft, implement, and adapt effective long-term strategies against intelligent adversaries at acceptable costs" had been declining for decades as the prolonged wars in Afghanistan, Iraq, and Syria after 9/11 confirmed.[39] In his 2000 memo Marshall noted that when Stephen Rosen had done an East Asian assessment in 1984 there had been no clear statement of the preferred future situation that the United States sought to achieve in the region, thereby forcing Rosen to posit his own strategy. Nevertheless, regarding his second idea, Marshall concluded that *if* a satisfactory statement of either a broad general strategy or strategies for specific areas (key functional competitions or important geographical areas) could be formulated, then a net assessment program could be structured around these strategies.

Neither of Marshall's two ideas, nor subsequent thinking about them, immediately produced a definitive list of future net assessments for ONA to undertake. As Marshall later wrote, in 2000 ONA still lacked an overall intellectual structure for what a post–Cold War net assessment program would be, and he believed it to be very important to have such an organizing framework. But as late as 2006 this problem had still not been conclusively resolved despite the progress that was made in the aftermath of the strategy review Donald Rumsfeld asked Marshall to conduct in 2001.

RUMSFELD'S STRATEGY REVIEW

One of the first things that Rumsfeld did when he began his second tour as defense secretary in 2001 was to ask Marshall to conduct a review of US strategy. The assignment was in many respects a perfect one for Marshall. Apart from his native talent as a strategist, for some years Marshall had sponsored a series of studies and workshops exploring the nature of strategy and new strategic concepts, including the development of alternative US defense strategies. Over the course of this work Marshall had become especially attracted to "core competency" strategies that looked to one's own deeply rooted strengths as the basis for enduring competitive advantage. Marshall turned, naturally, to this work when laying out the foundation for the 2001 strategy review. His diagnosis of the United States' military position that emerged from this review was that, at the dawn of the 21st century, the United States enjoyed a remarkably favorable geostrategic position with overwhelming military advantages in many areas. The guiding policy suggested by this diagnosis was to maintain (or possibly expand) US margins of advantage by investing preferentially in those areas of military competition judged most important to future American security. Marshall's central concept was that the United States should use its strong position to dissuade would-be competitors from entering some areas of military competition, while at the same time developing broad competences in areas that would provide hedges against the uncertainty about who exactly our adversaries would be, and what specific missions the U.S. military would be called upon to undertake.

If the Office of the Secretary of Defense and the military services could agree on a short list of core competencies, then ONA could structure a coherent assessment program based on them. After all, senior officials in the Pentagon would want to know how well the United States was performing in vital areas of military competition such as long-range precision strike and air dominance.

Unfortunately, as appealing as an advantage-based strategy appeared in 2001 and later years, it was resisted by the military services from the outset. The problem was building consensus on a relatively small number of areas of competition (probably fewer than ten) for preferential investment. But as C. K. Prahalad and Gary P. Hamel had observed in 1990 regarding the core competencies of corporations: "Few companies are likely to build world leadership in more than five or six fundamental competencies. A company that compiles a list of 20 or 30 purportedly "core" capabilities has probably not produced a list of core competencies."[40] The same was true of the Pentagon. When, in the midst of the 2001 strategy review, critics asked for a list of core competencies, ONA offered five notional candidates: air dominance, undersea warfare, space, robotics, and realistic training. Each of the military services immediately began objecting that several of their vital mission areas needed to be added. In the event, ONA efforts to reach consensus on core competencies proved so controversial that a proposed list of areas for preferential investment was dropped from the final iteration of the Rumsfeld strategy review and only appeared in the report's annex.[41]

In light of the lack of consensus on a sensibly short list of DoD's core competencies, Marshall came away from the 2001 strategy review feeling that more thinking was still needed on the future role and focus of ONA. Toward this end he had Barry Watts, then at the Center for Strategic and Budgetary Assessments (CSBA), run a one-day conference on the issue. Two main conclusions emerged from the conference. First, ONA's role would continue to be providing the defense secretary and other top Pentagon leaders with even-handed, diagnostic assessments of how the US military was doing in the most important areas of long-term competition. ONA's assessments would include force comparisons, key trends and asymmetries, uncertainties, the goals and strategies of the major powers (especially of adversaries), where the important competitions appeared to be headed in the future, and emerging strategic opportunities and problems.[42] Second, the net assessment program would be based on the strategy of maintaining or creating advantage, especially in DoD's current or future areas of core competency.[43] Still unresolved, at least in Marshall's mind, was specifying exactly the balances ONA should undertake.

As late as 2006 Marshall was still circulating memoranda soliciting views on what military competitions would be the best candidates as areas of enduring military advantage for the United States. A net assessment dealing with China's economic and military rise was an obvious and often suggested candidate. But in 2006 ONA had assessments underway on realistic training and robotics, and Marshall was planning to begin a space assessment.[44] By then, however, the protracted wars in Afghanistan and Iraq had gained the full attention of defense officials, the broader national security community, and the American public. These conflicts in the Middle East made it difficult for defense officials to focus on truly long-term strategies, especially ones that dealt with the growing importance of the Asia Pacific.

***

In 2018 *The Economist* calculated a geographic center of gravity for the global economy by taking an average of each country's latitude and longitude weighted by its GDP. The Economist Intelligence Unit estimated global economic centers of gravity for 1 AD, 1600, 1850, 1900, 1950, 1960, 1980, 2000, 2010 and 2018, and made a projection for 2025.[45] Connecting these data points produced the rough path that the world's economic center of gravity had taken since 1 AD. From 1800 to 1950 it moved steadily northwestward ending up in the north Atlantic off Greenland. But from 1950 to 2018 the direction was southeastward toward China, ending up in central Russia in 2018. The drift toward China since 1980 raises perhaps the most seminal question about long-term US strategy. As Marshall observed shortly before his death in March 2019, China under Xi Jinping clearly aspires by mid-century to become the dominant power in the Asia Pacific, if not the world's reigning superpower. But China's increasing dominance would threaten Beijing's Asian neighbors from the Philippines and Vietnam to South Korea, Japan, and Russia. In Marshall's view the first-order strategic question for the United States is whether it can devise (and execute!) a long-term strategy aimed at helping China's Asian neighbors preserve sustainable degrees of independence from Beijing.[46] One cannot help but suspect that the Office of Net Assessment is one of the few places in the US government that has the long-term vision to help promote such a strategy. Despite the problems that have emerged regarding ONA's role and focus since the Cold War ended, Marshall's conception of diagnostic net assessment remains a valuable— if not invaluable—Defense Department resource by framing the right questions.

Notes

1. Francis Fukuyama, "The End of History?" *The National Interest,* summer 1989.
2. The future security environment working group was led by Marshall and Charles Wolf, Jr. Two other groups, one on offense-defense (chaired by Fred S. Hoffman and Henry S. Rowen) and the other on technology (chaired by Charles Herzfeld), also published reports in support of CILTS. Membership in CILTS included Zbigniew Brzezinski, Samuel P. Huntington, Henry A. Kissinger, and John W. Vessey.
3. From February 1, 1972, to February 28, 1973, the US Air Force dropped more than 10,500 laser-guided bombs in Southeast Asia. Some 5,100 were direct hits while 4,000 others had a circular error probable of 25 feet. See Donald L. Ockerman, "An Analysis of Laser-Guided Bombs in SEA" (Nakhon Phanom Royal Thai Air Base, Thailand: Tactical Analysis Division, 7th Air Force, June 28, 1973), ii.
4. D. A. Paolucci, "Summary Report of the Long-Range Research and Development Planning Program" (Falls Church, VA: Lulejian and Associates, February 7, 1975), iii, 44–45.
5. William J. Perry, *My Journey at the Nuclear Brink* (Stanford, CA: Stanford University Press, 2015), 33–41. Other systems that underpinned Perry's offset strategy included the Sensor-Fused Weapon, the E-3 Joint Surveillance and Target Attack Radar System, and the Global Positioning System, which eventually enabled the all-weather Joint Direct Attack Munition.
6. Andrew F. Krepinevich, Jr. and Barry D. Watts, *The Last Warrior: Andrew Marshall and the Shaping of Modern American Defense Strategy* (New York: Basic Books, 2015), 197.
7. William E. Odom, "Soviet Military Doctrine," *Foreign Affairs* 67 (Winter 1988), 120.
8. N. V. Ogarkov, "The Defense of Socialism: Experience of History and the Present Day," *Red Star* [Красная звезда], May 9, 1984; trans. *Daily Report: Soviet Union,* vol. 3, no. 091, annex 054 (Washington, DC: Foreign Broadcast Information Service, May 9, 1984), R19.
9. Fred C. Iklé and Albert Wohlstetter, *Discriminate Deterrence: Report of the Commission on Integrated Long-Term Strategy* (Washington, DC: Commission on Integrated Long-Term Strategy, January 1988), 8.

10. Thomas A. Keaney and Eliot A. Cohen, *Revolution in Warfare: Air Power in the Persian Gulf* (Annapolis, MD: Naval Institute Press, 1995), 188–212.

11. Andrew F. Krepinevich, Jr., "The Military-Technical Revolution: A Preliminary Assessment" (Washington, DC: Center for Strategic and Budgetary Assessments, 2002), i. After Desert Storm the Soviets concluded the US military had demonstrated for the first time the "integration of control, communications, reconnaissance, electronic combat and delivery of conventional fires into a single whole," meaning that a reconnaissance-strike complex had been fielded. Defense Intelligence Agency, "Soviet Analysis of Operation Desert Shield and Desert Storm," trans. LN 006-92 (October 28, 1991), 32. While many elements of a reconnaissance-strike complex were evident during Desert Storm, integrating them into a near-real-time battle network proved to be an arduous enterprise even for the US military.

12. Michael G. Vickers and Robert C. Martinage, *The Revolution in War* (Washington, DC: Center for Strategic and Budgetary Assessments, December 2004), 2. Krepinevich earlier argued that genuine military revolutions produce "a dramatic increase—often an order of magnitude or greater—in the combat potential and military effectiveness of armed forces." See also Andrew F. Krepinevich, Jr., "Cavalry to Computer: The Pattern of Military Revolutions," *The National Interest* 37 (Fall 1994), 30.

13. Krepinevich and Watts, *Last Warrior*, 210–211.

14. Ibid., 211.

15. Andrew W. Marshall, "Some Thoughts on Military Revolutions," ONA memorandum for record (July 27, 1993).

16. Krepinevich and Watts, *Last Warrior*, 211–212.

17. Ibid., 214.

18. Theodor W. Galdi, "Revolution in Military Affairs? Competing Concepts, Organizational Responses, Outstanding Issues," CRS 95-1170 F (Washington, DC: Congressional Research Service, December 11, 1995), 10.

19. William A. Owens, "The Emerging US System-of-Systems," *Strategic Forum* 63 (February 1996).

20. Based on notes by James Blackwell from 1993 to 1998, there were six Dominating Maneuver workshops and nine Dominating Maneuver war games. In addition, an RMA roundtable and two Army After Next war games were held.

21. For an account of this experiment, see Andrew D. May, Christine Grafton, and James Lasswell, "The US Marine Corps and Hunter War-

rior: A Case Study in Experimentation" (McLean, VA: Science Applications International Corporation, August 30, 2001).

22. Jan M. van Tol, "Military Innovation and Carrier Aviation—The Relevant History," *Joint Force Quarterly* 16 (Summer 1997): 77–87; Jan M. van Tol, "Military Innovation and Carrier Aviation—An Analysis," *Joint Force Quarterly* 17 (Autumn/Winter 1997–1998): 97–109.

23. Williamson Murray and Allan R. Millett, eds., *Military Innovation and the Interwar Period* (Cambridge: Cambridge University Press, 1996).

24. The initial vision defining the scope of the games was set out by Michael G. Vickers in 1996 in "Future Warfare 2020." Vickers together with Robert C. Martinage, Robert O. Work, Thomas P. Ehrhard, Jan M. van Tol, et al. were principally responsible for the design and execution of the 20XX game series.

25. Andrew W. Marshall, "Some Thoughts on Military Revolutions—Second Version," ONA memorandum (August 23, 1993), 3.

26. Ibid., 4.

27. Lucas Kello, *The Virtual Weapon and International Order* (New Haven and London: Yale University Press, 2017), 18.

28. The SAIC team also included Dan Beck, Tom Banks.

29. In the case of discussing the RMA with the Israelis, this involved rekindling an earlier relationship with ONA that had begun in the 1970s.

30. Andrew W. Marshall and Charles Wolf, Jr., *The Future Security Environment: Report of the Future Security Environment Working Group, Submitted to the Commission on Long-Term Strategy* (Washington, D.C.: Department of Defense, October 1988).

31. Michael Pillsbury, *Chinese Views of Future Warfare* (Washington, DC: National Defense University Press, 1997), 3–57. With ONA's support Pillsbury published a second volume that discussed more than 600 quotes from the writings of over 200 Chinese authors published from 1994 to 1999. See Michael Pillsbury, *China Debates the Future Security Environment* (Washington, DC: National Defense University Press, 2000).

32. Pillsbury, *China Debates the Future Security Environment*, xv.

33. Welch analyzed Chinese over-the-horizon radar system at a time when such capabilities were generally dismissed. Mark Herman and Daniel DeMots of Booz Allen investigated projecting power against Chinese AA/AD systems.

34. Peng Guangqian and Yao Youzhi, eds., *The Science of Military Strategy* (Beijing: Military Science Publishing House, 2005), 17; and David M. Finklestein, "China's National Military Strategy," in Roy Kamphausen and

Andrew Scobell, eds., *Right Sizing the People's Liberation Army: Exploring the Contours of China's Military Strategy* (Carlisle, PA: Strategic Studies Institute, US Army War College, September 2007), 94, 104, 118.

35. Barry D. Watts, "Countering Informationized Operations in Peace and War," Center for Strategic and Budgetary Assessments, 2014, 1–2.

36. David Axe, "Report: China Tests D-26 'Carrier-Killer' Missile (Should the Navy Be Worried?)," *The National Interest*, January 30, 2019, available at https://nationalinterest.org/blog/buzz/report-china-tests-df-2 6-carrier-killer-missile-should-navy-be-worried-42827. See also Andrew S. Erickson, "Academy of Military Science Researchers: 'Why We Had to Develop the Dongfeng-26 Ballistic Missile," December 5, 2018, at http://www.andrewerickson.com/2015/12/academy-of-military-science-researchers-why-we-had-to-develop-the-dongfeng-26-ballistic-missile-bilingual-text-analysis-links/.

37. "China vs United States—A GDP Comparison," MGM Research, December 21, 2018, available at https://mgmresearch.com/china-vs-united-states-a-gdp-comparison/.

38. Andrew May, "RE: More on Analytic Themes," email to Barry Watts, August 23, 2002.

39. Andrew F. Krepinevich, Jr., and Barry D. Watts, "Regaining Strategic Competence" (Washington, DC: Center for Strategic and Budgetary Assessments, 2009), vi.

40. C. K. Prahalad and Gary Hamel, "The Core Competence of the Corporation," *Harvard Business Review* (May–June 1990), 83. In military terms, Prahalad and Hamel define core competencies as applying to a range of scenarios, providing significant military advantage, and being hard for competitors to imitate. Long-range precision strike is a good example of an area of military competition that meets these criteria.

41. Andrew D. May, remarks presented at a conference at the Jefferson Hotel in Washington, DC, March 11, 2003. Krepinevich and Watts, *Last Warrior*, 231–235.

42. Barry D. Watts, "Recommendations on the Future *Focus* of the Office of Net Assessment," May 20, 2003, 3–4.

43. Ibid., 5.

44. Ibid., 2.

45. "Well Under Way," *The Economist*, October 27, 2018, 85, available at https://www.economist.com/graphic-detail/2018/10/27/the-chinese-century-is-well-under-way.

46. Barry D. Watts, conversation with Andrew Marshall, February 6, 2019.

CHAPTER 4

NET ASSESSMENT
AND ITS CUSTOMERS

Thomas G. Mahnken

Scholarly opinions differ markedly on influence of the Office of Net Assessment. Some hold that it was critical. Andrew F. Krepinevich, Jr., and Barry D. Watts, for example, have concluded that it was highly influential organization.[1] Douglas J. Feith has credited Marshall with supporting the development of nuclear strategy, studying the organizational behavior of large bureaucracies, advancing concepts in understanding long-term peacetime competition, and exploring the prospect of radical changes in the character of war.[2] Graham T. Allison has argued that although Marshall's "record is classified, he is one of the towering figures in . . . defense thinking in the last era."[3] Still others have contended his role is exaggerated. Michael C. Desch considered him as "a public official who served too long . . . [pushing] his insights to their most hawkish extremes."[4] And Jeffrey Lewis thought him as someone who "wasn't particularly wise" and endorsed "pretty awful policy ideas."[5]

A comprehensive account of ONA successes and failures will not be feasible for some time because most of its products remain classified. This secrecy has been imposed by design because the mission was assisting officials, not satisfying the curiosity of scholars or the general public. Nonetheless, a preliminary judgment is possible. As an organization that responded to officials in the Pentagon, it is appropriate to give considerable weight to their views. Accordingly, the record of ONA can be evaluated through the eyes of its customers by exploring the value attached to net assessments by senior officials who found ONA useful in three ways. First, they valued its analysis. Schlesinger conceived ONA and depended on Marshall as a close advisor. Rumsfeld played a major role in institutionalizing the net assessment process in the Department of Defense by retaining Marshall. Harold Brown was a keen consumer who used its products to study the US-Soviet competition. Second, officials valued ONA as a purveyor of ideas. For example, while distancing themselves from ONA, Caspar W. Weinberger and Frank C. Carlucci made competitive strategies, which had been developed by Marshall, a pillar of US defense strategy during the Reagan years. Third, Secretaries have prized ONA as a convener of networks. Richard B. Cheney, for example, drew on ONA expertise to understand the Soviet Union and then Russia. Finally, there have been senior officials who did not see the value of net assessment. William S. Cohen, for one, expressed little interest in ONA but ultimately failed in his attempt to scuttle it. This pattern of influence is likely to remain true for future Secretaries of Defense.

PRODUCER OF ASSESSMENTS

National Security Decision Memorandum (NSDM) 224 on "National Net Assessment Process," signed by Kissinger in June 1973, created the Net Assessment Standing Committee chaired by Marshall representing the National Security Council Staff.[6] Within months, Kissinger approved

National Security Study Memorandum (NSSM) 186, which contained the terms of reference for the first net assessment. That study was intended to "evaluate the comparative costs to the US and the USSR to produce, maintain, and operate comparable military forces" and its initial focus was US and Soviet ground forces.[7] Next, Kissinger signed NSDM 239, "National Net Assessment Process" that transferred the responsibility for net assessments to the Pentagon. It also specified that ONA would continue to study US and Soviet ground forces as required by NSSM 186.[8]

Marshall moved to the Pentagon under Schlesinger to coordinate net assessment activities in the Pentagon, perform assessments directly for the Secretary, encourage the military services and others to perform assessments, and carry out long-term improvements in analytical tools and techniques.[9] ONA was established to serve the Secretary of Defense, and it served that purpose for Schlesinger as well as his immediate successors. He was particularly interested in assessing strategic nuclear forces, the NATO-Warsaw Pact balance, the maritime balance, and the military investment balance between the United States and the Soviet Union. ONA was initially small in size, consisting of a director, two military assistants, and two secretaries.[10]

The principal ONA customers were senior officials of the Department of Defense: first and foremost the Secretary of Defense. Its products were intended to assist in the management of strategic issues by highlighting important problems and opportunities in a timely way to permit senior leaders to do something about them.[11] Schlesinger found the bureaucracy as incapable of strategic thinking and looked to ONA on such matters. To meet his requirements, assessments had to be frank. Schlesinger instructed that they come directly to him without being coordinated by the bureaucracy and also did not impose a production schedule.[12] In that way, net assessment as practiced in the Pentagon became the antithesis of the original concept found in NSDM 224 of net assessment as an interagency process. Marshall thought that because most consequential decisions made by Secretaries of Defense dealt with the future, ONA needed to look out years or decades. He believed that net assessments should provide senior officials with early warning of emerging problems and opportunities and highlight neglected issues.[13]

Marshall became Schlesinger's personal advisor and saw him daily.[14] He performed a vital function: providing a no-nonsense, objective sounding board.[15] As Schlesinger recounted, "Andy would come to my office regularly. . . . I would take him on my trips to Europe, and Mary [his wife] and Andy would sit up in the cabin with my wife and myself. And so we have a lot of private communications. . . . A lot of this would be just sort of private briefings."[16] Marshall's relationship with Schlesinger afforded him considerable power. According to Schlesinger, "The Pentagon bureaucracy recognizes those who have the Secretary's ear from those who don't . . . [and] they treated Andy with kid gloves."[17] Schlesinger left the Pentagon in November 1975 and at the farewell ceremony Marshall was the only official below the rank of Assistant Secretary of Defense invited to stand with the Secretary of Defense on the dais.[18]

Rumsfeld became the youngest Secretary of Defense at the age of 43. His temperament and management style predisposed him to retain the position that Schlesinger established for him. He found it made sense to look at strategic issues in support of the Secretary of Defense.[19] Rumsfeld continued the agreement reached with Schlesinger: that ONA report directly to him and focus on diagnostic assessments.[20] It was logical for Marshall to be responsible to Rumsfeld because ONA products had implications that cut across the bureaucracy from policy and planning to acquisition and operations.[21] As Marshall would later recall: "After the first few weeks we did a lot of things for him and got along very well with him. I was very impressed with Rumsfeld."[22] Marshall discovered working for and with him easy.[23]

Marshall served as a personal advisor to Rumsfeld, who sent him requests for views on issues such as Soviet missile programs.[24] In December 1975, Marshall began to forward four or five page summaries on the strategic nuclear, naval, power projection, and NATO-Warsaw Pact balances. Rumsfeld asked not only for assessments of key balances but also special analyses of the Middle East, US and Soviet mobilization, détente, and strategic nuclear competition.[25] ONA work on the US-Soviet military balance proved useful to Rumsfeld. In his view, ONA indicated that the Soviet Union was gaining on the United States and, absent increased defense spending, "the projections of future trend lines did not bode well for the United States."[26]

Rumsfeld found ONA data useful in drafting his first posture statement. By one estimate, it was probably half written by the ONA staff.[27] He believed military trend data helpful for dealing with Congress while Robert Ellsworth, the Deputy Secretary of Defense, exploited the trend data in building support for conventional defense within NATO.[28] ONA under Rumsfeld also became a purveyor of ideas. Marshall and Commander James G. Roche, USN, drafted a memorandum in July 1976 for Rumsfeld on "Strategy for Competing with the Soviets in the Military Sector of the Continuing Political-Military Competition," drawing on previous work by Marshall while he was at RAND.[29] It offered some thoughts on how to develop strategy for competing with the Soviet Union in different areas over the long term.[30] However, Rumsfeld did not read the memorandum until later in the year, so it did not have a major impact on his thinking, particularly following the 1976 national elections, which saw Gerald R. Ford lose to Jimmy Carter.[31]

Just as it was hardly preordained that ONA would survive the transition from Schlesinger to Rumsfeld, the matter of whether it would outlast the Nixon and Ford administrations to exist under the Carter administration was uncertain. As it happened, Carter named Harold Brown as the Secretary of Defense who became the ideal ONA customer. He possessed imposing academic credentials and considerable national security experience. Although Marshall had known him for some time, they were not personal friends. As Marshall recounted: "When he came on board, I was asked to stay and in some ways the period under Brown was probably the time when ONA had the biggest kind of payoff."[32] Brown did not contemplate abolishing ONA. On the contrary, he was impressed because it "seemed analytical and strategic and thought ahead in a way that no other element in the Defense Department really took as its main mission."[33] And Marshall was providing the kind of longer-term strategic thinking that was needed.

Although Brown transferred ONA into the newly established Office of the Under Secretary of Defense for Policy, Marshall reported directly to him. While they did not often meet, Brown and Marshall communicated frequently in writing. Brown preferred to tackle strategic issues by reading papers and annotating those that he found useful with handwritten comments, notes, and guidance. As Marshall recalled, Brown "trained himself to be the most prodigious and efficient reader I have ever met. We did not send him lots of things, but we sent more to him than to any other secretary, partly because by the time he came in we were really up to speed."[34]

Brown agreed that assessments should be written and sent directly to him rather than being coordinated within the Pentagon. As he related later: "Andy was always able to come in directly and talk with me, and did present stuff to me directly without it being—and wrote stuff for me directly—without it having concurrence from a lot of other people."[35] In many ways, his tenure coincided with the highpoint in ONA activity. Marshall submitted eleven assessments to Brown compared with eight assessments for Weinberger, Carlucci, and Cheney from 1982 to 1991; and four assessments for Les Aspin, Jr., William J. Perry, and Cohen from 1992 to 2001.[36] ONA influenced the Carter defense program in a number of ways. For example, its undersea warfare assessment led Brown to increase US anti-submarine warfare efforts.[37] The NATO-Warsaw Pact balance also persuaded him to build sufficient NATO conventional forces to last 30 to 45 days in a conflict without escalating to nuclear warfare. ONA further convinced Brown of the need for NATO to leverage its technological advantage over the Soviet Union.[38]

ONA under Brown conducted work on the military balance in the Persian Gulf, including research by Dennis B. Ross, Edward N. Luttwak, and Stephen L. Canby.[39] ONA products also influenced the abortive decision by the Carter administration to withdraw the US Armed Forces from the Korean Peninsula. In fact, Brown recalled that the ONA study on the military balance in Korea convinced the President that pulling out would have dire consequences.[40] Although ONA continued to report to the Secretary of Defense, Marshall also fulfilled a number of requests from Under Secretary of Defense for Policy Stanley R. Resor and his successor, Robert W. Komer.[41] Another RAND veteran as well as friend of Marshall since the 1950s, Komer found its products helpful.[42] The ONA staff also built ties to the military services in this period.[43]

The paper by written Marshall and Roche in 1976 on "Strategy for Competing with the Soviets in the Military Sector of the Continuing Political-Military Competition" was originally prepared for Rumsfeld. It stimulated thinking on competitive strategies during Brown's tenure. He agreed with its conclusion that rather than seeking to counter threats, the United States must instead seek to exploit the weaknesses of the Soviet Union. In that situation, Moscow would be compelled to react to Washington rather than vice versa. As Brown noted:

> They started from a different premise: that is, stand back, we're in this competition which goes beyond the military, [and] what he does is going to depend on what he does, [so] what are our fundamental advantages, disadvantages, and how do you adopt strategies and take steps that rest on your competitive advantage? Although that's an obvious thing for any military strategist or any other kind of strategist to do, it doesn't come naturally from a bureaucratic set up. And it did come in many cases successfully from Andy Marshall's net assessment shop.[44]

The rationale for the B-1 *Lancer* bomber, which was designed to penetrate airspace at low altitude, was based partially on such considerations. Because the Soviet Union showed a great propensity to defend the Motherland against overflights, Marshall had good reason to expect that deploying nuclear-armed B-1s would reinforce Soviet decisions on making heavy investments in air defenses.[45] Overall, Brown found ONA products to be helpful. As he remarked some years later, "you can't single out a single sub-organization and say that it determined the policies, but you can say of Net Assessment that it had a very strong effect . . . on many key decisions."[46]

The US-Soviet strategic nuclear balance offered the most significant assessment that ONA undertook given the consequences of a failure in deterrence. Almost as critical was the NATO-Warsaw Pact balance given the possibility of conflict in Europe escalating to the use of nuclear weapons. Assessments of these balances were completed in the late 1970s and sent to Brown.[47] ONA also prepared other net assessments. For example, Commander Gerald W. Dunne, USN, completed one on US and Soviet command, control, and communications in 1978. It highlighted a weakness that needed to be addressed, provoking a surge in research on C3, which included five studies conducted by the Defense Science Board, improvements in C3 durability, and stimulus to focus attention on contemplating the relevance of the information revolution.[48]

As the experience of the Carter administration revealed, the ONA influence was a function of Marshall's relationship with the Secretary rather than the political views of the White House. Because of the relationship forged by Marshall with Brown, he enjoyed considerable influence, even in a dovish administration. By contrast, that influence was reduced during the ensuing years of the Reagan administration. Although many from the President down were predisposed to view the US-Soviet relationship in terms of competition, and the administration in many ways pursued a strategy in line with the conclusions of ONA analysis, its influence was somewhat attenuated during Weinberger's tenure, the first Secretary of Defense appointed by Reagan.[49]

Marshall had met Weinberger several times when the latter was the Director of the Office of Management and Budget in the Nixon administration but interacted very little once Weinberger became Secretary of

Defense. Weinberger seemed to have little interest in ONA, and he met with Marshall only a handful of times.[50] Weinberger gave the impression of being indifferent toward the sort of assessments produced for Brown. From Weinberger's point of view, the need to catch up to the Soviet Union did not require careful analysis of strengths and weaknesses.[51]

While previous Secretaries of Defense decided assessments should be performed internally, Weinberger and Casey agreed that assessments, "when undertaken, would be published under the joint auspices of the Secretary of Defense and [the] Director of Central Intelligence."[52] The initial study on the US-Soviet nuclear balance appeared as a two-volume document that was completed in November 1983.[53] The first volume consisted of an executive summary by Captain Charles C. Pease, USN, an ONA staff member, and Lawrence Gershwin, the National Intelligence Officer for Strategic Forces. It contained key judgments on the nuclear balance and was highly restricted when distributed because of its high level of classification. The second, longer volume contained details on the projected nuclear forces of the United States and Soviet Union. Marshall sent three other analyses in 1984 to Weinberger on the US-Soviet maritime and power projection balances and an East Asia assessment prepared by Stephen Peter Rosen. It is unclear whether Weinberger read them; if he did, he did not provide any feedback. Two years later, Marshall sent Weinberger an assessment of the NATO-Warsaw Pact military balance, which wound up being the last major study completed by the Office of Net Assessment during the Cold War.[54]

Given the limited interest shown by Weinberger in assessments, more than half of the ONA resources were devoted to projects associated with the Nuclear Strategy Development Group and the Commission on Integrated Long-Term Strategy (CILTS).[55] Additionally, ONA was requested to collect lessons from the US intervention in Lebanon.[56] Even though Weinberger seemed to be disinterested in assessments, Marshall remained in contact with Carlucci. At his behest, Marshall sent him memos on strategy and organization, which led to the creation of the

Strategic Concepts Development Center.[57] As the personal think tank of the Secretary, it was located at the National Defense University and headed by Phillip A. Karber who reported directly to Weinberger and the Chairman of the Joint Chiefs of Staff.[58] Marshall had greater contact with the Under Secretary of Defense for Policy, Fred Charles Iklé, under whom the ONA staff was moved in 1985.[59]

The notion of competitive strategies—presented first to Rumsfeld and then to Brown—had begun to take hold institutionally during Weinberger's tenure. In the annual report to Congress in February 1986, he announced competitive strategies would form a major theme for the remainder of the Reagan administration.[60] Three organizations were established to support the Competitive Strategies Initiative. The Competitive Strategies Council was chaired by Weinberger and included the Chairman, service secretaries and chiefs, undersecretaries, directors of both the National Security Agency and the Defense Intelligence Agency, and the Assistant Secretary of Defense for Program Analysis and Evaluation. Then came the Competitive Strategies Steering Group chaired by Allison and including the Director of Net Assessment, assistant secretaries for policy and international security affairs with representatives of the Undersecretary of Defense for Acquisition, service secretaries and chiefs, and the Director of the Defense Intelligence Agency. For day-to-day management of the initiative, Weinberger established the Competitive Strategies Office. He also established two interdepartmental task forces: one on competitive opportunities within the context of high-intensity conventional warfare in Europe, which proposed accelerated fielding of precision conventional munitions, wide-area sensors, and battle networks; and the other on non-nuclear strategic capabilities using precision munitions and long-range systems.[61]

When Carlucci succeeded Weinberger in 1987, he continued to institutionalize competitive strategies which was emphasized in his annual report to Congress.[62] Also, he was interested in the concept of net assessment, even though his tenure was too short to pursue it.[63]

By the time George H.W. Bush entered the White House in 1989, the Cold War and US-Soviet competition had ended. Secretary Cheney found less use in the ONA formal analysis than its network of expertise as he endeavored to understand the contours of the post–Cold War world. However, Under Secretary of Defense Paul D. Wolfowitz and I. Lewis Libby proved to be eager ONA customers.[64] Although Cheney did not request for analytical studies, Wolfowitz expressed interest in topics such as hardened targets and underground facilities.[65] Later, he recalled getting studies on China and the changing character of war that he found particularly useful.[66]

Marshall routinely interacted with Cheney on the Soviet Union and forwarded studies that were helpful to him.[67] Moreover, Wolfowitz and Libby arranged Saturday morning briefings on the Soviet Union for the Secretary that drew on the ONA network of expertise.[68] Libby related that when questions were posed on "the best guys to talk about the Soviet Union, and how strong is the Soviet economy, and what really is the role of the nationalities within the Soviet Union," ONA had been working on those questions for years and was prepared to respond.[69] More than most, Cheney searched for experts to obtain additional views and information.[70]

Although the end of the Cold War had called into question much of its traditional research agenda, ONA sent Cheney assessments of the military balance in Europe and Korea.[71] Moreover, its staff worked on assessments on proliferation in the developing world and how it could change the nature of power projection; the military balance in Asia, which Marshall at the time believed "has not been analyzed very much;" and the state of the so-called *military-technical revolution.*[72] It also continued work on the future security environment, which was begun about 1986.[73]

Ideas associated with a military-technical revolution or revolution in military affairs gained influence during the Clinton administration even as the direct influence of ONA waned.[74] Aspin's brief tenure saw ONA's access to the Secretary diminish. Marshall submitted the assessment on the military-technical revolution to Aspin in January 1993, with copies going to Walter B. Slocombe, the incoming Deputy Undersecretary of Defense for Policy and Allison, who had been named as the Assistant Secretary of Defense for Policy and Plans. Subsequently, Marshall was told his ideas would receive a better hearing if he worked through Allison rather than attempting to directly approach the Defense Secretary of Defense.[75]

Perry replaced Aspin when he stepped down in 1994. He backed the information revolution to transform the US Armed Forces, aspects of which he had kept an eye on as Under Secretary of Defense for Research and Engineering and then as the Deputy Secretary of Defense. In his view, previous experience more than ONA influenced his thinking. As he observed:

> Andy was writing about transformation, reform of defense. I spent my whole career as Under Secretary doing that. It wasn't that I had a problem with Andy, but the gospel he was preaching I was already converted to. I was already determined to do the reforms and did not need to be inspired to do them, the question was how to implement them. Andy is great at conceptualizing them, but I already had that concept and I was focusing on how to implement it."[76]

If ONA ideas such transforming the US Armed Forces to exploit an emerging revolution in military affairs found purchase during the early part of the Clinton administration without a close relationship with the Secretary, in the latter years of the administration ONA faced an existential threat. Secretary Cohen neither used ONA nor developed a relationship with Marshall. In fact, he decided in late 1997 to transfer ONA to the National Defense University in an effort to downsize the Pentagon.[77] His decision prompted letters of protest from Schlesinger, Rumsfeld, Brown, and Cheney as well as congressmen. Eventually, the pressure forced Cohen to relent: Marshall stayed in place as advisor to the Secretary of Defense for Net Assessment.[78] The ONA influence was marginal and conceptual based on initiatives such as the Revolution in Military Affairs.

With the inauguration of George W. Bush in 2001, Marshall found himself working again for Rumsfeld. Shortly after becoming Secretary of Defense, Rumsfeld invited Marshall to lunch in the Executive Dining Room at the Pentagon in a public show of support. As Rumsfeld noted, "I sought out someone whose advice I had valued during my first Pentagon tour: Andy Marshall was still working in the department, though his work was less in vogue during the prior Bush and Clinton administrations, in part because of his cautions on China and Russia."[79] Rumsfeld tasked Marshall to prepare a strategy review within a month. It outlined a strategy based on maintaining US military dominance for as long as possible.[80] Rumsfeld and Marshall met with the President in March 2001 to discuss the review. Bush was engaged and "very pleased" with the effort and urged them to continue developing the strategy.[81] In the words of the Under Secretary of Defense for Policy, the review called for greater attention to Asia and stressed the role of uncertainty in strategic planning, which "had a powerful effect on policy."[82]

Marshall did not propose another long-term ONA research agenda until 2004. When he did, three main balances were identified: a regional assessment of the military balance in Asia, which emphasized the requirement to hedge against the rise of China; a functional assessment of power projection in an anti-access/area-denial environment; and an assessment of the durability of the US advantage in realistic combat training. In addition, he included a series of studies designed to assist in the understanding of how advances in undersea warfare, the biological and life sciences, directed energy weapons, demographic decline in Russia, and possible natural calamities such as an AIDS epidemic in Asia, might affect the international security environment.[83]

* * *

Several conclusions stand out from this review of the influence of the Office of Net Assessment. First, it took a bureaucratic equivalent of three miracles for it to be established and then survive. It had to be created by Schlesinger, kept in existence for the balance of the Ford administration by Rumsfeld, and then preserved in the Carter administration by Brown. Without those miracles, ONA never would have had the influence that it subsequently acquired.[84] Second, its influence varied dramatically over the years. In general, ONA advised and assisted a number of Secretaries of Defense interested in strategy. It had greater difficulty performing that function when they were less than interested in strategic matters. Third, different Secretaries used ONA in different ways. Schlesinger, Rumsfeld, and Brown, were consumers of its analysis.[85] Others like Cheney saw value in its intellectual capital. Still others, such as Weinberger, Carlucci, Perry, and even Cohen, were consumers—sometimes consciously, sometimes not— of its ideas. More than assessments, this was perhaps the greatest ONA contribution. As Marshall put it: "My sense has been that, to the extent you can change the way in which a widening group of people think about a certain class of problems, that's maybe as much as you can expect to do."[86]

NOTES

1. Andrew F. Krepinevich, Jr., and Barry D. Watts, *The Last Warrior: Andrew Marshall and the Shaping of Modern American Defense Strategy* (New York: Basic Books, 2015).
2. Douglas J. Feith, "The Hidden Hand Behind American Foreign Policy," *Wall Street Journal*, January 23, 2015.
3. Jay Winik, "Secret Weapon," *Washingtonian* (April 1999), 48.
4. Michael C. Desch, "Don't Worship at the Alter of Andrew Marshall," *The National Interest* (January–February 2015).
5. Jeffrey Lewis, "Yoda Has Left the Building", *Foreign Policy* online.
6. National Security Decision Memorandum 224, "National Net Assessment Process," June 28, 1973.
7. National Security Study Memorandum 186, "National Net Assessment of the Comparative Costs and Capabilities of US and Soviet Military Establishments," September 1, 1973.
8. National Security Decision Memorandum 239, "National Net Assessment Process," November 27, 1973.
9. Interview with Andrew W. Marshall by Alfred Goldberg and Maurice Matloff (June 1, 1992), 19.
10. Ibid., 19
11. Krepinevich and Watts, *Last Warrior*, 103.
12. Ibid., 104.
13. Ibid., 103.
14. Interview with Marshall by Alfred Goldberg and Maurice Matloff (June 15, 1992), 21.
15. Interview with Phillip A. Karber by Thomas G. Mahnken and Andrew D. May (December 20, 2013), 3.
16. Interview with James R. Schlesinger by Andrew D. May and Barry D. Watts (February 8, 2006), 12.
17. Ibid., 12.
18. Interview with Karber, 5.
19. Interview with Donald Rumsfeld by Thomas G. Mahnken (September 16, 2014), 1–2.
20. Krepinevich and Watts, *Last Warrior*, 119.
21. Interview with Karber, 8.
22. Interview with Marshall (June 15, 1992), 11.

23. Ibid., 12.
24. Ibid., 11.
25. Krepinevich and Watts, *Last Warrior*, 121–22.
26. Donald Rumsfeld, *Known and Unknown: A Memoir* (New York: Sentinel, 2011), 224.
27. Interview with Karber, 6.
28. Ibid., 8.
29. Andrew W. Marshall, *Long-Term Competition with the Soviets: A Framework for Strategic Analysis*, R-862-PR (Santa Monica, CA: RAND Corporation, 1972).
30. James G. Roche and Andrew W. Marshall, "Strategy for Competing with the Soviets in the Military Sector of the Continuing Political-Military Competition," July 26, 1976.
31. Interview with Marshall, (June 15, 1992), 17.
32. Ibid., 17.
33. According to Brown: "It never occurred to me to eliminate it because it seemed to me fascinating and important. And perhaps the only place in the US government that did that kind of thing." Interview with Harold Brown by Andrew D. May (April 5, 2014), 2, 3.
34. Interview with Marshall, 20.
35. Interview with Harold Brown by Andrew D. May and Barry D. Watts (January 27, 2006), 3.
36. Krepinevich and Watts, *Last Warrior*, 130.
37. Interview with Brown (January 27, 2006), 5.
38. Ibid., 6.
39. See Dennis Ross, "Considering Soviet Threats to the Persian Gulf," *International Security* 6 (Fall 1981), 159–80. Ross was at the time an Assistant to the Director of Net Assessment.
40. Winik, "Secret Weapon," 46.
41. Interview with Marshall (June 15, 1992, 17); Frank Leith Jones, *Blowtorch: Robert Komer, Vietnam, and American Cold War Strategy* (Annapolis, MD: Naval Institute Press, 2013), chapter 12.
42. Interview with Karber, 10.
43. Ibid., 10, 12.
44. Interview with Brown (January 27, 2006), 5.
45. Krepinevich and Watts, *Last Warrior*, 131.
46. Interview with Brown (January 27, 2006), 7.
47. Krepinevich and Watts, *Last Warrior*, 148.
48. Krepinevich and Watts, *Last Warrior*, 148–49.

49. Thomas G. Mahnken, "The Reagan Administration's Strategy Toward the Soviet Union" In Williamson Murray and Richard Hart Sinnreich, ed., *Successful Strategies: Triumphing in War and Peace from Antiquity to the Present* (Cambridge: Cambridge University Press, 2014).

50. Interview with Marshall by Alfred Goldberg and Maurice Matloff (June 29, 1992), 3, 5; interview with Karber, 14.

51. Krepinevich and Watts, *Last Warrior*, 156.

52. Ibid., 159.

53. Secretary of Defense and Director of Central Intelligence, *US and Soviet Strategic Forces: Joint Net Assessment*, Executive Version, NI 83-10002X (Washington, D.C.: Central Intelligence Agency, November 14, 1983).

54. Krepinevich and Watts, *Last Warrior*, 176

55. Interview with Marshall (June 29, 1992), 12–14.

56. Ibid., 18.

57. Ibid., 4.

58. Krepinevich and Watts, *Last Warrior*, 163.

59. Interview with Marshall (June 29, 1992), 7.

60. *Report of the Secretary of Defense Caspar W. Weinberger to the Congress on the FY 1987 Budget, FY 1988 Authorization Request, and FY 1987–1991 Defense Programs* (Washington, D.C.: Government Printing Office, February 5, 1986), 85–89

61. See David J. Andre, *New Competitive Strategies Tools and Methodologies*, vol. 1, *Review of the Department of Defense Competitive Strategies Initiative, 1986–1990* (McLean, VA: Science Applications International Corporation, 1990). See also Daniel I. Gouré, "Overview of the Competitive Strategies Initiative" in Thomas G. Mahnken, editor, *Competitive Strategies for the 21st Century: Theory, History, and Practice* (Palo Alto, CA: Stanford University Press, 2012).

62. *Report of the Secretary of Defense, Frank C. Carlucci, to the Congress on the Amended FY 1988/FY 1989 Biennial Budget* (Washington, D.C.: Government Printing Office, February 18, 1988), 115–18.

63. Interview with Karber, 22.

64. Interview with Marshall by Alfred Goldberg and Maurice Matloff (July 2, 1992), 3.

65. Ibid., 7.

66. Interview with Paul D. Wolfowitz by Thomas G. Mahnken and Andrew D. May (February 12, 2014), 5.

67. Interview with Marshall (July 2, 1992), 1.

68. Interview with I. Lewis Libby by Thomas G. Mahnken and Andrew D. May (January 14, 2014), 3.
69. Ibid., 5.
70. Interview with Marshall (July 2, 1992), 4.
71. Ibid., 8.
72. Ibid., 6
73. Interview with Marshall (July 2, 1992), 5.
74. For example, see Andrew W. Marshall, "Some Thoughts on Military Revolutions," memorandum for the record, July 23, 1993; Andrew W. Marshall, "RMA Update," memorandum for the record, May 2, 1994.
75. Ibid., 216.
76. Interview with William J. Perry by Alfred Goldberg and Rebecca Welch (October 18, 2004).
77. William S. Cohen, *Defense Reform Initiative Report* (Washington, DC: Department of Defense, 1997).
78. Winik, "Secret Weapon," 45–55.
79. Rumsfeld, *Known and Unknown*, 293.
80. See Bradley Graham, *By His Own Rules: The Ambitions, Successes, and Ultimate Failures of Donald Rumsfeld* (New York: Public Affairs, 2009), 245; see also Krepinevich and Watts, *Last Warrior*, 232
81. Krepinevich and Watts, *Last Warrior*, 232.
82. Feith, "Hidden Hand."
83. Krepinevich and Watts, *Last Warrior*, 230–31.
84. As Marshall put it, ONA "probably never would have had the character that it had unless it had been started and perpetuated the way it was. The office was fortunate—first the Schlesinger period, when the basic role and mission were set, and then sustained very well under both Rumsfeld and Brown." Interview with Marshall (July 2, 1992), 10.
85. In Marshall's words, "I see the function of net assessment being to provide to top leadership a frank, well thought out, unbiased diagnosis of major problem areas and issues that they should pay more attention to." Ibid., 20.
86. Ibid., 10

CHAPTER 5

ASSESSING SOVIET MILITARY CAPABILITIES

John A. Battilega

The Office of Net Assessment identified, compared, and analyzed both strengths and weaknesses of US-USSR military capabilities and postures in support of strategic planning. The assessments included quantitative and qualitative factors, including identification of key military areas over which both sides competed, and a detailed understanding of the nature of that competition. What is more, asymmetric concepts, capabilities, and perspectives were crucial to assessments because they could represent dangerous vulnerabilities or sources of strength.[1] These assessments focused on trends with time horizons that provided comparative evaluations which looked 20 to 30 years into the future. Equally important were historical perspectives gained from studying the past. The net assessments were diagnostic rather than prescriptive, leaving to others the task of deciding what should be done in light of the conclusions reached by the assessments. Diagnostics stressed efforts to find relevant problems as well as opportunities for the United States.

ONA used different methods of evaluating military capabilities: head-to-head assessments (e.g., US armor versus Soviet armor), side-by-side assessments (e.g., Soviet air-to-air missiles versus US air-to-air missiles), major systems comparisons (e.g., Soviet versus US ICBM force), and comparisons of broader application of doctrine and military art (e.g., US electronic warfare versus Soviet radio-electronic combat). Moreover, assessments considered the impact of factors that influenced military power as a whole as well as the role of individual soldiers and indicators of Soviet effectiveness such as demography, economics, social issues, health, and environment. As a result, these comparative assessments could be either broad (e.g., the balance of forces in Central Europe) or more focused (e.g., command, control, and communications).

The net assessment process was not formulaic. Once a given subset of military capabilities was identified for comparison, details of the selected area determined the research methodology, organization of the assessment process, and form of the results. Both quantitative and qualitative methods were applied as needed. Although assessments dug as deep as possible, the process was careful and comprehensive. The scope of assessments included "forces, operational doctrines and practices, training regime, logistics, known or conjectured effectiveness in various environments, design practices and their effect of equipment cost and performance, and procurement practices and their influence on cost and lead time."[2] The assessments required in-depth understanding of Soviet internal operations, force capabilities, posture, approach to warfare, and trends.

This chapter surveys the requirements for understanding Soviet capabilities for the purpose of net assessment. Next, it considers procedures related to that understanding and representative asymmetries between US and Soviet approaches that informed net assessments. Then it discusses understanding the Soviet Union in terms of selected assessments conducted from 1974 to 1991. The chapter goes on to assess the lessons learned through an understanding of the Soviet Union. It concludes by looking at the implications for future net assessments. Moreover, an addendum to the chapter is included that elaborates the specific requirements for understanding the Soviet Union.

THE REQUIREMENTS

Taken at face value, net assessments compare the size of military forces. In fact, the collection of comprehensive and accurate data on force size over time turned out to be a major part of the net assessment process until the Cold War ended. As the US-USSR net assessment unfolded, many areas relating to Soviet forces emerged that required close study to understand their comparative military capabilities. Data collected and analyzed by the Intelligence Community became topics of research by governmental agencies, Federally Funded Research and Development Centers, corporations, academia, and even individuals.

Various dimensions of Soviet military affairs were crosscutting and influenced every aspect of its approach to warfare. They included the national security environment; the framework for application of military power; the influence of ideology on war; political and military objectives; military doctrine; key concepts of military science; the structure, content, and method of military art; the calculus of correlation of forces; the command economy; defense economics; societal and demographics; and the profile of the individual soldier. Additionally, there were important niche topics including perspectives on the United States, NATO, China, Japan, etc.; planning scenarios for future conflict; the historical style of war; command and control; nuclear doctrine; research, development, and acquisition; mobilization; training; logistics and maintenance; intelligence for internal control; power projection; quasi-military organizations; the role of the Communist Party; intangible factors in warfare; and the concept of a military-technical revolution.

Efforts at collecting data encountered two difficulties. The first involved an absence of data because of the closed nature of Soviet society. In time, this led to the expansion of intelligence sources to fill in the gaps. More significantly, it gradually became understood that a large volume of open-source literature existed with evidence on topics of interest. In addition, interviews with Russian émigrés and defectors revealed societal issues that contributed to actual military power which suggested programs to exploit them. The second issue concerned asymmetry. Moscow and Washington exercised military power differently. For the former, planning scenarios began with NATO attacking Eastern Europe while the latter envisioned the Warsaw Pact attacking NATO.[3] It became necessary to understand these differences and reflect them in assessments, which made avoiding mirror imaging key to evaluating Soviet perceptions of doctrine, capabilities, etc. Those questions related to deterring attacks on US and Western European forces, for instance, had to be understood in terms of the possible approaches employed by the Soviet Union.[4]

It was important to take the approaches of the Soviet Union at face value while not dismissing them because of functional differences with the United States. They had to be understood on the same terms that Moscow understood them. Only in this way could the intangible but extremely important aspects of Soviet decision-making during wartime be identified for consideration and appropriate action by the United States.

ASYMMETRIES

Three examples drawn from Soviet military art illustrate the asymmetries that were important to the net assessment process including the overall Soviet approach to warfare, the Soviet calculus of the correlation of forces, and the Soviet focus on centralized command and control.[5]

The underlying basis of the Soviet approach to warfare on all levels was scientific Marxism that implies believing objective laws govern processes such as warfighting. Similarly, the Soviets held that careful scientific study could create methods and criteria, based on the objective laws of war, that provided an objective basis for success. But sound methods alone do not insure victory. Military forces also have to operate properly. Hence, sound concepts and their execution based on such criteria might create objective conditions for victory.[6] Moreover, the Soviets thought military concepts and methods derived from objective laws offered a rationale for prescriptive plans that, if developed in advance and properly executed, would result in victory. The Soviet approach was opposite to the American view that saw warfare as an uncertain process, characterized by the fog of war and requiring the ability to adapt and prevail. Another relevant Marxist idea, derived from the German philosopher Georg Hegel, was the concept of the dialectic. According to his method, history proceeds as a result of conflict or struggle between opposites with the stronger winning out. The conflict, in turn, produces the conditions for a new dialectic and so forth.

A key derivative of this view is the concept of *sootnosheniye sil* (correlation of forces) that expresses the relationship between strengths of opposing sides in a conflict (that is, the two sides of the dialectic). According to Soviet thought, the result of a conflict (synthesis of the dialectic) is determined by the side with most strength. Victory belongs to the side with the best correlation of forces which determines the outcome of a conflict. Thus, interstate warfare was considered as a dialectic process. The major dimension of strength determining the outcome fell into political, economic, military, scientific-technical, and social (ideological) categories that developed major regimes of conflict and, in turn, was governed by the logic of the correlation of forces.

In the military sphere, the Soviet theories actually framed some basic laws of war in terms of the correlation of forces. For example, Soviet experts published an article in the journal of the General Staff, *Voyennaya Mysl'* (Military Thought), which argued that

> The correlation of belligerent forces (quantitative and qualitative) is an objective foundation on the basis of which troops accomplish

their assigned missions. . . . Since the outcome of war between
states (coalitions) depends on the correlation of their military
strength . . . each military action (engagement, battle, operation)
is predetermined by the same concrete conditions. In other words,
the law of dependence of the course and outcome of war on the
correlation of forces of the belligerents is in effect at all levels of
war and at every scale of war.[7]

The Soviets embedded this approach in military art. Hence, the overarching requirement in warfare called for achieving a "favorable correlation of forces at decisive places and times." The underlying approach to
combat saw this mandate as necessary and sufficient for success. There is
no such pervasive approach found in US military thinking. Approximate
estimates of the balance of forces sometimes are used as the initial basis
for planning operations by the United States, but they do not become the
focal point of the combat operations themselves.

The correlation of forces became the central focus of Soviet military
thought. The Soviets concluded that, if indices exist that yield correct
dimensions of comparative strength for a given form of combat, then
a clear relationship exists between the size of forces as measured by
those indices and the probability of success. The Soviet Union had a
well-developed calculus of the correlation of forces with three different
although related meanings. In general, it described the relationship
between opposing sides in dialectic struggles. In addition, it meant the
relationship of strengths between the opposing sides qualitatively and
quantitatively. The term also meant specific indices to gauge the probability of success. More narrowly, *sootnosheniye sil i sredstv* (correlation of
forces and means) typically described specific and numerically calculable
indices used in preparing and conducting war. The correlation of forces
denoted "the fighting power of opposing sides which permits a determination of the degree of superiority of one of them over the other."[8]

A family of indices captured strengths of different forms of combat.
Furthermore, there was a structure to apply those indices, monitor
success or failure in combat, and anticipate success or failure in the

future. The types of indices were the *quantitative*, which did not mean quantifiable but only some rough account of weapons, and the *qualitative*, which did not mean *subjective* but rather capabilities over and above weaponry. Some qualitative indices quantified human factors such as morale. For example, a quantitative index listed the number of tanks while a qualitative index for tank combat represented the number of tanks modified by the estimated rate of fire and the single shot probability of kill for the main gun against a representative target.

Calculating basic indices of the quantitative correlation of forces was standard practice for every operation and battle on the strategic, operational, and tactical levels. The basic quantitative correlation of forces, supported by norms derived from the analyses of historical battles, was key to success and future prospects for success.[9] As the Soviet Union developed improved methods, it was possible to formulate indices of the correlation of forces beyond the simply quantitative, namely, qualitative indices incorporating the additional characteristics of military force postures. The qualitative indices fell into different categories depending on the nature of the combat. This combined quantitative/qualitative index structure was superimposed on the structure and scale of combat to correlate forces which enabled deployment and disposition, precombat comparative loss estimates, overall future probabilities of success, and combat adjustments.

In the United States, force comparisons emphasizing the number of personnel and weapons have been used for programmatic trade-offs, trend analysis, arms control assessments, and even initial combat planning. However, calculations have been far less holistic with respect to military capabilities than those of the Soviet Union. In addition, there is no mandate to maintain specific levels of relative strength as a condition for victory. The Soviet approach to warfare included the prescriptions for success based on understanding objective laws of war. Also, military operations were conducted from the top down in hierarchical order. Furthermore, military art was based on the strategic, operational, and tactical levels. The largest activity was called the *theater strategic operation* executed across the *theater of military operations*. The efforts were subordinated to the latter and focused on parts of the theater of military operations while structured tactical combat actions were executed in each event. Their number and content changed over time. For example, Soviet plans by 1985 included 15 theaters of military operations, 3 theater strategic operations, and 14 operations executed with all combat functions. Canonical operations incorporated force mixes, preparation requirements, and estimated correlations of forces. The war plans orchestrated overall combat success under the centralized system of command and control.

Centralized planning was focused on the achievement of strategic goals that, in turn, led to a hierarchical scale of interrelated strategic, operational, and tactical missions. This approach to command and control was meant to ensure success on higher levels. The purpose of operational combat was guaranteeing strategic success though not necessarily in every mission, and tactical combat would ensure operational success but not in every battle. For example, the Soviet Union accepted tactical defeat if it enabled operational success. Tactical commanders were constrained by the parameters of the plan and major decisions were made centrally. To facilitate this process, the Soviets exercised a pervasive system of troop control to facilitate prescriptive plans to enable senior commanders to continuously direct subordinates in fulfilling their missions.

The Soviet predilection for centralized command was guided by historical and societal factors. The legacy inherited from Russia included a Tsar who exercised absolute power. The Communist Party continued that practice, extending control to all sectors. Individuals were expected to carry out directives to the letter. Officers grew up in a culture that did not promote individual decision-making until perhaps the teenage years. As a result, tactical officers regarded decision-making as an onerous task best left to others. Hence, the approach to command and control was suited to societal norms. What is more, enlisted ranks included unskilled men from agrarian backgrounds and non-Russian republics, stressing a need for centralized command and control.

By contrast the American view of war as an uncertain process characterized by friction and the fog of war leads directly to a preference for centralized command and control to establish a planned, but highly decentralized, system of command and control to execute combat starting with planning to define initial conditions. In addition, US officers belong to a society that values the free-market economy, Jeffersonian democracy, and the spirit of rugged individualism, which is emphasized from an early age. The Soviet Union exhibited many asymmetries compared to the United States. It was vital to identify them, understand them, and consider their consequences in war. Soviet asymmetries may have led to different uses of forces, more or less combat resources, and various modes of employment, levels, or timing. Hence comparative capabilities or strengths and weaknesses, as viewed by each side, directly reflected underlying asymmetries.

Selected Assessments

From 1974 to 1991, ONA focused on two types of the US-USSR military balance: regional and functional.[10] Initially, the most important involved the strategic nuclear, NATO-Warsaw Pact, and maritime balances.[11] In due course, the focus expanded. Regional assessments encompassed the NATO-Warsaw Pact, NATO-Warsaw Pact Central Front, NATO-Warsaw Pact European Northern Flank, and East Asia while functional assessments covered strategic nuclear forces; maritime; space; command, control, and communications; antisubmarine warfare; budget; and power projection. Each assessment incorporated whatever was known about key aspects of the Soviet Union at the time as they were developed. Two examples are geographic net assessments of the NATO-Warsaw Pact Central Front and the command, control, and communications (C3) net assessments. The former balance was done in 1978 and 1986.[12] It showed the progressions of knowledge on the Soviet Union and enabled the latter to become more complete. The latter balance illustrated functional net assessment and a different class of understanding than that required for assessing the Central Front.[13] Collectively, they illustrated the kinds of Soviet understanding that was important and the progress in understanding the same aspects over time.

The assessment of the NATO-Warsaw Pact balance in 1978 featured theater nuclear forces; conventional NATO-Warsaw Pact forces on the Central Front; air and air defense; naval forces; command, control, and communications; counter-C3; force deployment; sustainability; chemical operation; and radio-electronic combat. Besides force data, understanding critical aspects of the Soviet approach was incorporated in the assessment. A major theme involved an understanding of doctrine on high speed conventional ground attack and maneuver; camouflage, concealment, deception, and tactical surprise; coordinated early air, ground, and electronic warfare attack on key C3 targets; offensive airpower with extensive early interdiction of major NATO air bases; initial strikes on NATO nuclear delivery systems; employing nuclear weapons in combination with conventional weapons; operations conducted in a nuclear environment; special operations; and a careful orchestration of tasks utilizing centralized command and control.

The quantitative comparison was focused on tanks, artillery, antitank weapons, air defense, surface-to-surface missiles, and tactical aircraft. The qualitative comparison of force capabilities used Armor Division Equivalents to aggregate diverse combat forces.[14] Special issues offered the context for capabilities and operations including combat between NATO and the Warsaw Pact, modernization, the strategic nuclear balance, the NATO flanks, and deterrence.

An important Soviet trend was focused on growing interest in more limited nuclear options. Perceived Warsaw Pact asymmetries included highly centralized command and control; radio-electronic capabilities under coordinated attacks on NATO C3 assets using deception, jamming, and firepower; command and control as a distinct function; force sustainability employing unit versus individual replacements; and organization and conduct of air defense. The uncertainties of the Soviet approach included logistics and sustainability, training, command and control, detailed doctrine on several levels, delivery by aircraft of nuclear weapons, views of deterrence, scenarios that would result in war, deployment of tactical nuclear weapons, high-level decision-making, and a general lack of comparative data on the forces of both sides.

The 1986 NATO-Warsaw Pact balance used the same general lines of investigation as the 1976 assessment with an emphasis on aspects of the improved understanding of the Soviet Union gained from the previous eight years. This effort used a more comprehensive database of NATO and Warsaw Pact forces compared over time. Additionally, there was also new understanding of the significance to the Soviet Union of victory on the Central Front. That led to a decision that was focused on the area, although it resulted in an asymmetry due to the different way in which NATO and the Warsaw Pact organized combat operations across the entire theater.

The main assessment was focused on conventional ground and air forces of both sides. The major subordinate capabilities included air and ground force levels, sustainability (munitions and petroleum), command and control, operational concepts, and various warning scenarios and alert postures. Both maritime and nuclear forces were excluded, partially because of the insufficient understanding of how they may contribute to combat outcomes on the Central Front.

The research conducted for this assessment after 1978 led to a more detailed understanding of the Warsaw Pact Theater Strategic Operation to orchestrate combat activities. This established the ability to compare the NATO General Defense Plan with the Theater Strategic Operation and identify their respective strengths and weaknesses. Research also resulted in understanding the Soviet method for calculating military balances using combat potential scores, which enabled the capability to assess perspectives of the Warsaw Pact on quantity-quality force ratios for major concepts in the Theater Strategic Operation. Subsequently, these ratios could be compared with Armor Division Equivalent-based and other NATO methods that facilitate the understanding of the different views on aggregate capabilities and force adequacy for combat.

The research also resulted in improved understanding of Warsaw Pact logistics processes and planning factors that were incorporated into the assessment. Moreover, insights emerged on probable Soviet high-level perspectives on war in Europe that stressed pessimism in three ways: first, the ability for a conflict to remain conventional with a resulting failure of the combatants to achieve rates needed for success; second, the relative inferiority of Warsaw Pact versus NATO airpower; and third, the relative capabilities of NATO armor which the Soviet Union determined to be more capable than NATO assessments. Soviet assessments were focused on a *revolution in military affairs* with new advances in lasers and information technology that boosted the range of precision-strike weapons. However, the Soviets were pessimistic about their ability to succeed in this new era because of significant advantages in US information technology.

The assessment of the command, control, and communications balance was begun in 1976 and completed in 1978. Its focus was limited to C3 for strategic nuclear warfare as well as large-scale tactical and limited nuclear warfare. It compared both strategic and tactical C3 systems for defense and offense. The former resources involved facility hardening, airborne command posts, satellite communications, ground mobile communication, and survivability, while the latter dealt with counter-C3 (C-C3) doctrine, organization, targeting, antisatellite capabilities, concealment and deception, strategic nuclear and tactical warfare, and countermeasures. What is more, it also included command structures as well as tactical, theater nuclear, and alliance doctrine. Finally, comparisons of C3 capabilities for strategic nuclear warfare included national doctrine, strategic warning, tactical warning, readiness posture, and attack characterization. However, significant asymmetries existed. The

Soviet Union had designated C3 as a high-priority, separable warfare area with doctrine and methods to execute it in different scenarios. By contrast, the US approach was fragmented and focused on technology and less on protecting assets. Moreover, the Soviet approach was top-down, one-way, and unbending, based on preplanned options, while that of the United States was top-down, consultative, flexible, disjointed, and adaptive.

The conclusions were reached on C3 and counter-C3 priorities. The Soviets examined C3, developed tactical and strategic doctrine, and invested in both physical and electronic disruption systems. Soviet counter-C3 doctrine assigned a high priority to C3 targets. The US approach was fragmented and lacked integrated doctrine. The assessment found that a comparable US counter attack would be smaller, less integrated, and less effective. At the same time, both sides focused on protecting strategic C3 systems. The assessment also exposed needs for intelligence collection and research to understand Soviet C3 and counter-C3 processes including qualitative aspects. It also resulted in comprehensive C3 research to support future C3 assessments.

LESSONS LEARNED

The United States spent the last two decades of the Cold War striving to understand the Soviet Union for purposes of net assessment. Many organizations and people were involved. This work was guided by the results of and gaps in ongoing assessments as well as the requirement to stay abreast of changes in the Soviet Union. The asymmetries above and others came from a rigorous process that was learned, studied, and interpreted. Many activities, including the requirements for the US Intelligence Community, combined to generate knowledge that focused on analyzing key topics and also collecting and studying Soviet literature on intentions, doctrine, military art, basic concepts, future directions, and internal dynamics and processes. Other activities included translating references, monitoring trends (military-technical revolution), interpreting advances in weapons, investigating exercises, interviewing émigrés and defectors, interpreting social conditions, and examining past conflicts from World Wars I and II to Afghanistan (as well as the shooting down of KAL 007).

Several lessons can be learned from such an understanding. Basic lessons include realizing that it was not a simple problem. The initial objective of understanding the Soviet approach to war for the purpose of comparative assessment was oversimplified. Both unexpected dimensions and asymmetries existed that had to be identified and carefully worked out. It became a process of learning what to do and going about it by fits and starts. The process was partly evidence-based but mostly learning the ways that the Soviet Union conceptualized war and military operations with their unique precepts. Fusion meant approaching the needed knowledge like a jigsaw puzzle to be solved over time. The research was protracted and required attention to deliberate efforts to fuse piecemeal insights and move on. Many types of research were required that drew on various classes of evidence. Both persistence and endurance were essential to this process.

People were exceptionally important. The results and insights eventually obtained probably would not have been achievable without highly capable researchers who stayed with the problem for decades. This consistency allowed for efficient fusion and integration of knowledge as well as coalesced knowledge to take the next step from an advanced position. Dedicated analysts including researchers with Russian-language skills were key to this process, which made it easier to handle large amounts of relevant untranslated source material. It also helped to avoid technical errors which corrupted translations. In the realm of military science, common terms of art were given technical meaning as jargon. Precise translations were important in unscrambling concepts. Getting the Soviet approach right was important. Once understood, the pieces of the puzzle fit together and provided a rationale to fill in the gaps. Moreover, asymmetries surfaced at every turn. Compared with the US concept of war that included key ingredients and balance of forces, the differences had to be identified, understood, and incorporated in the assessment.

* * *

Decades of in-depth research on the Soviet Union that supported net assessments of the military balance suggests three lessons worthy of further consideration. The first lesson for assessments of the United States versus a potential adversary emphasizes key aspects of the latter in terms of the application of military power, including political, economic, social, environmental, and other factors influencing national power. In addition, it is necessary to examine their effect on combat operations. Moreover, asymmetries must be identified in order to modify assessments.

The next lesson in addition to fundamental data on an adversary requires answering some questions: What is the basic approach to warfare? What are the structures of military art? What cultural, ideological, and historical biases shape national security and combat operations? What is the approach to war planning and command and control? What are viewed as key uncertainties that must be resolved? What are the basic planning scenarios? What makes assessments easier to guide and conduct future research?

The third lesson is that it takes concerted efforts by language-trained analysts with military expertise to understand a given country. Moreover, some analysts must be knowledgeable about details of US approaches as well as the objectives and methods of net assessment to identify asymmetries and consequently interpret their implications.

In a global environment where the United States may be faced with a range of adversaries, it would be useful to identify a small set of countries as the enduring focus of future assessments and develop a process for sustained research on those dimensions relevant to them. In addition, it would be important to understand the basics on the countries previously discussed as well as the areas supporting warfare that change, including the maritime, space, cyber, and other domains in the global commons.[15]

ADDENDUM

UNDERSTANDING THE SOVIET UNION—SPECIFIC ASPECTS

Details on the Soviet Union important to net assessments were divided in two categories: topics underpinning the Soviet approach to warfare and topics informing the specific assessment. Those niche topics supporting the assessment process included the following:

- *national security environment*: Soviet leadership perceptions of the significant aspects and uncertainties of the environment and ways of dealing with it;
- *application of military power*: the division of the world into operational theaters, the use of strategic directions as bases for force posturing, creation of standard strategic operations and operational-scale operations which support war plans;
- *ideological influence on war*: Marx, Hegel, Engels, and Lenin; the dialectic ideology of change; scientific determinism; belief in objective laws governing warfare;
- *political and military goals*: the existence of national political and military goals as well as separate political and military goals for the theaters of military operation which in turn resulted in formulating combat plans for that theater;
- *military doctrine*: detailed structures and methods employed on the strategic, operational, and tactical levels; differences in each military service; approach to managing uncertainty; current developments and future trends;
- *military science*: the philosophical dialectic basis for warfare, objective laws of war, the concept of the correlation of forces, and other basic content of Soviet military science and its implications for warfare;
- *contents and methods of military art*: fourteen major operations which served as building blocks for warfighting, each with their own templates for action and associated derivative requirements; overarching strategic operations which guided their execution; subordinate standard tactical actions that were intrinsic to combat;

- *calculus of the correlation of forces*: nature and full dimensions of correlation of forces indices, incorporation of qualitative factors of warfighting, use in planning and combat;

- *command economy*: impact on military forces and operations, social conditions of armed forces personnel and national security posture; scope of economic infrastructure dedicated to military developments;

- *defense economics:* the primacy of the five-year planning structure, the burden of defense on the national economy, detailed structure and timing of the planning process for creating new weaponry;

- *society and demographics*: health care and medical factors, the aging and shortened life expectancy, addiction to alcohol and drugs, living conditions, ethnic tension including in the military, profiles of soldiers, differences among regions (republics), relations between central and regional governments, the psychology of Russian society;

- *profiles of Soviet soldiers*: background and education of officers, noncommissioned officers, and enlisted; hazing; lack of initiative; relations among the ranks; basic fears and attitudes; respect for authority; sources of tension between military and civilian personnel.

In addition, niche topics for each net assessment that proved to be helpful included:

- *Soviet views of adversaries*: American objectives, sensitivities, command and control, and nuclear doctrine; Western solidarity and capabilities; NATO vulnerabilities on the Northern and Southern flanks; the roles of China and Japan in future conflicts;

- *planning scenarios for future conflict*: contingencies related to wars that begin with or without nuclear weapons, linking war in the West (NATO) with war in the East (China);

- *historical style of warfare*: the strategic, operational, and tactical aspects of warfare which were demonstrated by key campaigns of World War II and resulting Soviet lessons;

- *command and control*: the overall command and control philosophy, centralized decision-making, quality of leadership, societal influences, automated troop control system;

- *nuclear doctrine and operations*: warfare involving nuclear and conventional forces, the concept of preemption, strategic defenses (air, missile, and civil) against nuclear weapons, operational concepts and target sets for nuclear forces;

- *research, development, and acquisition*: military technology, weaponizing technologies, and introducing systems and infrastructure devoted to innovations in weapons systems;

- *mobilization of society*: economic mobilization, preparation for war, civil defense, using camouflage, concealment, and deception to cover mobilization processes;

- *military training*: contents and the focus of military exercises, planning, and execution;

- *logistics and maintenance*: the district support system, structure and content of logistics processes and norms, equipment replacement to offset an absence of trained maintenance personnel at lower tactical levels;

- *intelligence services*: control at home, influence within the government, and role abroad;

- *power projection*: structure and operations of overseas bases and capabilities of maritime and air assets to rapidly project power;

- *quasi-military organizations*: the function of the Volunteer Society for Cooperation with the army, aviation, and fleet; Young Pioneers; Komsomol in military patriotic education and creating the new Soviet man;

- *educational process*: the levels and expertise for military personnel, regional differences, important educational institutions for the Soviet armed forces;

- *national security role of the Communist Party*: impact on the military and the view of the United States on the intentions and capabilities of the Soviet Union;

- *military processes in practice*: the successes and failures of military operations as well as use of forces or military infrastructure as well as the impact of psychological factors which impact on the performance of Soviet soldiers;

- *intangible factors in warfare*: influence of morale, allegiances, historical conditions such as experiences of past invasions;

- *consequences of a military-technical revolution*: implications of US reconnaissance strike for materials, stealth, information, and space technologies as well as the corollaries for both conventional force requirements and operations.

NOTES

1. The author conducted research on the Soviet Union in direct support of net assessments during the last 15 years of the Cold War. This chapter is based on his conclusions and does not reflect the views of the Department of Defense or the Office of Net Assessment. In addition, he wishes to thank Fritz W. Ermarth, Kar Pik Lau, Fred F. Littlepage, Thomas G. Mahnken, and S. Enders Wimbush for providing helpful comments on earlier drafts.

2. Andrew W. Marshall, "The Nature and Scope of Net Assessments," National Security Council, memorandum, August 16, 1972, 1.

3. See Barry D. Watts, "Notes from a Symposium on Net Assessment" (Washington, DC: Office of Net Assessment, May 22, 1990), 9.

4. Ibid., 7.

5. The discussion of asymmetries found in Soviet military art was taken from John A. Battilega, "Soviet Military Art: Some Major Asymmetries Important to Net Assessment," in *Essays on Diagnostic Net Assessment*, ed. Mie Augier and Barry D. Watts (Washington, DC: Center for Strategic and Budgetary Assessment, 2008), 145–59; and John A. Battilega, "Soviet Military Thought and the US Competitive Strategies Initiative," in *Competitive Strategies for the 21st Century*, ed. Thomas G. Mahnken (Stanford, CA: Stanford University Press, 2012), 106–27.

6. The belief in the existence of objective laws governing war does not necessarily imply rigid execution of combat. Rather laws establish fundamental relationships for success. This logic has a direct analog in the physical sciences. For example, physicists formulate mathematical relationships for physical processes such as Newton's Law. From this law, civil engineers generate parametric design tables to construct bridges. Engineers creatively use the tables. Newton's Law, on which design tables are based, stipulates that if engineers violate the relationships contained in the tables, the bridges will almost certainly collapse. The creativity or initiative of engineers has not been inhibited, but knowledge of Newton's Law, correctly applied to bridge building, saves them from disaster and allows them to design bridges that meet their intended goals.

7. V. Morozov and S. Tyushkevich, "The Objective Laws of War and Their Reflection in Soviet Military Science," *Voyennaya mysl'* 5 (May 1971).

8. See V. I. Belyakov, "Sootnosheniye Sil i Sredstv," *Soviet Military Encyclopedia*, 7 (1979).

9. During the early 1970s, basic quantitative indices were used in Soviet combat preparations. See Ghulam Dastagir Wardak, comp., Graham Hall Turbiville, Jr., ed., *The Voroshilov Lectures: Materials from the Soviet General Staff Academy*, 3 vols. (Washington, DC: National Defense University Press, 1989–1990). The author drew on material from the Voroshilov Military Academy. The Soviet Union expanded its calculations to include qualitative indices.

10. The list of major net assessment topics from 1974 to 1991 is taken from Watts, "Notes," 5.

11. Andrew W. Marshall, "The Future of Net Assessment," in *Essays on Diagnostic Net Assessment*, ed. Mie Augier and Barry D. Watts (Washington, DC: Center for Strategic and Budgetary Assessment, 2008), 324.

12. Descriptions of the NATO-Warsaw Pact assessments are based on the Director of Net Assessment, "The Military Balance in Europe: A Net Assessment" (March 1978); and Jeffrey S. McKitrick, "The NATO-Warsaw Pact Military Balance, 1986," in *Essays on Diagnostic Net Assessment*, ed. Augier and Watts, 196–206.

13. Gerry Dunne, "Cold War Net Assessment of US and USSR: Military Command, Control, and Communications," in *Essays on Diagnostic Net Assessment*, ed. Augier and Watts, 160–68.

14. One Armor Division Equivalent (ADE) is defined as the Weighted Unit Value (WUV) of a standard US armored division. The method was developed by the US Army for use in quantitative analysis. It starts by assigning Weapon Effectiveness Indicator (WEI) values to individual weapon systems based on their lethality, mobility, survivability, and other critical operational characteristics. A combat unit is scored by combining the WEI for its weapons systems based on specified weighting factors to produce a WUV. In the 1970s, this system of indices was used to compare trends in the aggregate combat capabilities of NATO versus Warsaw PACT forces.

15. Marshall, "The Future," 326.

CHAPTER 6

CONTRIBUTIONS OF MILITARY HISTORIANS

Williamson Murray

While considered as a futurist in the defense establishment, few people were aware of the interest Marshall gained for the application of military history in understanding national security affairs. During the years spent at the RAND Corporation, he concluded that historical perspectives were useful in tackling current and future challenges to the United States. Moreover, the nature of the Cold War suggested organizations change slowly. Thus, he concluded history provided insights of how nations adapt or fail to adapt in competitive situations. ONA gave Marshall opportunities to use historical case studies to examine issues that bedevil both strategists and defense planners. It is notable that his approach differed from that of other Pentagon officials. He believed studies could highlight similarities between current and past strategic events to address challenges posed by the Soviet Union. His approach corresponded to ideas attributed to Thucydides, the foremost historian and theorist of war who, in the fifth century BCE, recorded the conflict between Sparta and Athens through its twenty-first year in the *History of the Peloponnesian War.*

> It will be enough for me, however, if these words of mine are judged useful by those who understand clearly the events, which happened in the past and which (human nature being what it is) will, at some time or other and in much the same ways, be repeated in the future. My work is not a piece of writing designed to meet the tastes of the immediate public, but it was done forever.[1]

Voices from the Past

General James N. Mattis, USMC, echoed Thucydides in his response to students at the National War College who doubted the value of history. Senior leaders "do their troops a disservice by not studying (vice just reading) the men who have gone before us.... 'Winging it' and filling body bags as we sort out what works reminds us of the moral dictates and the cost of competence in our profession."[2] Overall, concern over the future requires an interest in the past. As MacGregor Knox noted, "historical experience remains the only available guide both to the present and to the range of alternatives inherent in the future."[3] Moreover, anyone seeking insights on the future must grasp political-military developments from an individual, organizational, or national point of view. Understanding the present necessitates appreciating *how* events came about.

Consequently, using history involves understanding the context of events in order to grasp the implications for the future. Simply rummaging through the past for case studies which appear on the surface to apply in theoretical constructs or present crises adds nothing to insights on the future. That, unfortunately, has been typical of many attempts by political science to use history. For example, invoking the analogy of Munich in support of US intervention in South Vietnam missed the fact Czechoslovakia was critical to the European balance of power while

Indochina did not occupy a similar position, setting aside the domino theory.[4]

Without some perspective on the unique history and culture of their nation, strategists and military leaders will be unable to judge where it stands. And, if they cannot figure out where it stands, no road to the future will suffice, as has often been demonstrated with disastrous results. A thorough understanding of the present based on history is the first step in intelligent thought about the future. But historical clues to the future often are buried in minutia, false narratives, sloppy analyses, and complex issues like making strategy, peacetime innovation, and adaptation to wartime conditions. As suggested elsewhere, understanding history requires studying the past over an entire career. Officers who made such a commitment include Generals William Slim and George S. Patton. But in the case of the uncommitted, history may suggest more dangerous ideas than a total ignorance of the past. The nonsense spouted by prophets of a so-called *revolution in military affairs* illustrates this dilemma. Adolph Hitler and Joseph Stalin read history but failed to grasp its complexities or ambiguities, only what agreed with their biases.

Ironically, while Marshall accepted the sentiment expressed by Thucydides on the past, the majority of academic historians did not. In the 1970s, when Marshall began promoting the use of history in thinking about the future, a disbelief in its utility represented a consensus among most historians that remains prevalent today. In the Ivy League, only Yale offers courses on military history but when faculty members teaching those courses retire, they are unlikely to be replaced. Duke, which once had a reputable program in military history, transferred an historian of grand strategy to business school because he could not get tenure in the history department.

While military historians once addressed their field, they rarely discussed its implications for strategists and policymakers. Yet political scientists willingly developed historical models, some with disastrous results. Barry Posen, considering French and German doctrine during the interwar period, made extraordinary claims that did not rely on documentary sources and also ignored most secondary sources in English as well as everything in French and German.[5] This criticism is not meant to disparage the writings of political scientists such as Eliot A. Cohen, Stephen Peter Rosen, and Aaron L. Friedberg who have carefully used history.

Only students who have read historical literature gain a sense of the causality, innovation, and adaptation that emerged in military affairs over the past centuries. Moreover, one must not forget that much of the secondary historical literature is riddled with distorted and misinterpreted events. Two cases exemplify the negative affect of such narratives. In order to garner support for the Cold War among former enemies, Germany created narratives of World War II that featured an apolitical Wehrmacht that did not commit war crimes. But historians debunked such myths in the 1980s particularly with regard to Germany. They also nixed stories of battleship admirals and the so-called *big gun club* controlling the US Navy in the interwar years.[6]

SOVIET HISTORICAL STUDIES

One of the last monographs written by Marshall at RAND, entitled *Long-Term Competition with the Soviets*, was published in 1972. He argued that US-USSR competition did not resemble arms races of the past, such as pre-World War I competition between Great Britain and Imperial Germany to build navies. Instead, he maintained that while interaction between Washington and Moscow existed, it was episodic. Moreover, internal factors seemed to be playing more critical roles than in earlier arms races. In particular, Marshall emphasized the need for comprehensive historical studies on the nature of previous episodes of US-USSR competition.

Marshall sponsored research by Ernest R. May, John D. Steinbruner, and Thomas U. Wolfe based on highly classified material, which indicated his willingness to use academics to examine contemporary history to elucidate insights for policymakers in efforts to deal with the US-USSR competition. The study represented the first but certainly not last attempt to use history to obtain greater insight into the wider strategic and assessment issues involved in US defense policies. In fact, Marshall began using more distant historic periods to shed light on contemporary problems. His relationship with May was fruitful. In the late 1970s, May assembled a group of historians to examine whether major powers and civil-military bureaucracies conducted net assessments in the years before World Wars II and I. The American and British academics compared approaches of selected nations to ponder the strategic and operational balances of the opposing forces. Meeting in Cambridge, they included Wilhelm Deist, John Erickson, William C. Fuller, Jr., John Gooch, Holger H. Herwig, Paul M. Kennedy, MacGregor Knox, Zara S. Steiner, D. C. Watt, and Samuel R. Williamson, Jr. Many had not met previously, but they forged relationships that would last for a lifetime. As a result, Marshall did a great service for strategy and military history.

The volume based on this conference did not quite achieve what Marshall intended, though most of the contributions examined intelligence organizations in periods leading to war.[7] Though they were scholarly, the issue of how net assessment was performed got little attention in spite of the fact Marshall clearly described the process that originally interested him.

While doing research on the Luftwaffe at Maxwell Air Force Base in 1980, an idea came to me for a study of issues involving the performance of military institutions during the first half of the twentieth century. In the following year, I approached Allan R. Millett, my colleague at Ohio State, who found the idea viable. Thus, I contacted Marshall indicating that military effectiveness of various nations in the twentieth century might be of interest. As a relatively junior academic with few publications, I did not anticipate a positive response. Within a week, however, he called to ask for a proposal for a study because it related to assessing US-USSR military effectiveness as well as relative alliance capabilities.

Unquestionably, historians could provide insights on the methods needed to calculate military potential in the contemporary world. It took almost a month to submit a proposal because no extensive thought had been given to the study. Only grappling with the problem of *military effectiveness* did its complexity appear. To avoid straying from the topic, guidance was issued. First nations were chosen, then a timeframe. Initially, the world wars were considered, but the study was later expanded to include the interwar period.

Selecting the nations proved easy, and after discussion four areas were chosen for analysis: the political, strategic, operational, and tactical levels in peacetime and war. The guidance for the contributors included specific objectives and methodologies to assess the capabilities of forces.[8] The success of this work influenced my further research. As pointed out in an article published by Millett and Murray after the volumes on military effectiveness appeared:

> Whether policy shaped strategy or strategic imperatives drove policy was irrelevant. Miscalculations in both led to defeat . . . even for some nations that ended the war as members of the victorious coalition. Even the effective mobilization of national will, manpower, industrial might, national wealth, and technological know-how did not save belligerents from reaping the bitter fruit of severe mistakes [at the political and strategic levels]. This is because it is more important to make correct decisions at the political and strategic level than it is at the operational and tactical level.[9]

In this sense, although German military effectiveness was impressive on the tactical level, it was catastrophic on the strategic level. That reality stayed with me an academic historian and in work as a defense consultant. It also served as a major theme in a number of later studies. The military effectiveness project proved that cooperation among historians in multiauthored works provided a useful approach to strategic and military problems without taking years or decades.

MILITARY EFFECTIVENESS

Whether provided by Marshall or others, support of all the projects sought to illuminate the past to enlighten future military leaders and strategists. Without that impetus, I would probably have remained entirely in the business of turning out works on military history that might or might not have had utility for thinking about the future. In any event, they would have lacked specific or targeted case studies made available from a long view of history. In other words, my study of the lessons from the past for military leaders and strategists resulted entirely from Marshall.

The three volumes of *Military Effectiveness* appeared in 1988 as Marshall recognized that history had more to say about uncertainty and ambiguities that marked the strategic environment at the end of the Cold War. After publishing these volumes, I approached Marshall about a basic problem of net assessment that May partially addressed in *Knowing One's Enemies.* Marshall was agreeable, which led to the publication of *Calculations, Net Assessment and the Coming of World War II.*[10] In 1989 at a meeting of the American Historical Society in Cincinnati, Marshall emphasized that the United States would confront multiple challenges more difficult than those faced in the Cold War. Moreover, in discussing issues that went beyond the project, he forecast the emergence of a multipolar world rather than the unipolar world that many pundits spouted, which would bring challenges that would not be easy or simple to solve.

After the project on military effectiveness, I started work on a multi-authored book without ONA support. It emerged from an experience at the Naval War College, where teaching strategy rested on case studies in lieu of the traditional approach as epitomized by Edward Meade Earle in *Makers of Modern Strategy,* which was replicated by Peter Paret in a less than successful edition of this classic on military leaders and theorists beginning in the modern era.[11] In 1987, however, Marshall endorsed a proposal for a multiauthored work focused on the *making* rather than the *makers* of strategy. With support from the Smith Richardson Foundation and Mershon Center at Ohio State, the project began that year and moved ahead by the time of the Cincinnati meeting. There Marshall voiced support for the project, suggesting that history would have much to say about the multipolar environment that emerged with the end of the Cold War.

The resulting book entitled *The Making of Strategy* was praised by Sir Michael Howard as the most important work on strategy to appear since *Makers of Modern Strategy* in 1943.[12] This led to a series of works published by Cambridge University Press that began with *The Making of Peace* followed by *The Shaping of Grand Strategy* and *Successful Strategies.*[13] Marshall played a role in only the last volume. In addition, a final volume on grand strategy and alliances was scheduled to appear with assistance from the Mershon Center. Whether Marshall or some other source funded the studies, he provided the intellectual impetus. As suggested earlier, it is doubtful that the studies would have appeared in their ultimate form without his support. His influence continues today. James G. Lacey recently conducted on a multiauthored study dealing with the long-term competition between the major powers with ONA support.

MILITARY INNOVATION

The demise of the Soviet Union did not usher in the anticipated peace dividend. The invasion of Kuwait resulted in an immense military buildup in the Middle East by the United States with the support of allied nations in late 1990 to early 1991. Many pundits forget the intense debates over the use of force against a supposedly battle-hardened Iraqi military that defeated Iran in a drawn-out war.[14] In fact, ground and air operations beat the supposedly effective Iraqi military with few casualties given some original inflated estimates. It was clear the US military was able to mount such operations because of technological advances in weaponry and battlefield tactics.

Marshall was among the first to recognize that a major paradigm shift occurred in the use of ground and air forces by understanding

Soviet thinking and called it as a revolution in military affairs instead of a military technical revolution. Unlike Admiral William A. Owens, USN (Ret.), who attributed extravagant possibilities to such a revolution, Marshall predicted the culmination of a long-term process through changes in technological, tactical, and conceptual dimensions of warfare going well beyond the incremental. As Marshall noted in the early 1990s, the revolution was only beginning. He argued that compared to the revolution in land warfare attributed to the British armor attack at Cambrai in 1917, the current revolution had only entered the initial stage. Distinct from advocates of a revolution, he realized that history could be useful in thinking about the implications of innovation at the time by examining major processes of change.

The third major project undertaken with ONA support developed the comparative study of particular innovations by leading organizations during the interwar period including armored and amphibious operations, strategic bombing, carrier aviation, and radar. It appeared to damp down wilder claims that a military technical revolution would change warfare by eliminating fog and friction. ONA declared the impact of changes in precision, computers, and communications as a military technical revolution. However, as more extreme views surfaced, it adopted the term *revolution in military affairs* which implied a nuanced approach. Toward that end, Marshall used case studies in seminars for senior military and civilian policymakers in the Pentagon.

Marshall's use of history led not only to a series of groundbreaking studies on the nature of change in the twentieth century, but also on how military historians have increasingly viewed the larger patterns of war and military institutions dating back to the sixteenth century or earlier. The study resulted in a book entitled *Military Innovation in the Interwar Period*.[15] Six years after that study appeared with ONA support, research began on the problems military institutions faced in adapting to the reality of war given enemy adaptation.[16] It took time to persuade Marshall that problems confronted in war and peace differed extensively, but his support facilitated the single-authored project that appeared 15 years following the military innovation study.

Marshall influenced studies ranging far beyond works on military innovation. He affected how military historians consider larger patterns of earlier innovation and adaptation. In addition to Murray and Millett, Harold R. Winton and David R. Metz edited works on military innovation in the interwar years.[17] As a result, interest grew in the subject including notable works by James S. Corum on the impact of Hans von Seeckt on the Reichswehr after World War I and David E. Johnson on US Army innovations in armored warfare and strategic bombing.[18]

Perhaps the most notable multiauthored study was published by Thomas C. Hone, Norman Friedman, and Mark D. Mandeles on the development of carrier aviation in the interwar years.[19] The evidence of the intellectual reach of Marshall can be found in a volume edited by Clifford J. Rogers, Jr., on the debates among historians over the military revolution.[20] Also, Geoffrey Parker published an important work on antecedents of military revolutions.[21] Actually, the insights by Marshall at the end of the Gulf War in 1991 resulted in a revolution in how historians viewed patterns of change in armies and navies of the past. A conference on the military revolution funded by Smith Richardson and held at Quantico in 1996 was attended by Marshall as well as Lieutenant General Paul K. Van Riper, USMC, and Major General Robert H. Scales, Jr., USA, and was particularly important for discussing the phenomena of military revolutions.

Four major military and social revolutions changed the Western way of war: the revolution that created the modern state and military of the seventeenth century, the Industrial Revolution that began in the mid-to-late eighteenth century, the French Revolution, and the merging of the Industrial and French Revolutions in World War I. These four upheavals are known as military revolutions. Smaller revolutions attended them such as the reinvention of the Roman system of drill by Maurice of Nassau and Gustavus Adolphus in the seventeenth century; the mobilization of manpower and resources by the French Revolution at the end of the eighteenth century; and the development of combined arms, modern steam-driven battle fleets, and carrier aviation in the twentieth century. The conference and post-conference deliberations resulted in the publication of *The Dynamics of Military Revolution*.[22] Again the guiding hand of Marshall became clear in convening a group of military historians to focus on a specific problem based on his insights of the significance demonstrated by the US military in the first Gulf War.

* * *

A dreadful irony may have occurred in efforts by Marshall and his collaborators to make history more accessible within the defense establishment. More than fifty years ago, when efforts began to turn net assessment into something other than an obscure process, history proved difficult for most senior officers to appreciate unless they had studied military history. With prodding from Marshall and others, using the knowledge of the past to indicate future possibilities became less difficult and sidestepping irresponsible thinking became easier. Influenced by Michael Howard, it became obvious to me that the military profession was not only physically but also intellectually demanding. One would not recognize the latter by the level of interest in education.

It is ironic that most senior officers do not care about education. Just how deeply the efforts by Marshall and the historians who attempted to utilize past experience as a signpost to the future has entered the collective mind of the US military is open to question. It was reported that Mattis asked his staff on arriving at Joint Forces Command who had interacted with the Office of Net Assessment. The reply was that no one had ever heard of it. That may be apocryphal, but the fact remains that no one in the command who touted a concept known as *operational net assessment* had bothered to learn what the term signified to Marshall.

Regrettably, professional military education without the Congressional oversight provided by Ike Skelton has reverted to the bad old days when the schoolhouse was the refuge of officers resting from a busy career.[23] Many improvements occurred because of Skelton, not the military services. It is no surprise that the US Armed Forces ignored the British lessons from suppressing rebellious Arabs in Mesopotamia in 1920 as well as their own lessons from Vietnam and Panama once the dust settled after invading and occupying Iraq. That would have required being aware of recent history. Except for a few general officers, that awareness did not exist. A visitor to Iraq in 2003 noted that only Generals James Mattis, David Petreaus, and Buford C Blount III seemed to recognize that an insurgency was unfolding. Ensconced in their tactical operations centers, other senior leaders were oblivious to signs that the combat veterans of the Vietnam War would have readily detected, but none of them had served in that conflict.

For years a dog-eared sign could be seen on the front desk in the Office of Net Assessment which proclaimed: "There is just so much stupidity that one individual can prevent." Eventually, the sign vanished into the inner sanctum but proved to be true. Marshall with his staff, associates, and collaborators made serious gains over the years in reversing that tide.

NOTES

1. Thucydides, *The History of the Peloponnesian War*, trans. Rex Warner (London; Penguin Classics, 1954), 48. On the importance of this work, see Williamson Murray, "Thucydides, Theorist of War," *Naval War College Review* 66 (Autumn 2013): 31–47.

2. Email to the author from James N. Mattis.

3. MacGregor Knox, "What History Can Tell Us about the 'New Strategic Environment,'" in *1995–1996 Brassey's Mershon Defense Annual: The United States and the Emerging Strategic Environment*, ed. Williamson Murray (Washington, DC: Brassey's, 1995).

4. See Williamson Murray, *The Change in the European Balance of Power, 1938–1939: The Path to Ruin* (Princeton, NJ: Princeton University Press, 1984).

5. Barry R. Posen, *The Sources of Military Doctrine: France, Britain, and Germany Between the World Wars* (Ithaca, NY: Cornell University Press, 1986).

6. On the former narrative, see Omer Bartov, *Hitler's Army, Soldiers, Nazis, and War in the Third Reich* (Oxford: Oxford University Press, 1991), and, on the latter, see Williamson Murray, "US Naval Strategy and Japan," in *Successful Strategies: Triumphing in War and Peace from Antiquity to the Present*, ed. Williamson Murray and Richard Hart Sinnreich (Cambridge: Cambridge University Press, 2014).

7. The study by Ernest May was *Knowing One's Enemies* (Princeton, NJ: Princeton University Press, 1986).

8. The guidance can be found in Allan R. Millett and Williamson Murray, *Military Effectiveness*, vol. 1, *The First World War* (London: Unwin Hyman, 1988), 1–30, as well as Allan R. Millett, Williamson Murray, and Kenneth H. Watman, "The Effectiveness of Military Organizations," *International Security* 11 (Summer 1986): 37–71.

9. Allan R. Millett and Williamson Murray, "Lessons of War," *The National Interest* 14 (Winter 1988–1989): 83–95.

10. Williamson Murray and Allan R. Millett, eds., *Calculations, Net Assessment and the Coming of World War II* (New York: Free Press, 1992).

11. See Edward Meade Earle, *Makers of Modern Strategy: Military Thought from Machiavelli to Hitler* (Princeton, NJ: Princeton University Press, 1943); and Peter Paret with Gordon A. Craig and Felix Gilbert, *Makers*

of Modern Strategy: Military Thought from Machiavelli to the Nuclear Age (Princeton, NJ: Princeton University Press, 1986).

12. Williamson Murray, MacGregor Knox, and Alvin Bernstein, *The Making of Strategy, Rulers States and War* (Cambridge: Cambridge University Press, 1994).

13. Williamson Murray and James Lacey, *The Making of Peace, Rulers, States, and the Aftermath of War* (Cambridge: Cambridge University Press, 2005); Williamson Murray, Richard Hart Sinnreich, and James Lacey, *The Shaping of Grand Strategy, Policy, Diplomacy and War* (Cambridge: Cambridge University Press, 2009); and Williamson Murray and Richard Hart Sinnreich, *Successful Strategies, Triumphing in War and Peace from Antiquity to the Present* (Cambridge: Cambridge University Press, 2014).

14. On this conflict, see Williamson Murray and Kevin M. Woods, *The Iran-Iraq War: A Military and Strategic History* (Cambridge: Cambridge University Press, 2014).

15. Williamson Murray and Allan R. Millett, eds., *Military Innovation in the Interwar Period* (Cambridge: Cambridge University Press, 1996).

16. Williamson Murray, *Military Adaptation in War: For Fear of Change* (Cambridge: Cambridge University Press, 2011).

17. Harold R. Winton and David R. Metz, *The Challenge of Change: Military Institutions and New Realities, 1918–1941* (Lincoln: University of Nebraska Press, 2000).

18. James S. Corum, *The Roots of Blitzkrieg, Hans von Seeckt and German Military Reform* (Lawrence: University Press of Kansas, 1992); and David E. Johnson, *Fast Tanks and Heavy Bombers: Innovation in the US Army, 1917–1945* (Ithaca, NY: Cornell University Press, 1998).

19. Thomas C. Hone, Norman Friedman, and Mark Mandeles, *American and British Aircraft Carrier Development, 1919–1941* (Annapolis, MD: Naval Institute Press, 1999).

20. See Clifford J. Rogers, ed., *The Military Revolution Debate: Readings on the Military Transformation of Early Modern Europe* (New York: Westview Press, 1995).

21. Geoffrey Parker, *The Military Revolution: Military Innovation and the Rise of the West, 1500–1800* (Cambridge: Cambridge University Press, 1988).

22. MacGregor Knox and Williamson Murray, eds., *The Dynamics of Military Revolution, 1300–2050* (Cambridge: Cambridge University Press, 2001).

23. Isaac Newton (Ike) Skelton IV represented the 4th district of Missouri from 1977 to 2011 and supported reforms of the professional military education system throughout much of his career.

CHAPTER 7

THE REVOLUTION IN MILITARY AFFAIRS

Dmitry (Dima) Adamsky

Contemporary military thought has been influenced by a hypothesis on transforming the nature of war known as an *information technology-revolution in military affairs* (IT-RMA). It provided the intellectual basis for the transformation of the US Armed Forces as well as an umbrella term for doctrine accompanying military innovations. Since the mid-1990s, many ideas that arose in the United States spread across the globe and the term *revolution in military affairs* was recorded in the military lexicon. Given the claim by Marxist theoretician Georgi Plekhanov on the role of individuals in history, the individual most closely identified with the RMA concept is Andrew W. Marshall. This chapter recounts the diffusion of the RMA concept, the development of IT-RMA in the US defense establishment, and contributions of Marshall and the ONA staff in promoting both enterprises. Reference to a revolution in military affairs and a military technical revolution signified radical innovation in defense circles. These revolutions include organizational structure as well as force deployment methods usually driven by technology that changed the conduct of war. Evoking the term *revolution* implies that change is profound rather than rapid, which means new methods of warfare are more powerful than older ones. Consequently, RMAs have rendered traditional forms of conflict obsolete. While most revolutions arise from technological advances, it takes more than such breakthroughs to drive RMAs and guarantee success.[1]

The United States and other nations claimed for decades that the most dramatic revolution in warfare since the nuclear age had begun. The IT-RMA integrated precision-guided munitions (PGMs); command, control, communications, computers, and information (C4I); and a variety of reconnaissance, surveillance, and target acquisition systems in ways that changed basic ideas on conventional war. With respect to military capabilities, the IT-RMA provides the means to strike with accuracy despite range, penetrate defenses with stealthy technology and unmanned vehicles, and communicate in the field to exploit the impact of joint force integration.[2]

In terms of organizational and operational concepts, classical ways of advancing on fronts with discernible lines and rear areas are gone; the number of platforms has become less relevant than networks and communications; military planning is focused on particular results instead of the attrition of hostile forces or the occupation of territory; maneuver of precise fire has replaced massive forces; sensor-to-shooter loops have been greatly shortened; both standoff and airpower capabilities have succeeded heavy ground units; and small mobile forces can operate over longer ranges with greater precision and lethality than in the past.[3]

The Gulf War in 1991 offered glimpses at the revolutionary potential of these capabilities. Nearly a decade later, Allied operations in Kosovo reinforced the value of so-called *information warfare*. Next, operations in Iraq and Afghanistan demonstrated that conventional wars may be fought with smaller, high-tech forces. The RMA concept spread widely and built a consensus on militaries as small, highly skilled joint forces that are rapidly deployable with information technology and versatility in conventional and counterinsurgency warfare.[4]

RMA Origins

The Revolution in Military Affairs can be traced to the mid-1970s as standoff, precision-guided munitions were introduced to military theory and practice in the United States and Soviet Union. As the attention of the United States returned to Europe after the Vietnam War, it was confronted by an ambiguous challenge: the realization of mutually assured destruction reduced the chance of a nuclear war but the Soviet Union remained predominant in the conventional balance of forces. To destroy second echelons deep in the rear, the United States needed to leverage standoff PGMs and over-the-horizon sensors, based on the introduction of advanced microelectronics.

Beginning in the mid-1970s, highly advanced technological achievements, particularly in the development of microprocessors, computers, lasers, and electronics, have enabled production of so-called *smart weapons*—including conventional munitions precision-guided to targets even at standoff ranges. Revolutionary concepts and technology on future war in Europe led to similar developments by the United States and NATO: namely, to strike deep against offensive, follow-on enemy forces. The US Armed Forces responded with deep-attack the doctrine called *AirLand Battle*, which depended on neutralizing follow-on echelons before they engaged NATO forces.[5] Destroying second echelon forces guided the evolution of tactics and weaponry. AirLand Battle envisioned Soviet second echelons in the offensive with standoff precision fire.

Deep attack required better air support and long-range fires. The creator of AirLand Battle, General Donn A. Starry, USA, thought the US military could fight the Soviet first echelon forces and regroup after surviving deep-strike bombardment and before a second echelon exploited any gains while seeking authority to use battlefield nuclear weapons. The NATO interest in a *follow-on forces attack* (FOFA) evolved from similar concerns and was fueled by emerging technology. Steps were taken in the 1970s to reduce the ratio of opposing forces reaching NATO defensive positions with conventional munitions. FOFA was intended to attack as far as possible in the rear as target acquisition and conventional weapons allowed. It was proposed to the NATO Military Committee in 1981 and AirLand Battle doctrine was released a year later.[6]

Admiral William A. Owens, USN (Ret.), attributed the prequel to the RMA to officials in the Pentagon during the late 1970s who considered the application of military technology and formulation of the so-called *offset strategy*. These efforts employed technological superiority to neutralize the overwhelming conventional advantages of Warsaw Pact forces using capabilities such as precision-strike weapons developed under projects sponsored by the Defense Advanced Research Project Agency (DARPA).[7] A budget was allocated to provide qualitative advantages for the US military to offset the quantitative superiority of the Soviet Union, a strategy that was pursued during the 1970s and 1980s. The core technological focus included land-, air-, and sea-launched precision-guided and standoff weapons such as terminally guided submunitions, smart bombs and guided missiles, and standoff land attack missiles; as well as command and control and automated reconnaissance and target acquisition projects such as the Airborne Warning and Control System, E-8 Joint Surveillance and Target Attack Radar System, Integrated Targets Acquisition and Strike System, and Standoff Target Acquisition System; programs that bolster anti-armor weapons (fire-and-follow and fire-and-forget antitank missiles); guidance devices based on the Global Positioning System; stealth technologies like the F-117 aircraft and naval stealth and standoff precision strike capabilities; and unmanned aerial vehicles. DARPA sought to integrate research and development of these capabilities in 1978 under a single project known as Assault Breaker. That project became the Smart Weapons Program which facilitated a period to develop new capabilities, which served as the formative RMA stage.[8]

WHAT OTHERS OVERLOOKED

AirLand Battle doctrine came about in order to counter Soviet second echelons deep in rear areas. For the US Army, it established the technological foundation of the RMA.[9] But the cultivation of the nucleus of the RMA concept occurred before its maturation. The offset response offered little more than the retention of a technological edge to blunt the armor of the Warsaw Pact. Although no advance in conceptualizing the existing paradigm on warfighting took place in the early 1970s, a few academics saw the future. Both MacGregor Knox and Williamson Murray claimed that the tactical emphasis of defense analysts in the Pentagon prevented them from recognizing anything of a revolutionary nature in emerging military capabilities.[10] While US technological capabilities to execute deep strikes with PGMs had advanced, the Soviets possessed a better understanding of the revolutionary impact of AirLand Battle and FOFA. It took almost a decade for the United States to grasp the changed view of the Soviet Union in the nature of warfare, which had established the reconnaissance-strike complex as the dominant architecture for combat operations.[11]

The US military developed technology and weaponry for nearly a decade without realizing their revolutionary implications. No effort was made to revisit the existing paradigms of warfare in futuristic terms. The military technical revolution conceptualized war prior to the procurement of technology and combat experience. The Soviets became the first to grasp this phenomenon as a discontinuity; they also coined the term *revolution in military affairs* and produced theoretical literature without developing new weaponry or technology. Although the United States had laid the technological groundwork, it was Soviet rather than American theorists who considered the long-term consequences of the RMA. By contrast to the West, which focused on narrow implications posed by weapons systems, the Soviet Union championed innovations representing discontinuity that was dubbed the *military technical revolution*. Beginning in the late 1970s, the Soviets had issued seminal literature on the MTR predating by nearly a decade the US and NATO efforts to address military-technological shifts. The Soviet Union harnessed the technological superiority of the West as the point of departure in the conceptualization of innovation.[12]

The technological and conceptual preconditions of the American RMA coincided with the misinterpretation of Soviet MTR concepts by the US Intelligence Community. In its estimate of perceptions of Western capabilities, intelligence analysts detected new directions in the thinking of the Soviet Union with an early, high degree of accuracy. After monitoring the Soviet quest for advanced technology, American experts began focusing on the operational essence of a MTR by experimenting with reconnaissance-strike and fire complexes. Additionally, they concluded that the Soviets found conventional weapons to be so accurate, lethal, and destructive that they were weighing their relative effects against the employment of nuclear weapons.[13]

A series of CIA estimates beginning in the early 1980s refers to so-called reconnaissance-strike organizations (RSO), which the Soviets had developed out of concern for the threat posed by the Assault Breaker initiative with its precision-guided, deep-striking, theater-level capability to engage follow-on Soviet echelons on the move.[14] Analysts found the Soviet RSOs consisted of an integrated triad of reconnaissance and target acquisition complexes, automated command and control elements, and long-range striking systems. They correctly envisioned operational (army) and tactical (division) levels as the main trends in Soviet force development. Further analysis of Soviet doctrine at the end of the Cold War indicated that the outcome of a future conflict would be determined by massed conventional PGMs and real-time reconnaissance and maneuver rather than massed armor.[15] As far as political, economic, and other factors went, the gap between the MTR concept and actual

Soviet capabilities was never bridged, though the theories later offered a looking glass for US strategic planners. After years of inattention, the United States studied the emerging vision in the Soviet Union of the military technical revolution which became known as the Revolution in Military Affairs. By assessing the Soviet perceptions of US power, Americans came to understand the importance of their own weaponry by the early 1990s.[16]

Soviet views of the discontinuities in military affairs together with a failure to comprehend the consequences were known for a decade. Only a few people, most notably Lieutenant General William E. Odom, USA, accepted the validity of the MTR concept and that it presented far more than simply another Soviet innovation.[17] Without having a date certain for the introduction of the American RMA, the period between the late 1980s to early 1990s can be identified as its starting point. Knox and Murray established that Marshall and his staff became the first members of the defense establishment to realize the consequences of Soviet literature on military technological revolutions and promote the concept of the Revolution in Military Affairs.[18]

General of the Army Makhmut Gareev, the President of the Russian Academy of Military Sciences, identified Marshall as a theoretical luminary who fully grasped the nature of the MTR and founded the American RMA.[19] The development in US capabilities was followed in the late 1980s by the conceptual birth of the RMA. While the technological groundwork was laid in the 1970s, the RMA remained an abstraction until a memorandum on the subject was distributed in the early 1990s by Marshall and Lieutenant Colonel Andrew F. Krepinevich, USA. Like British experimentation with armored forces in the mid-1920s, the US military was not thinking in terms of a revolution.[20] Only a small number of defense intellectuals perceived the advent of the RMA in the early 1980s. Albert Wohlstetter is generally considered to be the first prominent scholar to understand its influence on the nature of warfare. He referred to the phenomenon as a "revolution in the accuracies of unmanned weapon systems."[21] In the face of what was regarded as enormous inertia on the part of the US military, Wohlstetter, aided by Marshall and a few others, urged more thorough consideration of the strategic implications of the growing family of PGMs. In the view of Wohlstetter, the revolution in microelectronics opened vistas for both the application of force and ever-wider varieties of political and operational realities.[22]

ASSESSING THE SOVIET MTR

Interest in Soviet MTR theories gathered momentum with the end of the Cold War. The defining moment in efforts to persuade the defense establishment to conceptualize the nature of warfare came in 1987 when Wohlstetter co-chaired the Commission on Integrated Long-Term Strategy with Fred C. Iklé. The Commission report debated extending assessments beyond the Cold War military balance, even though the Soviet Union was still alive and kicking.[23] What is more, the report credited advances such as standoff PGMs, space, stealth, radar, and targeting capabilities. But it stated that while the Soviet Union appreciated the implications of the systems for modern warfare, the United States did not. To further its insights, the Commission convened a working group in 1988 which was cochaired by Marshall and Charles Wolf, Jr. It included members of the defense establishment and academe who were charged with projecting the probable contours of future military competition. The report stated that the Soviets had identified roughly the same technologies important for future war but considered them more systematically. Further, it stated that most if not all attention in the West was focused narrowly on highly accurate, long-range systems for raising the nuclear threshold and enhancing conventional deterrence.[24]

In contrast to the American approach, the report found that Soviet MTR writings tended to focus on new technologies that would be introduced and examine their tactical, operational, and strategic implications. The report asserted that the Soviets envisioned a more distant future than American experts, which suggested that they might have been correct in the assessment that the advent of new technologies would revolutionize warfare. The working group concluded that if indeed this progression was the case, transformation could affect some US force structures and command arrangements more profoundly than the introduction of nuclear weapons.[25]

Marshall replaced Wohlstetter during the late 1980s as the leading sponsor of an emerging paradigm of the future security environment. Building on previous work, ONA launched a more detailed assessment of the Soviet MTR vision in 1989. The preliminary lessons of the Gulf War further stimulated this research as the United States sought to conceptualize the form of warfare that characterized Operation Desert Storm. American experts claimed and the Soviets concurred that the defeat of the Iraqi forces represented a textbook example of conventional Soviet theater offensive doctrine. The victory encapsulated most of the principles developed in MTR systems. According to Marshal Nikolai Ogarkov, the most impressive military achievement of the US-led coalition was launching tightly synchronized, integrated joint assaults throughout the operational theater against strategic forces and centers of gravity to gain decisive results.[26] ONA analysis of the Soviet literature led to related questions: Did the Soviets think they witnessed a fundamental discontinuity? Was a revolution emerging? What critical issues must be prioritized?[27]

This MTR assessment in 1992 was followed by a more comprehensive effort the next year and perhaps is the best-known ONA document. It resulted in an apparent consensus that Soviet theorists had been correct since the late 1970s about the character of the emerging MTR. The net assessment confirmed the Soviet postulates that advanced technology, especially informatics and precision-guided weaponry employed at extended ranges, were taking military art to the level of revolution in the nature of warfare. Together with information warfare, the assessment identified reconnaissance-strike as a main determinant in future warfare.[28] Assessments conducted in 1992 and 1993 called for a major transformation. Advances in operational concepts and organizational innovation were seen as more enduring than in technology or weapons. Moreover, assessments stressed identifying effective weapons in the concept of operations. They criticized tendencies to use advanced technologies as force multipliers and also prioritized investigation and experiment with novel concepts of operations and deducing a new architecture of military power.[29]

In contrast to the technology-driven mentality of the defense establishment, Marshall and his associates stressed concepts and doctrine rather than the purely technological aspects of the RMA. They openly stated that although superior technology is desirable, the real competition is not technical but intellectual. The central task was finding innovative concepts of operations and organizations and then exploiting current and emerging technology. Because the term *MTR* gave too much weight to technology, the alternative term *Revolution in Military Affairs* was adopted. While ONA experts considered the term preferable, it was taken from Soviet literature.

Marshall emphasized the importance of US peacetime innovation that had been conducted since the early 1990s, a result of Soviet decline. He envisioned future challenges but in the peace that followed he advocated experimentation with new doctrines. By addressing the implications for strategic management, net assessment called implementing new concepts of both operations and organizations by enhancing professional military education and promoting systems to equip officers with the necessary expertise. A memorandum by Marshall and Krepinevich also offered the opportunity to establish activities in the Pentagon to develop knowledge on the RMA concept. They recommended that the military services assign their best minds to consider future warfare. After conducting historical studies for ONA, Millett and Murray found that "military institutions that developed organizational cultures where serious learning, study, and intellectual honesty lay at the heart of preparation of officers for war were those best prepared" for a war. In 1993–1995 the military services took part in ONA-financed and -run roundtables and wargames.[30]

THE IMPACT OF MARSHALL

A preliminary net assessment of a military-technical revolution became the point of departure for defense transformation. Marshall and his supporters not only managed to promote their ideas but actually implemented the RMA concept, which led to the most comprehensive reforms since the Vietnam War. One year after the memorandum by Marshall and Krepinevich circulated, five task forces were organized to explore the RMA and its consequences. From the mid-1990s, the term *RMA* established itself among specialists as an authoritative frame of reference within which the debate over the future of war unfolded. The RMA discourse of the 1990s became an "organizing principle of US defense modernization discussions." ONA not only stimulated IT-RMA debates, it facilitated diffusion of the concept within the military services, diverse segments of the defense establishment, and others interested in the changing nature of war. According to Barry Watts, the effort to think about future warfare led to substantial activity and a surge in literature from public and private institutions. Examples included the RMA task forces organized by Secretary Perry in 1994 to investigate concepts including combined arms (dominant) maneuver in theater warfare, deep precision strike, forward operations, special and peace operations, and innovation.[31]

The vision of the evolving RMA concept caused tremendous excitement within the defense establishment by 1995.[32] Moreover, the Quadrennial Defense Review in 1997 acknowledged the existence of the RMA while recommending the transformation of the US military.[33] Throughout this period, this vision shaped American military thinking. ONA commissioned historical studies on military innovation in the interwar years that resulted in carrier aviation, amphibious warfare, and blitzkrieg, and sponsored RMA wargames, conferences, etc.[34] The studies were inspired by questions on technological, conceptual, operational, and organizational factors in the twentieth century that led to peacetime changes in how militaries fight.[35] The RMA concept transformed the military between *Desert Storm* and *Iraqi Freedom*. According to Colin S. Gray, it formed the logical and practical consequence of the Revolution of Military Affairs.[36]

How did Marshall see what others missed? While General Odom and a few others grasped the basics of the Soviet MTR, Marshall and his staff outstripped the Intelligence Community and other components of the defense establishment in recognizing its meaning.[37] Both Marshall and Wohlstetter became the first Americans to instill discontinuities in military thinking. In addition, Marshall was perhaps the most prescient critic of CIA estimates of the Soviet military in the last decades of the Cold War.[38] His understanding was based on a reading of Soviet literature rather than summaries in intelligence reports. Since his time at RAND, Marshall had become convinced that Soviet military thought was fundamentally different. Within a context of net assessments of strategic nuclear and NATO-Warsaw Pact military balances, he had directed research on Soviet military theories, measures of effectiveness, and assessment methodologies.[39]

While most observers considered Soviet military literature as evidence of new technologies, Marshall found something different.[40] He later recalled that Soviet writings brought the notion of *revolution diagnostics* to his attention; it was a practice of studying the past to identify emerging forms of warfare that ultimately dominated military affairs. He thought it reasonable to embrace the notion of discontinuity as found in Soviet thinking as revolution. He viewed the declaration by the Soviet Union of the developing military technical revolution as "consciously experiencing a change in the nature of war. Usually, when one is situated in the middle of it, he is least aware of it. However, the earlier the military acknowledges the emergence of the change in the military regime, the more efficient defense management it will generate."[41]

Marshall usually agreed with the Soviet methodological-theoretical approach to the nature of war as well as the content of MTR analysis.

He indicated that, like innovation in the past (for example, German and British experiences in the interwar period), militaries did not consciously think about revolutions. In addition, he wanted to promote a diagnosis of the significant changes in the nature of war during periods that were familiar to Soviet military intellectuals. The Soviet literature of the 1970s emphasized the 1920s and 1930s as a period of change. RMA advocates cited this period as a frame of reference in pondering the emergence of discontinuity. Marshall wanted to encourage defense intellectuals to deliberately examine and pursue the revolution in military affairs, which maintained the ONA focus on strategic diagnosis and not prescription.[42] Marshall believed the right questions were more important than the right answers.[43]

Watts has maintained that "Marshall and Krepinevich were clear in their own minds that operational concepts and organizational adaptations were, if anything, more important than either new technology or getting it fielded in a significant number of systems."[44] Emphasizing the long timeframe and developing appropriate doctrine, organization, and operations versus focusing on technology alone distinguished their approach to the future RMA from the defense establishment and American culture in general. Marshall regarded the changes in warfare that occurred during the interwar years as combined-systems revolutions.

Though technological advances were necessary, the underpinning involved synergy among systems, doctrine, and organizational developments.[45] Subsequent criticism has refined the RMA concept. As Colin Gray stated:

> Despite the sophisticated and originally fairly tentative, essentially speculative view of Marshall and OSD Net Assessment, once the RMA idea became general property it was captured by a profoundly technological view of the revolution that seemed to beckon the Armed Forces into a new golden age of enhanced effectiveness. This technophilia was to be expected, given America's technological strengths, its military culture, and its preferred way of war.[46]

Technological lessons overshadowed conceptual, social, and cultural lessons. A list of examples that supported the argument by Marshall is compelling.[47] Because the US military did not come to terms with this challenge, "the Pentagon has probably not yet gotten even a third of the way down the road to mastering changes in the conduct of war" which were forecast in an assessment by Marshall in 1992.[48] Flawed thinking about the impact of technology on future wars not only occurred at the stage of paradigmatic change. H. R. McMaster indicated how the military often failed to understand the implications of the RMA concept. As a result, superficial thinking has corrupted American strategic and operational thinking in the ensuing decades.[49]

Another critique explored whether the transformation in the nature of warfare outlined by IT-RMA proponents constituted a revolutionary or evolutionary discontinuity in military affairs, an issue hotly debated after the publication of *Military Power* by Stephen D. Biddle. Some critics accused RMA proponents of being self-delusional, claiming they advocated a preferred type of warfare and assumed it was relevant. Using empirical data from US campaigns in both Iraq and Afghanistan, Biddle and other analysts found that ideas on defense transformation encountered difficulties in counterinsurgency and stability operations, and that the RMA concept even could be invalid in conventional wars.[50] Such critiques must be situated in a broader context because military innovation is a dialectical phenomenon. The IT-RMA concept is a brainchild of several epochs. It was born in the symmetrical-conventional Cold War contingency and, in turn, boosted as a peacetime innovation by facing different operational challenges. In due course, RMA ideas were tested and refined by a transformation under fire against dissimilar adversaries. Since the early 2000s, most IT-RMA militaries have deployed in situations that failed to realize visions of an idealized RMA and been compelled to adapt to the current environment.[51]

MODERN STRATEGIC THOUGHT

The historical record of the RMA and IT-RMA concepts demonstrates that theory and innovation develop by means of two complementary processes. One occurs when theoreticians imagine the future of warfare and outline a new theory of victory to achieve it. Such *anticipation* emerges in deductive ways and innovation evolves in a top-down mode. The other is a bottom-up innovation that is more inductive and reactive in nature and is dubbed *adaptation*. In peacetime anticipation involves imagination, systematic exploration, and holistic knowledge of the current nature of war. In combat it builds on the insights produced by friction and lessons learned from best practices. As it started, the IT-RMA was a tale of top-down innovation conceived as a peacetime endeavor but then evolved in war as a bottom-up adaptation. Various militaries largely innovated IT-RMA in the 1990s through such a process that emerged as defense transformation in the United States. By the mid-2000s, these militaries on both sides of the Atlantic found themselves on battlefields that differed from an idealized view of future war and required further innovation.

The focus on innovation through adaptation in current warfighting must not be undertaken at the expense of systematic thinking on future challenges and emerging military organizations. Much like wishful thinking, the lack of vision on changes in the nature of war can be dangerous. Without a commitment to developing new concepts and paradigms for future warfare, militaries can lose their relevance to the security environment. However, when new theories of victory are deduced by military thinkers and then meet the antithesis of war, adaptation will come into play. Best practices eventually find their way to the doctrine process and become codified as military theories that in turn confront the ultimate test of operational reality.[52]

Preserving a sensible balance between the two types of innovation is critical. Going to one extreme or the other could be devastating. An overemphasis on futurology is counterproductive. Campaigns of the last decade forced militaries, which transformed themselves along the lines of various IT-RMA models, to alter their visions of warfare and adjust to the security environment. Fascination with military futurology can lead to wishful thinking. Indeed, a number proponents of the IT-RMA outlined how they "would like to fight and then assumed that the preference was relevant." This self-delusion, of course, corrupted their ability to think critically.[53] Furthermore, scant investment in anticipating the future could be equally damaging. Military institutions need to contribute significant intellectual energy in developing a vision of a future war.[54] The fact that oracle forecasts are problematic must not dissuade analysts from undertaking modest but spirited intellectual efforts. While a fascination with the next imagined war may be dangerous, preparing for a specific war must start before it occurs. Otherwise militaries could become irrelevant to the security environment. Even if the appearance of a black swan cannot be predicted, imagining and anticipating its existence might be regarded as a contribution in itself.

The time might be ripe for the next round of anticipation. Today the early stages of several emerging military systems demand anticipation, like the strategic diagnosis outlined by Marshall. Consider questions formulated using the RMA diagnosis technique, some of which prolong the IT-RMA theme. What precision-strike capabilities, advanced sensors, and command and control systems might transform future battlefields? How would a conflict with several reconnaissance-strike complexes appear? Another possible focus of anticipation is proliferation. Current security concerns involve questions on emerging members of the nuclear-weapons club. Focusing on the behavior of nuclear proliferators offers another source of anticipation. Moreover, exploring the changing nature of war may focus on hybrid and cyber warfare. The former refers to conflicts in which state or nonstate actors adopt multiple strategic identities and the latter involves emerging cyber threats that alter traditional warfare and suggest other forms of anticipation.

* * *

The RMA combined an analytical framework introduced by the Office of Net Assessment with conceptual tools to explore questions related to innovation and systematic consideration of emerging challenges, which was unparalleled in modern strategic thought. Even if the IT-RMA concept was discredited, the principles development by Marshall would still be utilized around the world to diagnose transformations in the nature of war.[55] He stressed the RMA challenge was intellectual rather than technological, "which only sets the parameters of the possible and creates the potential for military revolution."[56] An innovation only appears when a military recognizes and exploits the opportunity to acquire new tools of war through organizational structures and force deployment. Earlier discontinuities in the nature of war are better recognized. Anticipating an RMA is not a talisman for victory, but any resulting transformation of capabilities is likely to enhance military effectiveness.[57] Accordingly, delaying transformation has the opposite effect. Mistakes can vary from ineffectiveness on the battlefield with tactical implications to strategic catastrophes with devastating consequences for national security.[58]

Notes

1. Andrew W. Marshall, statement before the Subcommittee on Acquisition and Technology of the Senate Armed Services Committee, 104th Congress, *Congressional Record* (Washington, DC: US Government Printing Office, May 5, 1995); Max Boot, *War Made New: Technology, Warfare and the Course of History, 1500 to Today* (New York: Gotham Books, 2006).
2. Michael G. Vickers and Robert C. Martinage, *The Revolution in War* (Washington, DC: Center for Strategic and Budgetary Assessments, 2004), 7.
3. Eliot A. Cohen, "Change and Transformation in Military Affairs," *Journal of Strategic Studies* 27 (September 2004): 397–405.
4. Chris C. Demchak, "Creating the Enemy: Global Diffusion of the Information Technology-Based Military Model," in *Diffusion of Military Technology and Ideas*, ed. Emily O. Goldman and Leslie C. Eliason (Stanford, CA: Stanford University Press, 2003), 307–10.
5. US Department of the Army, Field Manual 100-5, "Operations" (Washington, DC: Headquarters, Department of the Army, June 14, 1993).
6. See Dmitry (Dima) Adamsky, "Through the Looking Glass: The Soviet Military-Technical Revolution and the American Revolution in Military Affairs," *Journal of Strategic Studies* 31 (April 2008): 257–94.
7. Robert R. Tomes, *US Defense Strategy from Vietnam to Operation Iraqi Freedom: Military Innovation and the New American War of War, 1973–2003* (New York: Routledge, 2007), 96–126.
8. Ibid.
9. Richard H. Van Atta, Jack Nunn, and Alethia Cook, "Assault Breaker," in *Transformation and Transition: DARPA's Role in Fostering an Emerging Revolution in Military Affairs, Volume 2—Detailed Assessments*, ed. Richard H. Van Atta, Alethia Cook, Ivars Gutmanis, Michael J. Lippitz, Jasper Lupo, Rob Mahoney, and Jack Nunn (Alexandria, VA: Institute for Defense Analyses, November 2003), IV-1 to IV-40.
10. MacGregor Knox and Williamson Murray, *The Dynamics of Military Revolution, 1300–2050* (Cambridge: Cambridge University Press, 2001), 3; and Adamsky, *The Culture of Military Innovation*, chap. 3.
11. Jeffrey S. McKitrick, "The Revolution in Military Affairs," in *Battlefield of the Future: 21st Century Warfare Issues* (Maxwell Air Force Base, AL: Air University Press, 1995); Andrew W. Marshall, memorandum

for the record, "Some Thoughts on Military Revolutions—Second Version" (Washington, DC: Office of Net Assessment, August 23, 1993), 1.

12. Adamsky, *The Culture of Military Innovation*, chaps. 2 and 3.

13. Ibid., 62–64.

14. Van Atta, Nunn, and Cook, "Assault Breaker," IV–14.

15. US Central Intelligence Agency, "Warsaw Pact Nonnuclear Threat to NATO Airbases in Central Europe," NIE 11/20–6–84 (Washington, DC: Director of Central Intelligence, October 25, 1984), 41–42; "Trends and Developments in Warsaw Pact Theater Forces, 1985–2000," NIE 11–14–85/D (Washington, DC: Director of Central Intelligence, September 1985), 9–13, 29–33; "Trends and Developments in Warsaw Pact Theater Forces and Doctrine Through the 1990s," NIE 11–14–89 (Washington, DC: Director of Central Intelligence, February 1989).

16. Andrew W. Marshall, "Foreword," in *Diffusion of Military Technology*, eds. Goldman and Eliason, xiv; Marshall, "Some Thoughts."

17. Derek Leebaert, *The Fifty-Year Wound: The True Price of America's Cold War Victory* (Boston: Little, Brown, 2002), 507; Ronald E. Powaski, *The Cold War: The United States and the Soviet Union, 1917–1991* (New York: Oxford University Press, 1998), 233.

18. Knox and Murray, *Military Revolution*, 3.

19. See Jacob W. Kipp, "The Russian Military and the Revolution in Military Affairs: A Case of the Oracle of Delphi or Cassandra?" paper delivered at the MORS Conference in Annapolis, Maryland, on June 6–8, 1995; see also Sergei Modestov, "Serii Kardinal Pentagona Andrew Marshall—ideolog novoi amerikanskoi revoliucii v voennom dele," *Nezavisimoe voennoe obozrenie* 4, December 14, 1995.

20. Knox and Murray, *Military Revolution*, 4; James Der Derian, *Virtuous War* (Oxford: Westview Press, 2001), 29–32.

21. Andrew J. Bacevich, Jr., *The New American Militarism* (Oxford: Oxford University Press, 2005), 161–63; and Stephen Peter Rosen, "Net Assessment as an Analytical Concept," in *On Not Confusing Ourselves*, ed. Andrew W. Marshall, J. J. Martin, and Henry S. Rowen (Boulder, CO: Westview Press, 1991), 283–84.

22. Albert Wohlstetter, "Threats and Promises of Peace: Europe and America in the New Era," *Orbis* 17 (Winter 1974): 1107–44; "Between an Unfree World and None: Increasing Our Choices," *Foreign Affairs* 63 (Summer 1985): 962–94; and "The Political and Military Aims of Offensive and Defensive Innovation," in *Swords and Shields: NATO, the USSR, and New*

Choices for Long-Range Offense and Defense, Fred S. Hoffman, Albert Wohlstetter, and David S. Yost, (Lexington, MA: Lexington Books, 1987).

23. Krepinevich, *Military-Technical Revolution*, i–iv.
24. Notra Trulock III, "Emerging Technologies and Future War: A Soviet View," in *The Future Security Environment*, ed. Andrew W. Marshall and Charles Wolf, Jr. (Washington, DC: Department of Defense, October 1988), 143.
25. Marshall and Wolf, eds., *Future Security*, 34–35, 40, 42, 64, 69–71.
26. Stephen J. Blank, *The Soviet Military Views of Operation Desert Storm: A Preliminary Assessment* (Carlisle Barracks, PA: Strategic Studies Institute, US Army War College, 1991), 31–33; Shimon Naveh, *In Pursuit of Military Excellence: The Evolution of Operational Theory* (London: Frank Cass, 1997), 238, 330; Norman C. Davis, "An Information-Based Revolution in Military Affairs," in *In Athena's Camp*, John Arquilla and David Ronfeldt (Santa Monica, CA: RAND Corporation, 1997), 85; A. A. Kokoshin, *O Politicheskom smysle pobedy v sovremmen-noi voine* (Moscow: Editorial URSS, 2004), 36–37; Edward J. Felker, *Russian Military Doctrinal Reform in Light of Their Analysis of Desert Storm* (Maxwell Air Force Base, AL: Air University Press, 1995), 33.
27. Statement by Andrew W. Marshall at a CSBA roundtable on future warfare, March 12, 2002. Vickers and Martinage, *Revolution in War*, 12; Krepinevich, *Military-Technical Revolution*, i–iv.
28. Marshall, "Some Thoughts," 2–4; Krepinevich, *Military-Technical Revolution*, iii–iv, 5–7; Vickers and Martinage, *Revolution in War*, 10–13; Michael Horowitz and Stephen Peter Rosen, "Evolution or Revolution?" *Journal of Strategic Studies* 3 (June 2005): 439–40.
29. Krepinevich, *Military-Technical Revolution*, 8; Marshall, "Some Thoughts," 2–4.
30. Theodor W. Galdi, *Revolution in Military Affairs? Competing Concepts, Organizational Responses, Outstanding Issues*, Report to Congress 95–1170 F (Washington, DC: Library of Congress, Congressional Research Service, December 11, 1995), 9.
31. Barry D. Watts, *What Is the Revolution in Military Affairs?* (Arlington, VA: Northrop Grumman Analysis Center, April 6, 1995), 3–4.
32. Steven Metz and James Kievit, *Strategy and the Revolution in Military Affairs: From Theory to Policy* (Carlisle Barracks, PA: Strategic Studies Institute, US Army War College, 1995).
33. Thomas G. Mahnken, *Technology and the American Way of War* (New York: Columbia University Press, 2008), 177.

34. Barry D. Watts and Williamson Murray, "Military Innovation in Peacetime," in *Military Innovation in the Interwar Period*, ed. Williamson Murray and Allan R. Millett (New York: Cambridge University Press, 1996), 369–415.

35. Tomes, *Defense Strategy*, 24.

36. Colin S. Gray, *Out of the Wilderness: Prime Time for Strategic Culture* (Fort Belvoir, VA: Defense Threat Reduction Agency, 2006), 5.

37. See William E. Odom, "Soviet Force Posture: Dilemmas and Directions," *Problems of Communism* (July–August 1985): 1–2, 6–14, 40. This article represents a precise open-source account of the Soviet MTR published contemporaneously with the event.

38. William A. Owens with Edward Offley, *Lifting the Fog of War* (New York: Farrar, Straus and Giroux, 2000), 83–84.

39. Mahnken, *Technology*, 74–75; Watts, *What Is the Revolution?* 1–2.

40. Owens, *Fog of War*, 83; Watts, *What Is the Revolution?* 1–2.

41. Dima Adamsky, *The Culture of Military Innovation: The Impact of Cultural Factors on the Revolution in Military Affairs in Russia, the US, and Israel* (Stanford, CA: Stanford University Press, 2010), 73.

42. Der Derian, *Virtuous War*, 30–32. Stuart A. Whitehead, Director of the Integration Office for Battle Command at the US Army Training and Doctrine Command, argued that emulating Soviet holistic, synthetic, and nonlinear thinking could alter American military culture. See Williamson Murray, *Emerging Strategic Environment: Challenges of the Twenty-First Century* (Westport, CT: Praeger Publishers, 1999), 49.

43. McKitrick, "Adding to Net Assessment," 119.

44. Watts, *Six Decades*, 77; Watts, *What Is the Revolution?* 6; Galdi, *Revolution in Military Affairs?* 9.

45. Watts, *What Is the Revolution?* 6; Galdi, *Revolution in Military Affairs?* 9.

46. Colin Gray, *Recognizing and Understanding Revolutionary Change in Warfare* (Carlisle Barracks, PA: Strategic Studies Institute, US Army War College, 2006), 8.

47. Richard Lock-Pullan, "The US Way of War and the War on Terror," *Politics and Policy* 34 (June 2006): 374–99.

48. Barry D. Watts, "Evolving Military Affairs," *Defense News*, May 22, 2006.

49. H. R. McMaster, "On War: Lessons to Be Learned," *Survival* 50 (February–March 2008): 19–30.

50. Dmitry (Dima) Adamsky and Kjell Inge Bjerga, *Contemporary Military Innovation: Between Anticipation and Adaptation* (New York: Routledge, 2012), 5

51. Ibid., 4–5
52. Ibid., 189–90.
53. McMaster, "On War," 19; and H. R. McMaster, "Learning Contemporary Conflicts to Prepare for Future War," *Orbis* 52 (Fall 2008): 564–84.
54. Watts and Murray, "Military Innovation," 404–406.
55. Adamsky and Bjerga, 189–93.
56. Marshall, statement before the Subcommittee on Acquisition and Technology, 3–5; Watts, *What Is the RMA?* 5–6.
57. Richard O. Hundley, *Past Revolutions, Future Transformations: What Can the History of Revolutions in Military Affairs Tell Us About Transforming the US Military?* (Santa Monica, CA: RAND Corporation, 1999), 13.
58. Watts and Murray, "Military Innovation," 404–406.

Chapter 8

Understanding the Nature of "the Other"

Abram N. Shulsky

Among the practical methods of research utilized in strategic studies, net assessments are closely identified with systems analysis and intelligence. Like systems analysis, they seek to understand the actual or potential strength of one's own force posture and, like intelligence, the capabilities of potential adversaries. With regard to the United States and an adversary, assessments examine questions in the broadest possible terms. What is more, by focusing on the balance of forces and estimating their relative strength, the assessment process acts as a corrective to analysis of one side of a military balance. A net assessment not only endeavors to describe the balance of power but also trends influencing military balances over time. It must explain in dynamic terms the way in which each side of the balance operates and will likely interact. Finally, net assessments must compare the strengths of both sides as well as major trends in their military posture.

A maxim ascribed to Sun Tzu could serve as a catchphrase for the net assessment: "Know the enemy and know yourself; in a hundred battles you will never be in peril."[1] Situating demand for such knowledge might seem paradoxical because knowing oneself is taken for granted while understanding adversaries entails billions of dollars as well as a sizable effort. But knowledge of oneself is not a trivial pursuit. The defense establishment is complex and, for reasons of security, it may be difficult to gain information on its capabilities. For example, a joint effort by the Office of Net Assessment and the National Intelligence Council during the early 1980s was incomplete because the analysts lacked access to black programs including stealth aircraft and antisubmarine warfare.[2] In addition, the various components of the defense establishment are parochial when it comes to how they will perform together in war as well as how they will operate together. What is more, financial constraints may lead to solutions that are not considered during peacetime. For instance, countering improvised explosive devices with naval electronic warfare systems was not imagined prior to the enemy using them in Iraq but became vital to their defeat.[3]

Beyond matters of classification and compartmentalization in the Intelligence Community, it is always difficult to know how one will act in every situation beforehand. Whatever plans are made in advance, reactions in time of crisis are shaped by political pressures and perceptions of unfolding events. Thus, it is difficult to gauge the effectiveness of forces. For example, would the planners who looked at the balance of US and communist forces in East Asia in early 1950 have predicted a limited war scenario with hostilities confined to the Korean Peninsula?

INTELLIGENCE AND ASSESSMENTS

Whatever difficulties arise in knowing one's situation, the most laborious and costly part of a net assessment is gathering necessary information on an adversary. Therefore, as the principal source of information on potential adversaries, the Intelligence Community may appear to be the logical source of net assessments as well; however, this is not the case.

While the aims of policymakers should determine the range of information that intelligence agencies collect, those aims are often insufficient to provide useful guidance. Even in respect to known adversaries, policymakers may be unable to formulate priorities for collecting intelligence in a precise manner; given the nature of priority-setting exercises, the typical default position for policymakers involves asking for everything. No policymaker wants to go on record as claiming that a particular category of information warrants a low priority because it might prove later on to be crucial for understanding an adversary or dealing with a crisis.

One question essential about net assessment that senior officials should ask is the same one that Edward Koch, the former Mayor of New York City, often asked the good people of Gotham: "How'm I doing?" by which he meant, "improving or getting worse?" The question remains apt for competition between adversaries, particularly their military forces. Such queries are needed during peacetime when the outcome of conflicts is unavailable to disclose the capabilities of an adversary.

Yet, "How'm I doing?" should be asked even in regard to combat operations. It is quite difficult in counterinsurgencies to determine how well one is doing because hard-to-understand political factors often are far more important than the military ones. Remember criticism of using the term *body count* as a metric of success during the Vietnam War. Even in high-intensity conflicts, there might be room for net assessments to understand aspects of the struggle that do not immediately lead to results on the battlefield, namely, the relative development of productive capabilities on both sides regarding weapons systems and technological advantages.

Looking at the outcome of battles fought during the first half of 1942, the Allies seemed to be losing the war. But a true appreciation of the situation would have revealed that unparalleled American mobilization capabilities were likely to shift the actual balance against the Axis given sufficient time. Similarly, understanding the status of the secret competition of the United States and Great Britain versus Germany in developing the atomic bomb would have been significant in accurately evaluating the real balance between the protagonists.

A detailed understanding of relative situation vis-à-vis adversaries is important both in and of itself. Moreover, it supports development of so-called *competitive strategies* that seek ways to ensure that one's strengths are mobilized to maximum advantage while the weaknesses of the adversary are fully exploited. They attempt to channel ongoing competition in a favorable way, either by focusing the competition on an area where one has relative strength or by inducing the adversary to commit resources to defensive measures that are not threatening. As a result, they must explicitly take into account the responses of potential adversaries. Analyses that contribute to producing net assessments—which seek to understand the balance as well as the significance of one's actions from an adversary's point of view—supply the requisite insights.

This insistence on examining both oneself and one's adversary in the same study characterizes net assessments compared to other approaches for assessing an adversary. At the same time, net assessments embrace and indeed contribute to developing many techniques discussed in the relevant literature: techniques such as considering alternative competing hypotheses, gaming, red teams, and playing the devil's advocate.[4]

Even though the Intelligence Community embraces the lion's share of agencies capable of analyzing information collected from all sources in an organized manner, it is not positioned to offer the requisite answers. Superficially, intelligence analysis is entirely focused on "the other" and distanced from matters of policy, strategy, and resources. Thus, it can supply information on force structure, doctrine and plans, and strategic developments, but it does not tell policymakers what they must know: the capabilities of an adversary when pitted against US and its allies and the likely trends in understanding what such estimates mean for national security.

It might appear possible to obtain Red data from the Intelligence Community and place it in the first column and get Blue input from the defense establishment and list it in the second; Red and Blue being the standard shorthand terms for hostile and friendly forces. But would it provide the necessary comparative accounts of US and opposing forces? The short answer is no, given that understanding of the competition, the relevant categories, and criteria to be evaluated are not obvious. That is where net assessments come into the picture by providing understanding of the competition between Blue and Red and how it is likely to evolve. To do this, assessments must be familiar with each side because they react to "the other" to some extent in the course of making decisions. Thus, anyone who answers the proverbial question of "How'm I doing?" must be familiar with Red and Blue. Carl von Clausewitz came to a similar conclusion with the center of gravity and unravelling of an adversary when attacked. A vulnerability becomes this *center* only when it is possible to attack; thus, considering "the dominant characteristics of both belligerents is necessary in order to identify an enemy's center of gravity."[5]

INTELLIGENCE REQUIREMENTS

While intelligence is distinct from net assessment, it remains the essential source of information on potential adversaries. This places a major burden on the Intelligence Community because the intelligence requirements for net assessment are great and often involve detailed information on the political and military circumstances of the other side. In some cases, the questions posed by net assessment are not the ones intelligence would ordinarily address.

Furthermore, it is often impossible to identify intelligence requirements at the outset. Thus, the relationship between net assessment and intelligence cannot depend on a standard paradigm in which policymakers generate intelligence requirements and the information is provided in due course to fulfill them. Instead, the relationship must be interactive. Given the constant attempt to undertake net assessments that are comprehensive as well as feasible, it is impossible to pose all the questions requiring intelligence on any adversary. However, some questions important to net assessments rather than to other intelligence consumers can be posed.

One major class of questions concerns the Red perceptions of the situation and particularly its situation vis-à-vis Blue. An assessment of Red is crucial background in any attempt to predict its actions and understand why it takes them. From the point of view of intelligence, this is likely to be extremely difficult, at least in the typical situation when direct evidence is lacking such as written assessments and intercepted conversations. Analysts must be immersed in available data on past and current actions by Red and exercise their imagination in reconstructing perceptions of strategy, doctrine, weapons, etc., supporting them. Only in this way can the future actions of an adversary be reasonably predicted.

However, it is necessary to understand Blue, which is another reason net assessments must not remain exclusively within the realm of intelligence. While Red may misperceive or even be ignorant of things Blue is doing, it is also possible that Red will react to actions by Blue to which the Blue intelligence is not attentive.[6] Because of the difficulty in reconstructing the Red view of the situation, one tends to defer to the *rational actor model* that assumes rationality on the part of Red. But that means instead of answering a real question of how does Red assess its situation, an easier one is answered instead: if I were Red, how would I assess my situation.

A phenomenon known as *mirror imaging* assumes that Red weighs situations and reacts to them like Blue. In practice, this assumption corresponds to the rational actor model, even though analysts may believe that some actions by their side are not rational for political or other reasons. Amazingly this situation often does not lead analysts of Red to think Red's actions may be similarly distorted.[7] Net assessment emphasizes understanding decision-making by an adversary and to what extent it may be possible to find characteristic influences affecting the process. Thus, it seeks intelligence on all aspects of decision-making including the structure of the national security community and standard operating procedures. In a competition such as the Cold War, actions by the adversary will result from decisions made by bureaucracies with many competitors. For example, military services compete for available resources. One frequent complaint about defense programs is that for bureaucratic reasons the allocation of resources among the services has not been adjusted in light of the changing strategic environment.

Although senior political leaders will likely override the standard bureaucratic workings of national security institutions in a crisis, they can only devote their attention to a small number of questions. Most decisions governing military posture will be made elsewhere in the bureaucracy and reflect not only strategy but also competing organizations. As a RAND report originated by Andrew W. Marshall and Joseph E. Loftus had suggested in 1968, "it was more plausible that the Soviet posture evolved as a result of decisions taken within a large bureaucratic structure than as the output of a small set of individuals working in a highly consistent manner."[8]

Information on such bureaucratic practices may not be forthcoming from the Intelligence Community. For example, a memo in 1970 to Henry A. Kissinger about intelligence on matters including Soviet strategic forces, Marshall noted that the weakest point occurred

> . . . in judgments of intelligence analysts and estimators about plausible or likely Soviet behavior, in particular their understanding of the decision processes that influence Soviet military posture. The explicit or implicit assumptions and hypotheses concerning

the roots of Soviet behavior seem much too simplified, and rely too frequently upon a model of the Soviet government as a single unified actor pursuing an easily stated strategy.[9]

Similarly, decisions may be affected by cultural traditions. It was widely believed during the Cold War, for instance, that the Soviet Union had a predisposition to invest heavily in air defenses, notwithstanding its inability to counter a missile threat. Detailed knowledge of that predisposition would be important in understanding how Soviet forces were being developed. Additionally, one would have wanted to understand the significance of a related development, the organizational clout of the Air Defense Force within the Soviet Union.[10]

Other determinants of decision-making by an adversary may include available information and the ways experience affects behavior. For example, the reluctance of the British to introduce a convoy system to protect commercial shipping from German submarines threat in World War I resulted partly because of a lack of information on the number of ships to be protected. Thus, the Admiralty focused on vessels entering and leaving port instead of ships engaged in transatlantic trade and mistakenly concluded that it did not have resources to protect them all.[11]

Furthermore, decisionmakers can be overly influenced by experience and favor methods used successfully in the past whether or not those approaches remain appropriate. Machiavelli said that it is rare to find a man who is "sufficiently circumspect to know how to accommodate himself to [changed situations], both because he cannot deviate from what nature inclines him to, and also because, having always prospered by acting in one way, he cannot be persuaded that it is well to leave it."[12] One study of defensive preparations against Napoleon Bonaparte indicated that Russian leaders understood that he would attempt to replicate earlier battles by winning quickly and decisively, which could be countered by trading space for time.[13]

Understanding how an adversary makes decisions and especially how nonrational factors influence such decisions is important in developing competitive strategies which, even though conceptually different from net assessment, is a logical offshoot. Understanding decision-making as well as bureaucratic and other constraints may suggest measures by Blue that induce Red to devote resources to suboptimal or nonthreatening actions. This insight might enable Blue to gain a more favorable competitive position over the long run. Marshall sought to explain the nature of this situation during the early 1970s as expressed in the following way:

> It may be possible through US moves, based upon a superior understanding of the interaction process or other aspects of the competition [such as Soviet decision-making processes] to steer Soviet posture choices to some extent. In that case, US preferences would be operative. US preferences, all things considered, probably are that the Soviets expend resources on defensive rather than offensive systems.[14]

Because the Soviets were particularly sensitive to airborne threats, a disproportionate amount of resources could be diverted to air defense by developing US long-range bombers despite the fact missiles can be more cost efficient during all-out war. "One might suggest, for instance, that the Soviets assign a disproportionate disutility to a possible invasion of their air spaces."[15]

Another major area in which net assessment imposes requirements on intelligence relates to Red weaknesses which result from bureaucratic constraints or other causes. Although it might be assumed that the Intelligence Community will always report on weaknesses and strengths of any adversary, such information can go unreported unless determined efforts are made to focus on it. Experience has proven weaknesses are short-changed in intelligence analysis. For example, the Defense Intelligence Agency refused to discuss the weakness of Soviet tank forces in the 1970s on the grounds that if it existed, it would be fixed.[16]

Given attempts to produce *comprehensive* assessments of the strength of the United States and its adversaries, net assessments also tend to inquire into subjects that are of only minor interest to policymakers and thus be slighted by the Intelligence Community. For instance, an assessment of US and Soviet ground forces could not be limited to the number of weapons on each side and the speed and armor plating of tanks and the range of artillery. Instead, it had to explain how the weapons were to be used, resupplied, and repaired in an actual battle. But as Marshall observed: "Some aspects of Soviet forces important to net assessment have not had high priority in current intelligence efforts, in particular logistics and operational practices."[17]

DIFFICULT QUESTIONS

As a consumer of intelligence, net assessors may not appear different from other members of the government. But the questions that they pose to the Intelligence Community appear to cause particular difficulties. First and foremost, their questions are harder to answer than many others, especially given reliance on technical intelligence means. It is more difficult to address questions concerning bureaucratic and other motives behind the actions of adversaries than to either count or observe the performance of weapons systems being tested. Without access to the thinking of adversaries by means of espionage or communications intelligence, answering the questions of net assessors calls for large investments in analyses by highly trained experts.

Intelligence requirements for net assessments may not be positioned to command analytic resources within the Intelligence Community because they are necessarily diagnostic. Marshall described the objective of the new system of assessments in 1972: "It will highlight efficiency and inefficiency in the way we and others do things, and areas of comparative advantage with respect to our rivals. *It is not intended to provide recommendations as to force levels or force structures as an output* [emphasis added]."[18] This makes it difficult to compete for intelligence analysis against consumers who argue that answers to their questions directly inform decisions that high-level policymakers must address.

Thus, the Intelligence Community may slight other requests that are not identified with urgent policy issues.

Marshall recounted an instance when the Secretary of Defense, concerned with a building in Somalia that appeared to be a Soviet missile facility, asked him to serve as an intermediary to the Intelligence Community to learn how the Russians went about gaining access to such facilities. The Central Intelligence Agency balked at the request, claiming that it could respond better if told where the information would lead. Marshall remarked that the CIA failure to understand that the requested information, while not needed for a decision "next Thursday," was important to the process by which the defense establishment assessed the facility. This net assessment would then become part of the mental picture to which senior officials would refer in making their decision. Marshall regarded this refusal by the Intelligence Community as an illustration of the extent to which it failed to understand the national security decision-making process.[19]

That failure exemplifies an ongoing concern about intelligence: namely, the oft-noted trend for current requirements to overshadow and crowd out basic research. The fact that reforms over the years have called for redressing this balance in the Intelligence Community reveals ingrained emphasis that is focused on current requirements to the detriment of basic research. Also, many questions posed by net assessments demand information of a particular type such as perceptions of key adversary decision-makers. This means that setting priorities must be done more critically because considerable assets should be devoted to satisfactorily answering them.

Because net assessment is oftentimes concerned with long-term trends, it requires reliable and consistent data about the past as well as the present. Establishing trend data is difficult because in reporting it the Intelligence Community may not use either consistent definitions or standards. For example, it may not be apparent whether support vessels should be considered as warships. If changes in criteria are made by the

Intelligence Community from one year to the next, it is not likely the data from previous years will be adjusted to conform to the new criteria. Similarly, if something leads to changing estimates of a weapons system, intelligence analysts are unlikely to revise their earlier conclusions. Simply comparing previously available information on a weapon will not produce an accurate understanding of the progress made by an adversary.[20]

This characteristic situation appears to emerge from that fact that revised data on the past, although important in understanding trends, has no direct impact on current decision-making. In general, the Intelligence Community is resolutely oriented on the present and the future; it often underestimates historical analysis in understanding current situations. Even though this sort of analysis may seem more properly the function of academic research than intelligence analysts, relevant data may not be available in unclassified sources. Thus, this type of historical analysis has to be performed somewhere within the government.

Answering the questions posed by the net assessment process also necessitates specialized expertise in analyzing intelligence. For example, consider requirements for a net assessment of the missile forces possessed by the United States and a potential adversary. Analysts are needed who are familiar with missile technology *as well as* the culture or mindset of the adversary. Such expertise will not be found on street corners, but the Intelligence Community can hire individuals with the appropriate technical background and others who know the history, politics, culture, and language of the potential adversary. However, it is unlikely anyone can be recruited who is familiar with the missile industry or forces of the adversary. Therefore expertise must be developed in-house; it will take time to sufficiently immerse analysts in the way adversaries look at the world in order to think like their scientists, engineers, and military procurement officials.

This problem was observed during World War II by R.V. Jones, the noted British scientist and intelligence officer whose successes in countering the

German Luftwaffe are legendary. As he recalled, technological experts who thought like Germans were needed because technological expertise alone could be misleading. Analysts were key to dealing with advances such as radars that differed from the British developments or available expertise. As he explained:

> . . . it is difficult to overcome the prejudice that as we have not done something, it is impossible or foolish . . . our [technological] experts in examining German developments are no longer experts but novices. . . . From an intelligence point of view, it must always be borne in mind that the advice comes from a British, and not a German expert.[21]

One might expect the strengths and weaknesses of adversaries to be reported in the course of normal intelligence analyses but often it is not. In mulling the predisposition to understate the weaknesses and overemphasize the strengths of the Soviet Union, practitioners of net assessment discovered that it was presumed "the Soviets would be better than the United States at detecting their own weaknesses and that they would correct them over time."[22] Thus, while analysts must be alert to the possibility that adversaries will correct their weaknesses, they should also reflect on the extent to which they think the US military similarly corrects its weaknesses.

A reluctance to focus on the weaknesses of an adversary may derive from several factors. The oft-noted tendency for worst-case analysis leads to the neglect of weaknesses. Given that underestimating an adversary is more likely to create problems for one's own forces—and thus for intelligence analysis—than overestimating it or erring on the side of caution, this neglect is perhaps explicable. Missing an opportunity to exploit weakness is likely to go unnoticed; in any case, it will not lead to a crisis. The same cannot be said of failing to identify the strength of an adversary; bureaucratic caution leads to an unwillingness to be forthright.

The mindset common within the Intelligence Community is found throughout the national security apparatus and results in far greater attention being paid to defending against challenges than exploiting opportunities. In a sense, this attitude indicates the view of decision makers. The establishment of the net assessment in the early 1970s responded to a fear that the United States might be unable to retain its superiority over the Soviet Union. Given the geopolitical position that the nation has occupied in the world for decades, it is understandable that American policy makers, and hence intelligence analysts, were more focused on threats to the status quo instead of identifying strategic opportunities and pursuing them to strengthen it.

By virtue of its comprehensive approach, net assessments ask questions that cross ordinary bureaucratic lines in the Intelligence Community. Thus, political and economic analyses have to be added to the strictly military analysis to piece together the required understanding of adversaries. Forcing the various disparate parts of the intelligence analysis world to coordinate on a coherent overall picture of an adversary can be harder than it might initially seem.

Intelligence collection has been defined in terms of disciplines or the so-called *ints* which include espionage or human sources (*humint*), interception and decryption of communications (*comint*), and remote photography or imagery (*imint*) plus technical means. Recent attempts have given open-source collection equal status with *ints*, and it has been designated as *osint* to validate the process. Just like Monsieur Jourdain in *Le bourgeois gentilhomme* by Molière who delighted in learning that he had been speaking prose for his entire life, many ordinary newspaper readers can take pride in the fact they have been *osint* collectors without realizing it.

At their most difficult, the sorts of questions which net assessment asks require insight into the adversary's way of thinking. To some extent, the necessary information can be gleaned from the established *ints* (particularly if open source collection is included among them). However, it also has proved beneficial to use all sorts of unconventional sources of information. For example, during the Cold War, émigrés from the Soviet Union (especially after Soviet Jews were allowed to emigrate in large numbers during the 1970s) were a potentially valuable source of information on a range of topics relevant to the questions posed by net assessment. Information from émigrés was crucial to the process that led the Central Intelligence Agency in the mid-1970s to double the estimate of defense outlays as a percentage of Soviet GNP. That ratio would become essential to understanding constraints on the Soviet military in response to US developments.

But making use of such information can be difficult for two reasons. First, there have been distinctions in the Intelligence Community between collection and analysis whereby the Central Intelligence Agency separates the directorates responsible for operations and intelligence. While in principle collection is driven by analytic requirements, this division of labor reduces flexibility in the system as collectors are organized into specific *ints* and focused on improving the quality as well as the amount and type of information gathered. Second, the Intelligence Community recruits personnel directly from colleges with the expectation that they will spend their careers in the field or at least in public service. Thus recruits may be unaware of extragovernmental sources of information and less likely to have contacts among individuals in other walks of life. This situation may be compared to the Office of Strategic Services (OSS), the forerunner of the CIA, which benefited from the lateral entry of people with diverse backgrounds. Given that the need to build up its capabilities arose when most Americans were eligible for wartime service, the OSS recruited men and women from many walks of life including its head, William J. Donovan, who previously had worked as an attorney in government and on Wall Street and built international contacts in addition to being the most highly decorated veteran of World War I.

INTELLIGENCE CHALLENGES

Efforts have been made by the Intelligence Community to meet periodic challenges and take appropriate steps whenever possible. The value of opportunity analysis to policymakers has been discussed sometimes: that is, the systematic focus on not only opportunities but also threats. This is a potentially difficult area for intelligence activities. For one thing, it appears to breach the wall between intelligence and policy because identifying weaknesses as opportunities will imply a policy opinion; that is, the potential value of exploiting the vulnerability. In principle, identifying an opportunity is not equivalent to recognizing that its exploitation would be good from a policy point of view. Nevertheless, identifying and analyzing various courses of action suggests that some are more promising than others. Therefore this type of procedure involves political risks that the Intelligence Community tends to be reluctant to accept.

The Intelligence Community also has addressed the inherent bureaucratic rigidity found in the division of intelligence collection among *ints*. One such initiative has been the formation of centers that merge collection and analysis under one institutional umbrella with respect to given topics such as counterterrorism. Another initiative has been establishing issue managers under the auspices of the Director of National Intelligence who are responsible for overseeing as well as improving collection of information with respect to topics and countries. Imaginative issue managers are incentivized and capable of collecting information from unconventional sources, which are particularly useful in conducting their analyses.

Other initiatives could address the need for area or country specialists to be trained to think more strategically. The preparation of net assessments by the Red team would require analysts to be steeped in Red strategic culture and consider its situation, problems, and opportunities. Such analysis must reconstruct Red knowledge of Blue using open source material and incorporating insights provided by counterintelligence regarding Red intelligence collection on Blue.

Closer interaction between net assessors and intelligence analysts is beneficial as well; the latter understand the type of information required for net assessment and its importance. Thus, net assessors can gain a better understanding of competing views from the Intelligence Community before they are homogenized in the coordination process. Both the assessors and analysts seek to know the nature of "the other" even though the former apply it to specific products: "a very clear description of the comparative situation of ourselves and our rivals" according to Marshall.[23] This type of net assessment or the military balance could refer to competition with adversaries or specific areas such as naval forces which constitute subsets of competition. Another by-product of assessments is competitive strategy which contrasts strengths and vulnerabilities.

Efforts to conduct a strategic analysis of the situation of an adversary require information on its characteristic mindset, strategic culture, and bureaucratic institutions and constraints. This type of insight combines strategic analysis and an appreciation of the peculiarities of the thought processes and conduct of an adversary. In piecing together such a picture, one noteworthy pitfall is mirror imaging—the tendency demonstrated by intelligence analysts to act on the assumption adversaries evaluate that situation in the same way as Americans and then would react in similar ways. This exhibition of unconscious self-deception reveals the failure to determine whether the analysis contains specific US perspectives or is universally applicable.

The Intelligence Community takes the problem of mirror imaging seriously in part because of the fact that the expertise available to analysts of any particular national security issue is Blue expertise in the first instance. Unless the possibility of an adversary considering national security issues differently from the analysts is explicitly highlighted, they are unlikely to realize the fact simply by connecting the dots. It is improbable that enough data points will be available to force analysts to reconsider the premise; only when the possibility of Red perceptions differing from Blue is posed will analysts be inclined to perceive a distinctive Red approach and mindset.

Although the problems associated with mirror imaging have been aired in the literature on intelligence, less attention has been given to the apparently opposite possibility that analysts can regard adversaries only in terms of cultural biases and forgetting that they can react to strategic affairs in unexpected ways. For example, some observers were surprised by the Iraqi invasion of Kuwait in 1990 because it went against traditional interaction among Arab states, which consists of subversion, proxies, and terrorism but not the use of military force.

Net assessments underscore the need for Red expertise—that is, analysts with knowledge of the subject and the way Red does things. No discipline trains people in this manner. But one technique that may help is strategic gaming. If analysts who understand Red strategic culture are combined with technical experts to assess problems, they can develop insights on how Red may deal with issues. Giving weight to the strategic imperatives faced by an adversary and its ways of thought and operational constraints provides the balance that is characteristic of the manner in which the net assessment approach strives to understand "the other" in context.

NOTES

1. Sun Tzu, *The Art of War*, trans. Samuel B. Griffith (Oxford: Oxford University Press, 1963), 84.

2. See Andrew W. Marshall, "1969–75," interview 7–21 (December 14, 1993). Transcription by Kurt Guthe; the number 7 designates the seventh interview and is followed by a page number).

3. Melissa Nelson, "Navy Specialists Lead IED Fight," *USA Today*, March 20, 2008.

4. See Richards J. Heuer, Jr., *Psychology of Intelligence Analysis* (Washington, DC: Center for the Study of Intelligence, 1999). See also Robert Jervis, *Perception and Misperception in International Politics* (Princeton NJ: Princeton University Press, 1976).

5. *On War*, book 8, chapter 4, as cited in Stephen Peter Rosen, "Net Assessment as an Analytic Concept," in *On Not Confusing Ourselves: Essays on National Security Strategy in Honor of Albert and Roberta Wohlstetter*, ed. Andrew W. Marshall, J. J. Martin, and Henry S. Rowen (Boulder, CO: Westview Press, 1991), 286.

6. Marshall, "1969–75," interview 7–21 (December 14, 1993).

7. On decisions by actors as imperfectly rational at best, see Stephen Peter Rosen, "Competitive Strategies: Theoretical Foundations, Limits and Extensions," in *Competitive Strategies for the 21st Century: Theory, History and Practice*, ed. Thomas G. Mahnken (Stanford, CA: Stanford University Press, 2012), 12–16.

8. Andrew W. Marshall, "The Improvement in Intelligence Estimates Through Study of Organizational Behavior," D-16858-PR (Santa Monica, CA: RAND Corporation, March 15, 1968; declassified January 14, 1977), 1.

9. Memorandum from the Consultant to the National Security Council [Marshall] to the Assistant to the President for National Security Affairs [Kissinger], "Intelligence Inputs for Major Issues: A Substantive Evaluation and Proposals for Improvement," in *Foreign Relations of the United States, 1969–1976*, vol. 2, *Organization and Management of US Foreign Policy, 1969–1972*, Document 206; available at http://history.state.gov/historicaldocuments/frus1969-76v02/d206.

10. Gordon S. Barrass, "US Competitive Strategy during the Cold War," in Mahnken, *Competitive Strategies*, 77–78.

11. Rosen, *Competitive Strategies*, 13–14.

12. *The Prince*, XXV.
13. Dominic Lieven, *Russia Against Napoleon* (New York: Viking, 2010), as discussed in Rosen, *Competitive Strategies*, 18–19.
14. "Long-Term Competition with the Soviets: A Framework for Strategic Analysis," R-862-PR (Washington, DC: RAND Corporation, April 1972), 34.
15. James G. Roche and Andrew W. Marshall, "Strategy for Competing with the Soviets in the Military Sector of the Continuing Political-Military Competition" (July 26, 1976), 10.
16. Marshall, "1969–75," interview 5–42 (December 14, 1993).
17. Andrew W. Marshall, "The Nature and Scope of Net Assessments" (Washington, DC: National Security Council, March 26, 1972), 2.
18. Ibid., 1.
19. Marshall, "1969–75," interviews 5–54 and 5–55 (December 14, 1993).
20. See Rosen, "Analytic Concept," in *On Not Confusing Ourselves*, 292.
21. R. V. [Reginald Victor] Jones, *The Wizard War: British Scientific Intelligence, 1939–45* (New York: Coward, McCann and Geoghegan, 1978), 457–58.
22. George E. Pickett, James G. Roche, and Barry D. Watts, "Net Assessment: A Historical Review," in *On Not Confusing Ourselves*, 168.
23. Marshall, "Net Assessment," 1.

CHAPTER 9

ANALYTICAL TOOLS
AND TECHNIQUES

Jeffrey S. McKitrick

Studies known as *net assessments*—what also may be called *strategic assessments*—are intended to identify and analyze issues, trends and asymmetries, and challenges and opportunities found in functional or regional military competition. They include top-level studies delivered to decision-makers in the Department of Defense. They are diagnostic rather than therapeutic, describing the nature of problems without proffering solutions. The typical assessments of military balances are complex and must be broken down to further analyze land, sea, and air forces. Only critical areas are selected for attention. For example, naval forces may have been omitted in net assessments of the European theater during the Cold War because air-land battle on the Central Front appeared to play the key role in determining the outcome of a conflict.

No universal template or formula exists for net assessments. The organization and approach of assessments are unique and based on major factors in the assessment area. Nevertheless, each assessment begins with a section on how to consider the area that provides a foundation for the process. Often assessments are structured around US national security objectives in that area. Research questions must be developed, the answers to which help form judgments on the nature of the military balance in an area. Assessments might pose questions on comparative ground and air forces on the Central Front; what those capabilities portend for a day-to-day, surprise attack scenario; what they look like under an extended mobilization scenario; what capabilities existed ten years ago; or what capabilities might plausibly exist ten years in the future.

The selected analytic tools and techniques must assist in addressing the research questions. These tools are physical entities typically developed by someone other than assessors that are applied to questions at hand. Analytic techniques are human activities or events that usually are developed by assessors that deal with specific questions, which form the basis of assessments. Because assessments normally are focused on the theater or strategic level of war, selected tools and techniques must function on that level or in the aggregate. For example, detailed analyses of weapons systems, while useful to some elements of the defense establishment, are less helpful to assessments, notwithstanding exceptions when only a few highly classified systems exist.

Net assessments must deal with uncertainty, not only because they seek to characterize and analyze the future that is inherently unknowable but also because warfare and military competition are human endeavors fraught with misunderstanding, mistakes, emotions, intangibles, and deceit—the fog of war portrayed by Carl von Clausewitz. Thus, the analytic tools and techniques used in developing assessments must deal with uncertainty, identifying where major uncertainties lie, and at least seeking to bound them even if it is impossible for assessors to resolve them.

Building a *competitor's assessment* is critical in a good net assessment. It provides insight on the intended employment of forces by a competitor that offers a basis to select contingencies for the combat outcomes of wargames. It also provides insight on the objectives of a competitor, enabling the assessors to understand when a competitor may likely go to war and what it will take to win. Because deterrence represents a strategic objective, it serves as a means to evaluate how well the United States does in achieving that objective. But it is difficult because it requires detailed information that a competitor will necessarily attempt to conceal.

This chapter identifies some of the tools and techniques used to address key questions, deal with uncertainties, and contribute to developing net assessments. Not every tool and technique is helpful to assessments. Moreover, because the nature and structure of some military competitions are understood better than others, some analytical instruments are more useful in studies and less so in others. Four tools and six techniques with broad if not universal application to assessments are examined below. However, tools and techniques focused on unique net assessments such as using parity in purchasing power to equate the military investments of competitors are excluded. Those tools examined include databases, models, simulations, and intelligence reports while the techniques are all-source literature, historical case studies, interviews by subject matter experts, seminars workshops, etc., alternative scenarios or futures, and wargames.

DATABASES

To assess the capabilities of opposing military forces in a given regional or functional area, one must begin with a baseline of data. Such databases would appear to be the simplest of tools and readily available, but they are not. Unclassified data such as that found in the *Military Balance*, the annual publication issued by the International Institute for Strategic Studies, are useful but insufficient for several reasons. First, many nations do not disclose information on their military capabilities. Thus, unclassified data may be incomplete or inaccurate. Second, assessors must sort and categorize opposing forces based on the analytic framework chosen for the assessment, and the unclassified databases are more likely to be more highly aggregated. In the NATO-Warsaw Pact military balance, for example, comparisons of air and ground forces on both sides focused on the Central Front where they were situated or intended to be deployed. But unclassified data normally groups forces by country rather than area of deployment. Third, databases rarely extend long enough to enable comprehensive trend analysis. Finally, institutions producing databases regularly change how forces are categorized, making year-on-year comparisons problematic.

Even classified databases often can be inadequate because of organizational issues. Since the Intelligence Community maintains databases on foreign militaries and the Pentagon gathers data on US and allied militaries, that information cannot be combined in one database because of varying rules, categories, and methods of estimating forces. Thus, a major ONA activity has been developing and maintaining databases. An initial effort occurred in 1972 with the development of a NATO-Warsaw Pact database when the White House requested an assessment of the balance in Europe. Such databases may categorize hardware by type, quantity, and year deployed. Tradeoffs exist between levels of detail and degrees of aggregation. The greater the specifics, the more precise the database—and the more difficult it is to utilize. Computers alleviate the difficulty but they do not eliminate it. To be useful in analyzing trends of relative force capabilities over time, databases should go back 10 to 20 years (or to the beginning of the military competition being assessed, if not very old) and project out 10 to 20 years. Both approaches are problematic. Often the detail sought for early forces is unavailable in classified or unclassified documents. And neither the Department of Defense nor the Intelligence Community make detailed force estimates extending out 10 to 20 years. Thus, databases must be based on judgments of the past and future using available information such as planned and programmed US force data.

Databases could be expanded to include nongovernmental and commercial systems as well as military systems, for example, in support of assessments of space. Because so many militaries around the world use commercial satellites to conduct their operations, a space database would have to include them. Other types of databases may be useful for specific areas. For example, there were indications Moscow may have been investing more in its military than Washington during the Cold War. A database capturing annual investments by both sides could have identified such an asymmetry, how large it was, and what the trend was over time. Similarly, early deaths and low birth rates indicated the dwindling manpower pool available for military service in the Soviet Union. Demographic data could have quantified the shrinkage, the approximate years of low points in manpower, and the prospects for recovery. Given the larger amount of information needed in assessing cyber warfare, developmental work on Big Data databases may prove to be useful for operational and long-term trend analysis. It is likely cyber databases will be classified over privacy concerns as well as intelligence sources and methods.

MODELS

Military capabilities or processes are modeled to gain insights on relative force capabilities with particular attention to potential combat outcomes on both sides of a conflict. For example, some historical studies indicate *rules of thumb* force ratios needed for attacks in combat operations are three to one for unfortified positions and six to one for fortified positions. Early models of force ratios basically counted and compared numbers of weapons systems such as tanks through the technique popularly known simply as *bean counting.*

More refined models developed by the Soviet military sought to capture qualitative aspects of weapons systems by assigning them scores based on technical and tactical features such as the thickness of tank armor or the range of guns. The results yielded combat potential scores for each system. The Soviets found that the quantitative-qualitative ratio between the two sides, based on extensive operational research and analysis, was correlated to the rate of advance of their ground forces. The rate was linked to the assessed probability of achieving operational objectives along the Central Front. Similar methods such as the US Army Weighted Equipment Index/Weighted Unit Values and the Force Modernization Model utilized by TASC, Inc., formerly known as The Analytic Sciences Corporation, Inc., fell into some disrepute, possibly because they were oversold. Models only offer insights when employed with other analytic tools to improve judgments on combat outcomes.

Examining multiple models and how each one depicts change in military force ratios that appear over time improves their utility. The ratios are likely to differ for various of reasons and are particular to each model. But if the trend of each model seems to go in the same general direction at roughly the same rate, the outcome would give assessors increased confidence in the judgment made about the overall trends in the balance. Two other types of models may be useful in assessing particular aspects of a balance. Models of command and control structures indicating organizational relationships between subordinate units and commands can help in understanding the operational concept of an adversary as form often follows function. For example, in assessing the military balance in Europe during the Cold War, it was useful to understand that the Warsaw Pact had a Baltic Front under its Western Theater-Strategic Command. Because of location, that Front was clearly intended to seize ports in the NATO rear, potentially delaying or even stopping the resupply and reinforcement from America of forces critical to NATO strategy.

Moreover, understanding that the Baltic Front was assigned to the Western rather than the Northern Theater-Strategic Command of the Warsaw Pact revealed an operational asymmetry, as NATO included the Baltic region in Allied Forces North. The resulting dissimilarity of command structures could have made it more challenging for NATO to defeat the Baltic Front because it would have had to coordinate operations across major command boundaries, which are difficult and uncertain propositions under combat conditions.

A second category of potentially useful models includes the communications networks of an adversary. Understanding those networks can help develop models of command and control structures because the forces of an adversary cannot exercise command and control without the supporting communications. Moreover, understanding communications networks can assist in developing operational plans to both target networks and disrupt command and control, which has become critical as cyber threats expand in significance.

SIMULATIONS

While databases and models provide insights on outcomes of combat operations, they obviously do not furnish complete answers. How opposing forces are organized and employed significantly influences outcomes. For example, the German Army did not have more or better tanks than the French in 1940. Analysis of the Battle of France found that assessing the force ratios (numerical comparisons) or the combat potential ratios (quantity adjusted for quality) would have resulted in a stalemate comparable to World War I. But, in the event, the Wehrmacht won a rapid victory by employing armor together with ground-attack Stukas in radio contact and deployed under a more effective theater-operational concept.[1] To better understand that difference between the opposing forces, a dynamic model or simulation is needed to factor in the forces being deployed.

Simulations are mathematically based, typically computerized, and intended to display the outcome of interaction between two or more opposing forces. Because they are computer based, multiple events can be conducted within a short timeframe by varying the parameters to examine which factors can be more influential on the outcome. For instance, the analysts might change the assumptions about the absolute and relative mobilization of two sides prior to an attack. They might replicate a surprise attack when Side A receives two days for mobilization and Side B has four days. Or they might explore longer periods of mobilization that might occur during a crisis with one side having three weeks and the other four weeks.

Because organizations typically develop simulations for their particular needs rather than assessments, analysts must explore and understand the limits and settings of a given simulation. Even then shortcomings in current simulations cannot be overcome by adjusting the parameters. Simulations normally use different measures of effectiveness such as the loss-exchange ratio or front-line movement to determine outcomes. But such measures do not capture the intricacies of human behavior or decision-making. Nor are other intangibles such as morale, leadership, or the impact of surprise captured adequately in most simulations.

Nonetheless, short of analyzing real conflicts—which contains its own analytic difficulties such as the accuracy of reports and unique events and personalities—simulations offer one way for analysts to obtain insights on combat outcomes. As with models, the inherent inadequacy of simulations can be overcome to a certain extent by employing multiple simulations using the same inputs such as forces, locations, times of attack, etc., and then examining the similarities and differences to find out why the outcomes of combat turned out in a certain way.

Over the years, ONA employed models and simulations developed by several organizations inside government such as the Army Concepts Analysis Agency and the Supreme Headquarters Allied Powers Europe. Models and simulations by organizations outside government such as the RAND Corporation and TASC, Inc. also were employed.

INTELLIGENCE

Because a key part of assessments depends on understanding how adversaries view the balance, it stands to reason that reviewing intelligence reports forms a basis for doing so. Of course, there are multiple intelligence agencies and differing levels of classifications with varying degrees of specificity and relevance to given assessments. Intelligence gathered by the military tends to be focused on technical aspects of an opposing service; for example, the US Navy concentrates on Russian or Chinese naval capabilities. The members of the Intelligence Community also differ in their respective approaches to collection and analysis which makes reporting on the capabilities of adversaries vary. Accordingly, assessors should examine reports from multiple agencies and then select the most useful for the assessment at hand. Friendly intelligence agencies also can provide useful information but habitually look at fewer adversaries than the United States with its global interests; despite this, friendly nations gather information often overlooked by the Intelligence Community. But caution should be exercised because foreign nations may seek to influence US national security policy with misleading intelligence reports.

Among the most helpful intelligence for net assessment are the reports focused on doctrine and exercises that indicate enemy intentions. Regrettably for some nongovernmental users, such intelligence may be highly classified due to sources and methods. Even government assessors may be unable to obtain compartmentalized intelligence reports that require special permission to access because of sensitive ways in which it is collected. Problems of retrieving information include restricted Special Access Programs of the military services and defense agencies. While not analytic tools per se, they may be potentially important in producing comprehensive and accurate assessments. Frequently, they are research and development programs for new weapons systems or classified operations that might change military judgments if known.

ANALYTICAL TECHNIQUES

A combination of classified and unclassified documentation constitutes what is called *all-source* literature. Reports from governmental agencies, academe, FFRDCs (like RAND and the Institute for Defense Analyses),

Congressional Research Service, etc., are potentially helpful. Biographies of significant individuals and major historical works bearing on net assessments can be examined for critical information. Foreign military journals and manuals also provide insights on adversary thinking and planning, but getting the material translated and distributed is time-consuming and sporadic. For example, an article written by Marshal Nikolai Ogarkov in 1984 that appeared in the military journal *Krasnaya Zvezda* (Red Star) provided insights on the thinking of the Chief of the Soviet General Staff on revolutions in military affairs and the nature of warfare.

Beijing also publishes considerable literature on its armed forces and warfighting that is generally underappreciated, most probably because of the language barrier. Organizations such as the China Maritime Studies Institute at the Naval War College gather, translate, and analyze documentation on this critical area of military competition. Other activities inside and outside of government have proved especially useful over the years. Moreover, classified foreign literature such as *Voyennaya mysl'* (Military Thought) published by the Soviet General Staff was useful in the net assessment process. Because of its sensitivity, access to the material was restricted. Even though redacted, numerous editions of *Voyennaya mysl'* have been declassified and posted online by the National Security Archive at The George Washington University.

Case Studies

Although similar to literature reviews, historical case studies are focused on a specific issue or problem. Furthermore, they are not exploratory but instead tailored to satisfy the analytical needs of the assessor in several ways. First, it is often difficult to comprehend the various factors at work as events unfold. Contrary to conventional wisdom, the gift of hindsight is not always 20/20 because unknown influences come into play. Nevertheless, the passage of time results in more information becoming available for the development of historical case studies to better understand what really occurred.

Moreover, case studies are useful in relating problems that comprise assessments. In that context, studies may illuminate aspects of a problem that otherwise can be overlooked. They are based on the principle that the past is prologue. Analysis of what has happened in a specific case in the past may proffer understanding of how it shaped current situations or problems. Moreover, in addition, it may yield insights on the evolution of a problem in order that decision-making can be understood within a broader framework. For instance, a case study of the German advance in 1940 into France supported the ONA assessments of the military balance during the Cold War. Numerous books, articles, reports, etc., have appeared on this campaign since World War II, but the study differed by addressing a specific question: how can an operational concept be utilized to achieve overwhelming force advantages at a crucial point in both time and space? In this case it was the concept of *blitzkrieg* that enabled the German Army, despite the approximate parity of the opposing forces along the Maginot Line, to mass superior forces capable of bypassing French defenses and defeating them within six weeks. The historical case study prepared under contract provided how this operational innovation actually worked for the first time.

What is more, a catchall category of studies exists which is known as *topical studies*. Since the ONA mission involves exploring every dimension of warfare, studies are often conducted on given topics to inspire others to undertake similar research. For example, because the revolution in military affairs was identified by Ogarkov, ONA examined its development for several years to obtain insights on various areas including cyber and space warfare, which caused the military services to conduct their own studies of revolutions in military affairs.

Studies also can be conducted to encourage and support investments in particular areas. For example, late in the last century studies and games considered the development and employment of precision-strike forces.

Those activities indicated that such forces could be useful and, in many situations, could become major factors in the course and outcome of an engagement or campaign. The results encouraged those Americans who advocated precision-strike forces, and subsequently such forces were acquired and employed in a number of military operations.

Biological factors in physical, cognitive, and socio-emotional performance in warfare led to ONA studies on human performance that fostered research and development by various defense agencies while other studies supported particular assessments. Demographic studies of the Soviet manpower indicated that it was shrinking; others revealed an aging Japanese population with its expending social welfare programs that were crowding out defense spending; others found that China—with up to 32 million more males than females—was confronted with potential social discontent.

Subject Matter Experts

Frequently the knowledge to needed to prepare net assessments rests with individuals and is not documented in the literature, which leads to two questions: where do you find experts and how do you know how to determine their expertise? The answer to the first question is casting a wide net. The military services, think tanks, academe, and private sector have experts knowledgeable about US military doctrine and capabilities. In addition, members of intelligence agencies, worldwide churches, international corporations, and émigrés communities are sources of information on foreign military programs. The second question requires processes of trial and error. Trusted experts might recommend another individual like themselves. In the final analysis, it comes down to a matter of judgment like net assessments. Care should be taken to not discard individual commentaries because they appear to originate from strange people.

There are two useful types of subject matter experts (SMEs): the functional experts familiar with nuclear weapons, communications, logistics, etc., and regional or country experts. Usually, it is easier to identify the former because they deal with numbers and technology while the latter consider human behavior and cultural factors. But even functional SMEs might be misled. Other countries view and evaluate technologies differently, and unless those differences are discovered, assessments may be off the mark. For example, it was found the Soviets valued tanks with guns that fired tank rounds and missiles more than those that only fired tank rounds. Although the Soviet Union was deploying tanks with such guns, the United States considered M551 Sheridan armored vehicles, which fired tank rounds and missiles, second rate and thus they were not fielded to army units.

Caution must be exercised in selecting regional and country SMEs. While most are informed about political matters, they may have limited military expertise. Some of them, after years of immersion in their subject, lose objectivity regarding national objectives. Nevertheless, regional or country SMEs are invaluable in understanding the strategic culture and decision-making of adversaries. Russian émigrés assisted ONA efforts by describing the social, cultural, economic, and political dynamics of their countries of origin as well as clarifying significant variables.

WORKSHOPS, SEMINARS, AND CONFERENCES

Experts are convened to examine individual problems or sets of problems. The nature of these problems determines which experts to invite and which format is best suited to elicit the desired information. Workshops are the smallest groups and can include only eight to twelve participants convened for one to three days. They may consider topics such as scenarios for upcoming games and provide expert advice in support of draft reports and briefings. Seminars are the next largest groups and usually comprise fifteen to twenty individuals and last from one to three days. They are more useful in gaining insights on specific topics. Given their size, the group dynamics of the seminars make it difficult for some participants to remain engaged. Large groups challenge moderators in shaping discussions and reaching useful conclusions. However, seminars can lead to sharing insights if the moderators seek information instead of conclusions. For example, ONA-organized service roundtables explored the revolution in military affairs in the 1990s. These were attended by active and retired officers who distilled institutional thinking on the subject. Conferences are the largest activities with twenty to forty individuals. In many ways they attempt to capture the wisdom of a wider audience. Often conferees break into small workshops and then reassemble in plenary sessions for presentations, questions, and comments—but not for discussions.

Successful workshops and seminars require moderators adept at managing group dynamics. Often experienced academics have such abilities and can serve as effective moderators in net assessment workshops and seminars. Conferences usually do not require moderators because as a rule serious discussions will take place within subgroups, and a skillful master of ceremonies will suffice in plenary sessions. Finally, a way should be provided to identify and document the results of these activities. Conferences often result in publishable papers, though workshops and seminars typically do not. As a result, smaller gatherings must have knowledgeable rapporteurs to document the proceedings. From time to time, attempts are made at recording and transcribing these events, but experience has shown that not to be particularly useful as it generally results in too much information to take on board and digest.

ALTERNATIVE SCENARIOS AND FUTURES

Varying boundaries using alternative scenarios to influence outcomes offer helpful components of wargames and stand-alone exercises. For example, one might use different teams in games with different warning times for an attack as a way of exploring how sensitive combat outcomes can become with respect to available mobilization time. As a stand-alone, exercises with alternative scenarios similar to those conducted by Royal Dutch Shell can identify large issues that warrant detailed research and analysis. Alternative futures are used in wargaming to set initial conditions based on the notion that they would differ enough from present or current forecasts to explore *what ifs* with implications for the future. For example, what might occur if Japan was not allied with the United States and a conflict broke out in Northeast Asia, or what might occur if Iran built nuclear weapons and decided to mount a conventional attack on Saudi Arabia?

WARGAMES

A final technique conducted by different organizations for various purposes is the wargame. For example, to establish the adequacy of force structures, the Pentagon holds Title 10 wargames that involve hundreds of participants and cost millions of dollars. They differ from games played as an analytic technique in support of assessments which are smaller, cheaper, and multipurpose, and intentionally do not evaluate service programs.[2] Generally, net assessment wargaming is useful in examining nonquantitative aspects of warfare, particularly the impact of operational concepts on the outcome of combat. They expose military officers to new ideas as well as proffer insights on the uncertainty or fog of war. In addition, they can indicate how warfare may differ in the future by developing force structures and contingency planning. For a time in the 1980s and 1990s, ONA was interested in other types of games as a means to examine alternative futures. But those wargames lost their appeal because they depended on players who understood the strategic thinking of competitors but who were difficult to find.

Several types of wargames support net assessment. One type examines the potential combat outcomes of theater-level campaigns. They can examine a base case using the canonical scenario, expected forces, operational concepts, and game changes (like mobilization scenarios) to identify critical variables at play. Also, different past, current, and future force structures can be gamed to discover which trends occur in relative combat capabilities. Wargames can also analyze specific problems such as power projection and escalation control. They can highlight asymmetries in operational approaches and provide a sense of advantages and disadvantages. What is more, they can examine new operational and organizational approaches like the nearly 60 ONA-sponsored games on the revolution in military affairs during the 1990s.[3] However, wargaming can only offer insights, not answers. Because wars and battles are complex human endeavors, it is helpful to break up analytic questions for wargames into sets of questions and examine them as a series of three or more games. Two aspects of wargames are worth highlighting: thinking like Red and selecting players. Finding participants who can *think* Red is problematic. Relatively few players have studied how potential adversaries think about warfare and can accurately portray how they might act in a wargame. Too often players on the Red Team mirror image what they think Red would do based on their experience gained in the US military, which is not accurate or helpful. This approach is not confined to wargamers but attributable to a cultural bias which ignores what an adversary might really do. Blue teams are often surprised by things good Red teams do that they would never consider doing. As a former ONA member expressed it, no wargame exceeds the capabilities of the players. There is a chance of obtaining good results when good players are found, but no chance exists of achieving good outcomes without them.

* * *

The Office of Net Assessment has experimented with newly developed tools and techniques over the years because it was not clear which would prove to be the most helpful. That approach takes time and sustained effort, something displayed by the ONA staff in the past and which must be continued in the future. Improved tools and techniques must be developed to better understand the strategic calculus of adversaries and more effectively deter them. Models and simulations must be enhanced, particularly by taking account of the human factor of performance in combat aptitude and outcomes. Nonetheless, tools and techniques can only offer inputs and insights, not answers and certainly not assessments. Net assessments are informed by the judgments that the assessors reach in bringing together everything known to them which is combined with several other elements that they may have only suspected.

NOTES

1. Phillip A. Karber et al., "Assessing the Correlation of Forces: France 1940" (McLean, VA: BDM Corporation, June 18, 1979).
2. For the best descriptions, see Peter P. Perla, *The Art of Wargaming* (Annapolis, MD: Naval Institute Press, 2011) and Robert G. Angevine, "Gaming the Future: Insights on Wargaming from the RMA Wargames of the 1990s" (Rosslyn, VA: Scitor Corporation, August 2011).
3. Robert G. Angevine, "The RMA Reconsidered: Insights on the Revolution in Military Affairs from the RMA Wargames of the 1990s" (Rosslyn, VA: Scitor Corporation, December 2011).

Conclusion

The Future of Net Assessment

Andrew D. May

The purpose of this short, final chapter is to put forward some ideas for how analysts might structure a program of net assessments appropriate for the United States and for the United States Department of Defense in particular. After some preliminary argument about the character of effective net assessments, it offers two candidate frameworks for structuring portfolios of net assessments, either of which could be useful but which would likely lead in very different directions analytically. Finally, it will outline some of the most salient characteristics of an organization that might attempt to undertake assessments of any sort.

Mostly I will write about the kinds of assessments I know—net assessments focused on military competition and intended to help the U.S. Secretary of Defense—but I hope that at least some of the chapter may be more broadly applicable to other sorts of assessments for other customers. Because of my current position, I have been vague in discussing some aspects of the subject at hand. More specifically, nothing contained herein should be construed as official policy of the Department of Defense or an indication of projects that the Office of Net Assessment is undertaking today. Instead, the observations outlined are grounded in my understanding of the history of ONA work and how the net assessment process was originally conceived.

THE CHARACTER OF FUTURE NET ASSESSMENTS

It may be useful to describe the kind of net assessments that are needed and likely to be of future value to senior leaders. As with classic net assessments of the Cold War era, future assessments should not concentrate exclusively or even primarily on predictions of who might win a conflict, or what war would look like if it started tomorrow, but rather on delineating broader goals for each competitor and assessing how each stands in the ability to achieve their goals. Thus, the assessments should be structured to assist senior officials in guiding the competition and identifying management issues to include opportunities for improving the US position or complicating the life of the adversary. This is an important distinction from national intelligence estimates and most of the analyses conducted by think tanks and other organizations. For net assessments to be valuable to the Secretary, they should be conceived and structured as management tools, aiming not to declare what the nation should do but to provide issues appropriate to the specific customer or group of customers responsible in a direct way for managing governmental activities.

At the military-operational level, special attention should be paid to factors like military doctrine, training, skill level, and operational competence; factors that history indicates matter as much or more than the technical characteristics of weapons systems, but which are often short-changed for various reasons in formal and informal comparisons. These aspects of militaries can be difficult to assess and also difficult to compare in peacetime. On the other hand, they cannot be avoided, and so difficult and frequently unsatisfying work must be undertaken.

Toward the end of this chapter I will offer a few ideas about the kinds of analytic efforts that may be required, and the sorts of organizations that may be best suited to that work.

Probably the most obvious and perhaps the most compelling way to structure a body of net assessments is around the long-term competition with a specific adversary. This of course was the approach during the first two decades of the Office of Net Assessment, during which time the bulk of the office's most analytically rich assessments were completed. It makes sense to consider returning to this approach to revive the analytic traditions of the Office. Some debate on what competitor on which to focus is necessary to structure the assessments. Today, the most obvious candidate is China, which for decades has demonstrated its intentions to compete with the United States and which has become an increasingly potent military threat. In this case analysts must disaggregate the broader military competition into manageable pieces, which must be worked out over time. As the US approach to competing with China becomes more salient, the important geographic and functional aspects of the competition will become more clearly defined, and relevant assessment areas may become more obvious.

There are several functional competitions that seem especially promi-nent today (which I will have to leave to the reader to discern for himself) and in time new functional areas might begin to take on more importance, as the Chinese military seeks out new missions or as the character of warfare evolves. It is possible to imagine, for example, a comparative power projection net assessment, or a net assessment focused on long-range precision strike. Geographically oriented assessments are harder to structure at the moment, because it is still not clear where the equivalent of the Central Front will be (if there is one at all), but such theater balances will be an important means of pulling together some of the more disparate functional assessments and providing senior leaders with a sense of how the relevant militaries stack up at the theater level. In the competition with the Soviet Union, theater assessments were among the most useful conducted by the Office of Net Assessment. These assessments integrated functional areas and provided a sense of the possible character of conflict at the operational level, often illuminating aspects of the contest that did not emerge from functional assessments. Determining what theaters might be appropriate for a US-China net assessment will be difficult and will require experimentation in construct and method.

Military oriented assessments of this sort would probably need to be complemented by other sorts of analyses. As was the case in the Cold War, militaries will need to be evaluated as enterprises with varying capacities for innovation (technological as well as organizational and conceptual), differing approaches to command and control, and sometimes wide disparities in operational competence. Such functions are difficult to monitor and more difficult to measure, but these are so obviously important that even preliminary or rough answers may be useful. To the extent that good net assessments should help identify opportunities to build upon enduring strengths on our side, or exploit fundamental weaknesses besetting the other, those undertaking net assessments focused on China should also study the problems China may face in mounting and sustaining a real challenge to the United States: doing so will require an economic foundation, some societal cohesion, some shared commitment to national goals, and so forth. The emphasis in this work should not be to find ways to dismiss the challenge that China may pose to the United States, but instead to find weaknesses that may hamper its ability to compete, and that may provide opportunities for the United States.

The renewed attention being given to long-term competition with Russia suggests an argument for undertaking a set of net assessments focused on this contest. Here, more thought is required on what the competition will look like over the next several decades. As its economy falters and Russia faces sustained and possibly irreversible difficulties associated with demography, public health, and other issues, it is difficult to envision Russian ambitions developing to rival those of the former

Soviet Union or China today. On the other hand, geopolitical ambitions—together with the investment in military resources including nuclear weapons and undersea warfare—mean that Russia will continue to pose a serious threat in some ways. Furthermore, even in areas in which it is not leading, Russia may challenge other regional militaries that have underinvested in their own defense. Consequently, some set of US-Russia net assessments could be illuminating. Like the situation with China, it will be necessary to disaggregate the broader competition into components that focus on key functional areas, regions, or theaters central to long-term competition.

The final candidate for competitor-based assessments is the long-term contest between the West and Radical Islam. Here there are obvious problems in identifying the real competitor, describing the history and plausible future course of the competition, and articulating plausible goals for either side. It is not even clear that there is a single competition or competitor around which net assessments could be structured. Yet the turmoil in the Islamic world might persist for decades or longer, and if the United States seeks to play the same global role as it has for the last 70-plus years, it will likely continue to encounter the radical, Jihadist elements of that world. It also seems clear that our progress in assessing or even understanding this competition so far has been very poor and that we lack, as a military and as a country, any developed framework for assessing how we are faring, or how we may fare in the future. In this light, it is reasonable to argue that there is room for comparative assessments in this area, designed to help shed light on these problems and identify emerging problems and (especially) opportunities for improving our performance.

STRATEGY-BASED ASSESSMENTS

There is another, different type of assessment that is worth at least some brief examination. These are what might be called strategic assessments, rather than net assessments. Here I have in mind assessments that are focused less on a specific competitor and more on the overall U.S. position in some set of especially important military areas. Assessments of this sort might be appropriate for an analyst or group of analysts that has decided that there is no single competitor substantial enough to organize around. In this case, it might make sense to structure assessments around a set of warfare areas that are determined to be especially important, or areas that for one reason or another the U.S. wishes to retain an especially pronounced lead. Foundational work would be required to establish a good set of these areas, but some initial candidates are nuclear, undersea, the military exploitation of space, and global precision strike.

For strategic assessments, analyses could be structured with less attention to any single specific adversary but instead a more general look at the U.S. position against all potential adversaries. Such assessments might also be designed to identify potential changes in the character of these warfare areas—brought on by the introduction of new technologies or as a consequence of broader changes in the operational environment— that could undermine longstanding U.S. strengths. Assessments such as these might at least initially be closer to threat assessments, in the sense that they are most likely to raise threats or problems relevant to the maintenance of advantage, rather than opportunities. Over time it may be possible to do more to identify opportunities—either investments that could be made early on to reinforce an existing strength or insights into problems adversaries are likely to face—to help make these assessments more well-balanced.

Another type of strategy-oriented assessment could be used to support a different kind of national security strategy. For example, in the next 10 or 20 years the Nation could shift its basic strategy and role in the world by not concentrating on the retention of global military superiority that it has enjoyed for two decades but instead on defending interests in the Western Hemisphere or limited geographic area. To support this strategy, assessments could be structured around a set of functional balances such as missile defense, sea control, or strategic nuclear weapons. To infer goals for the United States in these competitions will be difficult and take time, but through preliminary attempts at trial and error it should be possible to structure assessments useful to senior leaders in order to monitor the position of the United States on a subset of critical warfare areas.

Organizing for Net Assessments

The kinds of assessments I have described are obviously very demanding analytically. They call for making extremely difficult judgments about aspects of military competitions that are poorly defined and for which there is no real hope of developing transparent, reproducible, or methodologically straightforward conclusions. In most cases, even if the sorts of factors that should be tracked and measured were known, the relevant data may not be collected or organized in ways to make it useful for structuring comparisons. Outside of the government, few institutions are focused on the Chinese military, making informed forecasts on the ways in which it might function at the operational level. The United States does not produce enough linguists; locating defense analysts with Chinese-language skills is difficult. Whereas we once had a large pool of Russia military analysts (some better than others), numbers have dropped markedly since the end of the Cold War, and today there are far too few skilled analysts with a deep understanding of Russian ways of thinking and fighting. The situation is even worse for the contest with Radical Islam; here as a nation we still struggle to talk openly about important aspects of the competition. Nearly twenty years after 9-11 we still do not have institutions dedicated to producing the sorts of analysts needed to make expert judgments about the goals of Radical Islamists, possible future instantiations of the Jihadi impulse, or the nature of realistic goals for the U.S. military in this competition.

This does not mean, however, that the situation is hopeless. We can see from the Cold War experience, as well as other episodes, that sustained study and close analytic attention can chip away at very large, seemingly intractable problems. Below I will offer some of my ideas about the attributes of organizations that are likely to make the most progress.

Effective long-term work will call for organizations with stable budgets and leadership, bureaucratic protection, and privacy to undertake risky projects to examine impolitic questions with latitude to make slow progress on difficult questions. These features are necessary preconditions but not sufficient alone. Really, when we think about the responsibilities that a good net assessment function will have, we should think about a different class of characteristics that will largely determine whether or not such a function—whether it is in or out of government—will actually produce the sort of analytic work that has defined the net assessment approach for the past several decades. It is helpful to think of these things are responsibilities, rather than attributes, because they are all costly, and undertaking them will be difficult, or possibly even painful.

One of the most important things such organizations can do is dedicate themselves to uncovering, promoting, and encouraging heretical ideas and people. Although cultural detractors grouse endlessly about the divergence in America, politicization, and the chasm between political parties, the main feature of the defense analysis community is fundamental consensus; consensus about the major problems, consensus about the kinds of things possible in this world, and consensus about the sane range of solutions. The problem, which many people know but do not acknowledge, is that the consensus is often wrong in important ways. Crises that nobody anticipated suddenly emerge or adversaries behave in unanticipated ways or people begin experimenting with solutions that would have been rejected as outlandish months or years earlier. More people are needed who will entertain ideas that may be wrong; who are comfortable questioning commonly held truths to suggest, for example, that the economy of the Soviet Union may be weak or that prevailing notions of how oil is created may be wrong.

It is difficult to find—particularly at main-line organizations such as the FFRDCs and prominent consultancies—people who have radically different views, different backgrounds, different casts of mind, and who can help think about aspects of the world or of the future that others do not. As we all know, people who think differently about the world and who are unconventional in their analysis are often unconventional in other ways. They dress, speak, and comport themselves differently. They might say or do things that embarrass a large organization that cultivates its brand, as Herman Kahn and Laurent Murawiec aggravated RAND leadership or as Warren Nutter scandalized his academic colleagues. We can all think of examples today of intelligent, original, and sometimes difficult people who are sidelined because of who and what they are. The challenge for net assessment work is to keep these people working; to accept the risk of embarrassment, to tolerate eccentricities, and to accept work that is sometimes a hit but sometimes disastrous. The organizations that maintain that they want the net assessment approach to continue to flourish will have to do their part here.

A second important activity will be to continue to undertake long-term analytic campaigns against large, difficult problems. One way to look at ONA history is as a story proving that things that appear unknowable—such as the size of the Soviet defense burden when little reliable data exists for the numerator or the denominator—could be made to yield to sustained analytic effort. It might take a decade or more and progress might be slow, but fewer impossible problems exist than one might think at first. This means, among other things, that analysts and organizations must be willing to pay the opportunity costs associated with such campaigns; they must be willing to *not* dedicate their effort to the new Secretary's most prominent initiative and *not* break away to study lessons learned from a current conflict. This can be just as hard as tolerating heretics: there is money lost, fame lost, and the prospect of influence lost in ignoring the dominant issues of the day. Donors, bosses, and others will want to know what an organization has done to obtain influence and will want to draw a line—a short, straight one—between analytical work and new visions, policies, and programs. Those people focused on long-term problems have to justify that not all work yields immediate results. Again, the organizations that support the net assessment process will have to accept bearing the costs.

A third responsibility is supporting methodological innovation and experimentation. Here we have a dual problem. Part of the problem is the tendency in some quarters to think in narrow terms about what net assessment is or is not, or those supporting methodologies that are or are not appropriate to the conduct of net assessments. The other part is a business problem: organizations get good at doing particular things, come to know how quickly and well they can be done, and become attached to them. Experimentation is costly and risks cost overruns, blown deadlines, and embarrassing failures. Looking back, there is little doubt that as a way of tackling problems assessments have drawn on games, modeling, game theory, scenario development, historical studies, etc. Some have paid off and others did not, but new analytic methods will be developed or existing approaches modified; the best possible work will demand a willingness to continue to try new things.

One final responsibility, and one that is probably less costly but nevertheless rarely accepted, is being focused on an actual, identifiable customer; to craft management documents rather than hogwash about whole-of-government solutions or platitudes about what the Nation must do. If there is one fundamental feature of good net assessment work that I think is poorly described in the existing literature on the concept, it is this. Yes, good assessments are valuable because they are comparative and diagnostic, but also because they are oriented to helping senior decision-makers cope with managing the defense establishment in protracted competition with adversaries. These officials as a class and the Secretary of Defense most of all, usually get very little in the way of good management advice from their organizations. They get appeals for decisions to be made and recommendations about new policies to promulgate, but generally they do not receive much help on thinking through the businesses the Department is in or ought to be in, how the DoD is faring in those businesses, or the directions in which they may need to move in order to maintain a favorable military balance. This is what makes net assessments, when done well, more practical and more useful than other DoD reports or more general Government documents such as National Intelligence Estimates. They are not intended for general edification but to serve as management tools to help senior officials. Work with this sort of orientation demands a measure of discipline and attentiveness, but is more focused and ultimately more powerful.

* * *

It should be clear that there is still a great need for the continued application of the net assessment approach; that the country is engaged in a series of competitions that remain poorly understood and for which our senior leaders need good, even-handed, forward-looking assessments of how we are faring and where we might have opportunities to improve our competitive position. It also suggests, I hope, that this future may be characterized by both expansion and experimentation; that there are new kinds of problems and new kinds of competitions emerging for which the net assessment approach might be useful, and areas into which we should push for this approach to be applied. As we do this, we will need to continue to experiment with new supporting methods, new analysts, and new organizations, in the hope that even as some or many turn out to be failures, some or even a few will help U.S. officials extend the remarkably strong competitive position our Cold War leaders left us.

SELECT BIBLIOGRAPHY

Adamsky, Dmitry. *The Culture of Military Innovation: The Impact of Cultural Factors on the Revolution in Military Affairs in Russia, the US, and Israel.* Stanford, CA: Stanford University Press, 2010.

———. "Through the Looking Glass: The Soviet Military-Technical Revolution and the American Revolution in Military Affairs." *Journal of Strategic Studies* 31 (April 2008): 257–94.

———, and Kjell Inge Bjerga, eds. *Contemporary Military Innovation: Between Anticipation and Adaptation* (New York: Routledge, 2012).

Allen, Thomas B. *War Games: The Secret World of the Creators, Players, and Policy Makers Rehearsing World War III Today.* New York: McGraw-Hill, 1987.

Andre, David J. "Competitive Strategies: An Approach Against Proliferation." In *Prevailing in a Well Armed World: Devising Competitive Strategies Against Weapons Proliferation*, edited by Henry D. Sokolski, 3–25. Carlisle Barracks, PA: Strategic Studies Institute, US Army War College, March 2000.

———. "New Competitive Strategies Tools and Methodologies, Review of the Department of Defense Competitive Strategies Initiative, 1986–1990." Washington DC: Competitive Strategies Office, Office of the Undersecretary of Defense for Policy, 1990.

Aronsen, Lawrence. "Seeing Red: US Air Force Assessments of the Soviet Union, 1945-1949." *Intelligence and National Security* 16 (Summer 2001): 103–32.

Aspin, Les. "Debate over US Strategic Forecasts: A Mixed Record." *Strategic Review* 8 (Spring 1980): 22–43, 57–59.

Augier, Mie. "Thinking about War and Peace: Andrew Marshall and the Early Development of the Intellectual Foundations for Net Assessment." *Comparative Strategy* 32, no. 1 (2013): 1–17.

Blaker, James R. "Understanding the Revolution in Military Affairs: A Guide to America's 21st Century Defense." Defense Working Paper 3. Washington, DC: Progressive Policy Institute, January 1997.

Battilega, John A. "Soviet Views of Nuclear Warfare: The Post-Cold War Interviews." In *Getting Mad: Nuclear Mutual Assured Destruction*, edited by Henry D. Sokolski, 151–74. Carlisle Barracks, PA: Strategic Studies Institute, US Army War College, November 2004.

Betts, Richard K. "Is Strategy an Illusion?" *International Security* 25 (Fall 2000): 5–50.

——— . "US National Security Strategy: Lenses and Landmarks." Paper delivered at a conference entitled "Toward a New National Security Strategy," convened by the Woodrow Wilson School of Public and International Affairs in Princeton, NJ, on May 21–22, 2004.

Beyerchen, Alan. "Clausewitz, Nonlinearity, and the Unpredictability of War." *International Security* 17 (Winter 1992–1993): 59–90.

Biddle, Stephen D. "The Gulf War Debate Redux: Why Skill and Technology Are the Right Answer." *International Security* 22 (Fall 1997): 163–74.

——— . *Military Power: Explaining Victory and Defeat in Modern Battle.* Princeton, NJ: Princeton University Press, 2004.

——— . "Military Power: A Reply." *Journal of Strategic Studies* 28 (June 2005): 453–69.

——— . "Victory Misunderstood: What the Gulf War Tells Us About the Future of Conflict." *International Security* 21 (Fall 1996): 139–79.

Bower, Joseph L., and Clayton M. Christensen. "Disruptive Technologies: Catching the Wave." *Harvard Business Review* 73 (January–February 1995): 43–53.

Bracken, Paul. "Net Assessment: A Practical Guide." *Parameters* 36 (Spring 2006): 90–100.

——— , Linda S. Brandt, and Stuart E. Johnson. "The Changing Landscape of Defense Innovation." *Defense Horizons* 47 (July 2005): 1–8.

Bright, James R., ed. *Technological Forecasting for Industry and Government: Methods and Applications.* Englewood Cliffs, NJ: Prentice Hall, 1968.

Brodie, Bernard. "The Development of Nuclear Strategy." *International Security* 2 (Spring 1978): 65–83.

Carafano, James Jay, Frank J. Cilluffo, Richard Weitz, and Jan Lane. "Stopping Surprise Attacks: Thinking Smarter About Homeland Security." *Backgrounder* 2026. Washington, DC: Heritage Foundation, April 23, 2007.

Cetron, Marvin J., and Christine A. Ralph. *Industrial Applications of Technological Forecasting: Its Utilization in R&D Management.* New York: Wiley-Interscience, 1971.

Chu, David S. C., and Nurith Berstein. "Decisionmaking for Defense." In *New Challenges, New Tools for Defense Decisionmaking*, edited by Stuart E. Johnson, Martin C. Libicki, Gregory F. Treverton, 13–32. MR-1526-RC. Santa Monica, CA: RAND Corporation, 2003.

Cockell, W., J. J. Martin, and G. Weaver. "Core Competencies and Other Business Concepts for Use in DoD Strategic Planning." McLean, VA: Science Applications International Corporation, February 7, 1992.

Cohen, Eliot A. "A Bad Rap on High Tech: The GAO's Misguided Missile Against Gulf War Weaponry." *Washington Post*, July 16, 1996.

———. "Net Assessment: An American Approach." Memorandum 29. Tel Aviv: Jaffee Center for Strategic Studies, Tel Aviv University, April 1990.

———. "Stephen Biddle on Military Power." *Journal of Strategic Studies* 28 (June 2005): 413–24.

———. "Revolution in Warfare." *Foreign Affairs* 75 (March–April 1996): 37–54.

———. "Toward a Better Net Assessment: Rethinking the European Conventional Balance." *International Security* 13 (Summer 1988): 50–89.

———, and John Gooch. Military Misfortunes: *The Anatomy of Failure in War.* New York: Free Press, 1990.

Congressional Budget Office. "US Ground Forces and the Conventional Balance in Europe." Washington, DC: US Government Printing Office, June 1988.

Connelly, Matthew, Matt Fay, Giulia Ferrini, Micki Kaufman, Will Leonard, Harrison Monsky, Ryan Mutso, Taunton Paine, Nicholas Standish, and Lydia Walker. "'General, I Have Fought Just as Many Nuclear Wars and You Have': Forecasts, Future Scenarios, and the Politics of Armageddon." *American Historical Review* 117 (December 2012): 1431–60.

Cote, Owen R., Jr. "The Politics of Innovative Military Doctrine: US Navy and Fleet Ballistic Missiles." PhD diss., Massachusetts Institute of Technology, September 1995.

Courtney, Hugh, Jane Kirkland, and Patrick Viguerie. "Strategy Under Uncertainty." *Harvard Business Review* 75 (November–December 1997): 67–79.

Davis, Paul K. "Rethinking Defense Planning." New York: John Brademas Center for the Study of Congress, New York University, December 2007.

Eisenhardt, Kathleen M., and Shona L. Brown. "Time pacing: Competing in Markets that Won't Stand Still." *Harvard Business Review* 76 (March–April 1998): 59–69.

Engerman, David C. *Know Your Enemy: The Rise and Fall of America's Soviet Experts.* New York: Oxford University Press, 2009.

Epstein, Joshua M. "Dynamic Analysis and the Conventional Balance in Europe." *International Security* 12 (Spring 1988): 154–65.

——— . "The 3:1 Rule, the Adaptive Dynamic Model, and the Future of Security Studies." *International Security* 13 (Spring 1989): 90–127.

FitzSimonds, James R. "The Coming Military Revolution: Opportunities and Risks." *Parameters* 25 (Summer 1995): 30–36.

——— , and Jan M van Tol. "Revolutions in Military Affairs." *Joint Force Quarterly* 4 (Spring 1994): 24–31.

Flournoy, Michèle A., ed. *QDR 2001: Strategy-Driven Choices for America's Security*. Washington, DC: National Defense University Press, 2001.

Freedman, Lawrence. "A Theory of Battle of a Theory of War." *Journal of Strategic Studies* 28 (June 2005): 425–36.

———. *US Intelligence and the Soviet Strategic Threat*. Princeton: Princeton University Press, 1986.

Freier, Nathan P. Known Unknowns: Unconventional "Strategic Shocks" in *Defense Strategy Development*. Carlisle Barracks, PA: Strategic Studies Institute, US Army War College, November 2008.

———. *Toward a Risk Management Defense Strategy*. Carlisle Barracks, PA: Strategic Studies Institute, US Army War College, August 2009.

Friedberg, Aaron. "A History of US Strategic 'Doctrine'—1945 to 1980." *Journal of Strategic Studies* 3 (December 1980): 37–71.

Heng, Yee-Kuang. "The Return of Net Assessment." *Survival* 49 (Winter 2007–2008): 135–52.

Galdi, Theodor W. "Revolution in Military Affairs? Competing Concepts, Organizational Responses, Outstanding Issues." CRS 96-1170. Washington, DC: Congressional Research Service, Library of Congress, December 11, 1995.

Gates, Robert M. "A Balanced Strategy: Reprogramming the Pentagon for a New Age." *Foreign Affairs* 88 (January–February 2009): 28–40.

Grissom, Adam. "The Future of Military Innovation Studies." *Journal of Strategic Studies* 29 (October 2006): 905–34.

Heuser, Beatrice. "Victory in a Nuclear War? A Comparison of NATO and WTO War Aims and Strategies." *Contemporary European History* 7 (November 1998): 311–28.

Hitch, Charles J., and Roland N. McKean with contributions by Stephen Enke, Alain Enthoven, Malcolm W. Hoag, C. B. McGuire, and Albert Wohlstetter. "The Economics of Defense in the Nuclear Age." R-346. Santa Monica, CA: RAND Corporation, March 1960. [Published by Harvard University Press in 1960.]

Horowitz, Michael and Stephen P. Rosen. "Evolution or Revolution?" *Journal of Strategic Studies* 28 (June 2005): 437–48.

Jervis, Robert, Richard Ned Lebow, and Janice Gross Stein. *Psychology and Deterrence.* Baltimore, MD: Johns Hopkins University Press, 1985.

Kaplan, Fred. *The Wizards of Armageddon.* Palo Alto, CA: Stanford University Press, 1991.

Karber, Phillip A. "Net Assessment and Strategy Development for the Secretary of Defense: Future Implications from Early Formulations." Paper delivered at a conference entitled "Net Assessment: Past, Present, and Future," convened by the Center for Strategic and Budgetary Assessments in Washington, DC, on March 28–29, 2008.

——— , "Net Assessment for SecDef: Future Implications and Early Formulations." *Potomac Papers* 13, no. 2 (n.d.).

——— , A. Grant Whitley, Mark L. Herman, and Douglas R. Komer. "Assessing the Correlation of Forces: France 1940." BDM/W-79-560-TR. McLean, VA: BDM Corporation, June 18, 1979.

Keaney, Thomas A. "The Linkage of Air and Ground Power in the Future of Conflict." *International Security* 22 (Fall 1997): 147–50.

——— , and Eliot A. Cohen. *Revolution in Warfare? Air Power in the Persian Gulf.* Annapolis, MD: Naval Institute Press, 1995.

Keegan, John. *Intelligence and War: Knowledge of the Enemy from Napoleon to Al-Qaeda.* New York: Alfred A. Knopf, 2003.

Kent, Glenn A. "Concepts of Operations: A More Coherent Framework for Defense Planning." N-2026-AF. Santa Monica, CA: RAND Corporation, August 1983.

——— , David Ochmanek, Michael Spirtas, and Bruce R. Pirine. OP-223-AF. "Thinking About America's Defense: An Analytic Memoir." Santa Monica, CA: RAND Corporation, 2008.

Kotter, John P. "Leading Change: Why Transformation Efforts Fail." *Harvard Business Review* 73 (March–April 1995): 59–67.

Krepinevich, Andrew F., Jr. *The Army and Vietnam.* Baltimore, MD: Johns Hopkins University Press, 1986.

——— . "Cavalry to Computer: The Patterns of Military Revolutions." *The National Interest* 37 (Fall 1994): 30–42.

——— . "Defense Investment Strategies in an Uncertain World: Strategy for the Long Haul." Washington, DC: Center for Strategic and Budgetary Assessments, 2008.

——— . "The Military-Technical Revolution: A Preliminary Assessment." Washington, DC: Center for Strategic and Budgetary Assessments, 2002.

——— . *7 Deadly Scenarios: A Military Futurist Explores War in the 21st Century.* New York: Bantam Books, 2008.

——— , and Barry D. Watts. *The Last Warrior: Andrew Marshall and That Shaping of Modern American Defense Strategy.* New York: Basic Books, 2015.

Larson, Eric V., David T. Orletsky, and Kristin J. Leuschner. "Defense Planning in a Decade of Change: Lessons from the Base Force, Bottom-Up Review, and Quadrennial Defense Review." MR-1387-AF. Santa Monica, CA: RAND Corporation, January 1, 2001.

Leppingwell, John W. R. "The Laws of Combat?" *International Security* 12 (Summer 1987): 89–134.

Lerner, Jennifer S., and Philip E. Tetlock. "Accounting for the Effects of Accountability." *Psychological Bulletin* 125 (1999): 255–75.

Liao, Kai. "The Pentagon and the Pivot," *Survival* 55 (June–July 2013): 95–114.

Loftus, Joseph E. "Strategy, Economics and the Bomb." *The Scientific Monthly* 68 (May 1949): 310–20.

Mahnken, Thomas G., ed. *Competitive Strategies for the 21st Century: Theory, History, and Practice.* Palo Alto, CA: Stanford University Press, 2012.

——— . *Technology and the American Way of War Since 1945.* New York: Columbia University Press, 2008.

——— . *Uncovering Ways of War: US Intelligence and Foreign Military Innovation, 1918–1941.* Ithaca, NY: Cornell University Press, 2002.

——— , and Barry D. Watts. "What the Gulf War Can (and Cannot) Tell Us About Future of Warfare." *International Security* 22 (Fall 1997): 151–62.

Marshall, Andrew W. "Long-Term Competition with the Soviets: A Framework for Strategic Analysis." R-862-PR. Santa Monica, CA: RAND Corporation, April 1972.

——— . "Problems of Estimating Military Power." P-3417. Santa Monica, CA: RAND Corporation, August 1966.

——— . "A Program to Improve Analytic Methods Related to Strategic Forces." *Policy Sciences* 15 (November 1982): 47–50.

——— , J. J. Martin, and Henry S. Rowen, eds. *On Not Confusing Ourselves: Essays on National Security Strategy in Honor of Albert and Roberta Wohlstetter.* Boulder, CO: Westview, 1991.

May, Ernest R. *Strange Victory: Hitler's Conquest of France.* New York: Hill and Wang, 2000.

McGray, Douglas. "The Marshall Plan." *Wired Magazine*, February 11, 2003.

McKitrick, Jeffrey S. "Adding to 'Net Assessment.'" *Parameters* 36 (Summer 2006): 118–19.

Mearsheimer, John J. "Assessing the Conventional Balance: The 3:1 Rule and Its Critics." *International Security* 13 (Spring 1989): 54–89.

——— . "Numbers, Strategy, and the European Balance." *International Security* 12 (Spring 1988): 174–85.

——— . "Why the Soviets Can't Quickly Win in Central Europe." *International Security* 7 (Summer 1982): 3–39.

——— , Barry R. Posen, and Eliot A. Cohen. "Correspondence: Reassessing Net Assessment." *International Security* 13 (Spring 1989): 128–79.

Mazaar, Michael J. *The Revolution in Military Affairs: A Framework for Defense Planning.* Carlisle Barracks, PA: Strategic Studies Institute, US Army War College, June 10, 1994.

Mintzberg, Henry. "The Fall and Rise of Strategic Planning." *Harvard Business Review* 72 (January–February 1994): 107–14.

Mowthorpe, Matthew. "The Revolution in Military Affairs (RMA): The United States, Russian and Chinese Views." *Journal of Social, Political, and Economic Studies* 30 (Summer 2005): 137–53.

Murdock, Clark A. *Future Making: Getting Your Organization Read for What's Next.* Stevensville, MD: Murdock Associates, 2007.

Murray, William S. "A Will to Measure." *Parameters* 31 (August 2001): 134–37.

Murray, Williamson. *The Change in the European Balance Power, 1938–1939: The Path to Ruin.* Princeton, NJ: Princeton University Press, 1984.

Newmyer, Jacqueline [Deal]. "The Revolution in Military Affairs with Chinese Characteristics." *Journal of Strategic Studies* 33 (August 2010): 481–504.

Perla, Peter P. *The Art of Wargaming: A Guide for Professionals and Hobbyists.* Annapolis, MD: Naval Institute Press, 1990.

Porter, Michael E. "The Comparative Advantage of Nations." *Harvard Business Review* 68 (May–June 1990): 73–93.

Posen, Barry R. "Is NATO Decisively Outnumbered?" *International Security* 12 (Spring 1988): 186–202.

——— . *The Sources of Military Doctrine: France, Britain, and Germany Between the World Wars.* Ithaca, NY: Cornell University Press, 1984.

Possony, Stefan T. *Tomorrow's War: Its Planning, Management and Cost.* London: W. Hodge, 1938.

Prados, John. *The Soviet Estimate: US Intelligence Analysis and Russian Military Strength.* Princeton, NJ: Princeton University Press, 1986.

Prahalad, C. K., and Gary P. Hamel. "The Core Competence of the Corporation." *Harvard Business Review* 68 (May–June 1990): 79–91.

Press, Daryl G. "Lessons from Ground Combat in the Gulf." *International Security* 22 (Fall 1997): 137–46.

Richter, Andrew. "The Revolution in Military Affairs and Its Impact on Canada: The Challenges and Consequences." Working Paper 28. Vancouver: Institute of International Relations, University of British Columbia, March 1999.

Roche, James G., and Barry D. Watts. "Choosing Analytic Measures." *Journal of Strategic Studies* 14 (June 1991): 165–209.

Rosen, Stephen Peter. "The Impact of the Office of Net Assessment on the American Military in the Matter of the Revolution in Military Affairs." *Journal of Strategic Studies* 33 (August 2010): 469–82.

———. "Systems Analysis and the Quest for Rational Defense." *The Public Interest* 76 (Summer 1984): 3–27.

———. *Winning the Next War: Innovation and the Modern Military.* Ithaca, NY: Cornell University Press, 1991.

Schlesinger, James R. "Quantitative Analysis and National Security." *World Politics* 15 (January 1963): 295–315.

———. "Uses and Abuses of Analysis." *Survival* 10 (October 1968): 334–42.

Schroden, Jonathan J. "Measures for Security in a Counterinsurgency." *Journal of Strategic Studies* 32 (October 2009): 715–44.

Schwartz, Peter. *The Art of the Long View: Planning for the Future in an Uncertain World.* New York: Currency Doubleday, 1991.

Skypek, Thomas M. "Evaluating Military Balances Through the Lens of Net Assessment: History and Application." *Journal of Military and Strategic Studies* 12 (Winter 2010): 1–25.

Stalk, George, Jr. "Time—The Next Source of Competitive Advantage." *Harvard Business Review* 66 (July–August 1988): 41–51.

Tetlock, Philip E. "Theory-Driven Reasoning about Plausible Pasts and Probable Futures in World Politics: Are We Prisoners of Our Misconceptions?" *American Journal of Political Science* 43 (April 1999): 335–66.

Tilford, H. Earl, Jr. *The Revolution in Military Affairs: Prospects and Cautions.* Carlisle Barracks, PA: Strategic Studies Institute, US Army War College, June 23, 1995.

US Department of Defense, Joint Chiefs of Staff, Force Structure, Resources, and Assessment Directorate (J-8). "Capabilities-Based Assessment (CBA) User's Guide, Version 2." Washington, DC: Joint Chiefs of Staff, December 2006.

US General Accounting Office. "Operation Desert Storm: Evaluation of the Air Campaign." GAO/NSIAD-97-134. Washington, DC: National Security and International Affairs Division, General Accounting Office, June 12, 1997.

Van Creveld, Martin. *Command in War.* Cambridge, MA: Harvard University Press, 1985.

——— . *Fighting Power: German and US Army Performance, 1939–1945.* Westport, CT:

Greenwood Press, 1982.

——— . *Supplying War: Logistics from Wallenstein to Patton.* Cambridge: Cambridge University Press, 1977.

——— . *The Transformation of War.* New York: Free Press, 1991.

van Tol, Jan M. "Military Innovation and Carrier Aviation—The Relevant History." *Joint Force Quarterly* 16 (Summer 1997): 77–87.

——— . "Military Innovation and Carrier Aviation—An Analysis." *Joint Force Quarterly* 17 (Autumn–Winter 1997–98): 97–109.

Wack, Pierre. "Scenarios: Shooting the Rapids." *Harvard Business Review* 63 (November–December 1985): 139–50.

——— . "Scenarios: Uncharted Waters Ahead." *Harvard Business Review* 63 (September–October 1985): 73–89.

Watts, Barry D. "The Maturing Revolution in Military Affairs." Washington, DC: Center for Strategic and Budgetary Assessments, 2011.

Willis, Gordon, David Ashton, Gordon and Bernard Taylor, eds. *Technological Forecasting and Corporate Strategy.* New York: American Elsevier Publishing, 1969.

Winik, Jay. "Secret Weapon." *Washingtonian Magazine* 34 (April 1999): 45–55.

Yusuf, Moeed. "Predicting Proliferation: The History of the Future of Nuclear Weapons." Policy Paper 11. Washington, DC: Brookings Institution, January 2009.

About the Contributors

Dmitry (Dima) Adamsky is a professor at the School of Government, Diplomacy and Strategy at the IDC Herzliya University, Israel. His research interests include international security, cultural approach to IR, and American, Russian and Israeli national security policy. He has published on these topics in *Foreign Affairs, Security Studies, Journal of Strategic Studies, Intelligence and National Security, Studies in Conflict and Terrorism,* and *Cold War History.* His books *Operation Kavkaz* and *The Culture of Military Innovation* (Stanford University Press) earned the annual (2006 and 2012) prizes for the best academic works on Israeli security. His latest book *Russian Nuclear Orthodoxy* (Stanford University Press, 2019) is about religion, politics, and strategy in Russia.

John A. Battilega was the Senior Technical Director at Leidos, director of the Foreign Systems Research Center at Science Applications International Corporation, and the President of John Battilega Associates. Earlier, he served as a Military Assistant in the Office of Net Assessment. Dr. Battilega was appointed to both the Defense Science Board and the Board of Directors of the US Military Operations Research Society, and also taught at the University of Denver.

Thomas G. Mahnken is the President and Chief Executive Officer of the Center for Strategic and Budgetary Assessments and a Senior Research Professor in the Paul H. Nitze School of Advanced International Studies. Previously, he served as the Deputy Assistant Secretary of Defense for Policy Planning and held the Jerome Levy Chair at the Naval War College. Dr. Mahnken's publications include *Competitive Strategies for the 21st Century.*

Andrew W. Marshall served as the Director of the Office of Net Assessment within the Office of the Secretary of Defense from 1973 to

2015. Prior to being appointed to the National Security Council Staff during the Nixon administration, he was employed in the Economics Department at the RAND Corporation. He was honored as one of the "Top 100 Global Thinkers" by *Foreign Policy* magazine in 2012.

Andrew D. May is the Associate Director of the Office of Net Assessment and teaches in the Center for Security Studies at Georgetown University. Earlier, Dr. May contributed to various projects on net assessment at Science Applications International Corporation before joining the Office of the Secretary of Defense. His doctoral dissertation concerned strategic thought at the RAND Corporation.

Jeffrey S. McKitrick is a Research Staff Member at the Institute for Defense Analyses, and previously worked as the Director of Security Assessment and Authorization at the Science Applications International Corporation. He also taught in the Department of Social Sciences at the US Military Academy and served as a Military Assistant in the Office of Net Assessment. He is the author of The JCS: Evolutionary or Revolutionary *Reform.*

Williamson Murray is Professor Emeritus of History at The Ohio State University and has taught at the Naval War College, Marine Corps University, and London School of Economics and Political Science. In addition, Dr. Murray was the Harold K. Johnson Professor of Military History at the US Army War College and held the Charles Lindberg Chair at the Air and Space Museum. He co-edited *Military Innovation in the Interwar Period.*

James G. Roche was named as the Secretary of the Air Force by President George H. W. Bush. Formerly, he held senior executive positions with Northrop Grumman. A retired naval officer, Dr. Roche also served as a Military Assistant in the Office of Net Assessment, on the Defense Policy Board and the Policy Planning Staff at the Department of State, and with the Senate Select Committee on Intelligence.

Stephen Peter Rosen is the Beton Michael Kaneb Professor of National Security and Military Affairs at Harvard University and has been the Master of Winthrop House at Harvard College. Dr. Rosen directed the John M. Olin Institute for Strategic Studies at Harvard and taught at the Naval War College. He also has served as a Civilian Assistant in the Office of Net Assessment and on the National Security Council Staff.

Abram N. Shulsky is a Senior Fellow at the Hudson Institute and previously worked for the Under Secretary of Defense for Policy. Earlier, he worked at RAND and as a consultant to the Office of Net Assessment. Dr. Shulsky also served as the Director of Strategic Arms Control Policy within the Office of the Secretary of Defense and as the Minority Staff Director for the Senate Select Committee on Intelligence.

Barry D. Watts served as the Director of Program Analysis and Evaluation at the Pentagon and the Director of the Northrop Grumman Analysis Center. He was a Senior Fellow at the Center for Strategic and Budgetary Assessments and a Military Assistant in the Office of Net Assessment. Mr. Watts contributed to the Gulf War Air Power Survey and taught in the Center for Security Studies at Georgetown University.

INDEX

Cambria Rapid Communications in Conflict and Security (RCCS) Series

General Editor: Geoffrey R. H. Burn

The aim of the RCCS series is to provide policy makers, practitioners, analysts, and academics with in-depth analysis of fast-moving topics that require urgent yet informed debate. Since its launch in October 2015, the RCCS series has the following book publications:

- *A New Strategy for Complex Warfare: Combined Effects in East Asia* by Thomas A. Drohan
- *US National Security: New Threats, Old Realities* by Paul R. Viotti
- *Security Forces in African States: Cases and Assessment* edited by Paul Shemella and Nicholas Tomb
- *Trust and Distrust in Sino-American Relations: Challenge and Opportunity* by Steve Chan
- *The Gathering Pacific Storm: Emerging US-China Strategic Competition in Defense Technological and Industrial Development* edited by Tai Ming Cheung and Thomas G. Mahnken
- *Military Strategy for the 21st Century: People, Connectivity, and Competitipauon* by Charles Cleveland, Benjamin Jensen, Susan Bryant, and Arnel David
- *Ensuring National Government Stability After US Counterinsurgency Operations: The Critical Measure of Success* by Dallas E. Shaw Jr.
- *Reassessing U.S. Nuclear Strategy* by David W. Kearn, Jr.
- *Deglobalization and International Security* by T. X. Hammes
- *American Foreign Policy and National Security* by Paul R. Viotti

- *Make America First Again: Grand Strategy Analysis and the Trump Administration* by Jacob Shively
- *Learning from Russia's Recent Wars: Why, Where, and When Russia Might Strike Next* by Neal G. Jesse
- *Restoring Thucydides: Testing Familiar Lessons and Deriving New Ones* by Andrew R. Novo and Jay M. Parker
- *Net Assessment and Military Strategy: Retrospective and Prospective Essays* edited by Thomas G. Mahnken, with an introduction by Andrew W. Marshall

For more information, visit www.cambriapress.com.